The International Arms Trade

The International Arms Trade

RACHEL STOHL AND
SUZETTE GRILLOT

polity

First published in 2009 by Polity Press
Reprinted 2012

Polity Press
65 Bridge Street
Cambridge CB2 1UR, UK

Polity Press
350 Main Street
Malden, MA 02148, USA

ISBN-13: 978-0-7456-4153-9
ISBN-13: 978-0-7456-4154-6 (paperback)

A catalogue record for this book is available from the British Library.

Typeset in 10 on 13 pt FF Scala
by Servis Filmsetting Ltd, Stockport, Cheshire
Printed and bound by MPG Books Group, Bodmin, Cornwall

For further information on Polity, visit our website: www.polity.co.uk.

Contents

Acknowledgements

Any undertaking of this magnitude would not be possible without the considerable assistance of friends and colleagues around the world. We would, therefore, like to thank a number of people who contributed significantly to this project. Rhea Myerscough and Sara Rafferty served as invaluable researchers, editors and sounding boards throughout this process. Doug Tuttle, Jonah Leff and Camilla Kardel stepped in to provide additional research and helpful suggestions in the book's final stages. Kerri Shadid, Lessa Keller-Kenton, Brooke Hammer and Holly Presnell also provided much-needed research support. We would also like to thank numerous colleagues at the Center for Defense Information at the World Security Institute and the University of Oklahoma, for supporting this endeavour. In addition, Emma Hutchinson and Louise Knight at Polity have been incredibly supportive and helpful in the development and production of this manuscript. We have been extremely fortunate to work with such talented and encouraging women. While numerous colleagues have assisted in the production of the book, we alone are responsible for its content. Lastly, we thank and acknowledge our families, without which such projects would never see light nor be as fulfilling. We thus deeply thank Quentin, Sophia and Samuel Baird, Pat Lannon and Hannah Grillot for their unconditional love and unending patience as we undertook this project.

Acronyms

AECA	Arms Export Control Act
APLs	Anti-Personnel Landmines
ATT	Arms Trade Treaty
AU	African Union
BERR	Business, Enterprise and Regulatory Reform
BIS	Bureau of Industry and Security
BMS	Biennial Meeting of States
CAT	Conventional Arms Transfer Talks
CCL	Commercial Control List
CCW	Convention on Prohibitions or Restrictions on the Use of Certain Conventional Weapons Which May Be Deemed to Be Excessively Injurious or to Have Indiscriminate Effects
CFE	Conventional Forces in Europe Treaty
CIEEMG	Commission for the Study of Military Equipment Exports
CIFTA	Inter-American Convention Against the Illicit Manufacturing of and Trafficking in Firearms, Ammunition, Explosives and other Related Materials
CMC	Cluster Munitions Coalition
COCOM	Coordinating Committee for Multilateral Export Controls
COSTIND	Commission on Science, Technology and Industry for National Defence
CRS	Congressional Research Service

CTFP	Counterterrorism Fellowship Programme
DCS	Direct Commercial Sales
DDTC	Directorate of Defence Trade Controls
DESO	Defence Export Services Organisation
DHS	Department of Homeland Security
DOD	Department of Defense
DRC	Democratic Republic of the Congo
DSCA	Defense Security Cooperation Agency
DSEI	Defence Systems & Equipment International
DTRA	Defence Threat Reduction Agency
DTSI	Defence Trade Security Initiative
EAPC	Euro-Atlantic Partnership Council
ECA	Export Control Act
ECO	Export Control Organisation
ECOSAP	Economic Community of West African States Small Arms Project
ECOWAS	Economic Community of West African States
EDA	Excess Defence Articles
ELN	National Liberation Army, Colombia
EU	European Union
EXBS	Export Control and Related Border Security Assistance
FAO	United Nations Food and Agriculture Organisation
FAR	Armed Forces of Rwanda
FARC	Fuerzas Armadas Revolucianarias de Colombia
FBI	Federal Bureau of Investigation
FMS	Foreign Military Sales
FY	Fiscal Year
GAO	Government Accountability Office
GDP	Gross Domestic Product
HMRC	Her Majesty's Revenue & Customs
IANSA	International Action Network on Small Arms
ICBL	International Campaign to Ban Landmines
ICE	Immigration and Customs Enforcement

IDPs	Internally Displaced People
IEDs	Improvised Explosive Devices
ITAR	International Traffic in Arms Regulations
LURD	Liberians United for Reconciliation and Democracy
MANPADS	Man-Portable Air Defence Systems
MFA	Ministry of Foreign Affairs
NATO	North Atlantic Treaty Organisation
NGOs	Nongovernmental Organizations
NISAT	Norwegian Initiative on Small Arms Transfers
NRA	National Rifle Association
NSPD	National Security Policy Directive
OAS	Organization of American States
OECD	Organization for Economic Cooperation and Development
OSCE	Organisation for Security and Cooperation in Europe
PAC-3	Patriot Advanced Capability-3
PCASED	United Nations Programme for Coordination and Assistance on Security and Development
PDD	Presidential Decision Directive
PoA	United Nations Programme of Action to Prevent, Combat and Eradicate the Illicit Trade in Small Arms and Light Weapons in All Its Aspects
PSSM	Physical Security and Stockpile Management
QSC	Quadripartite Select Committee
RevCon	United Nations Conference to Review Progress Made in the Implementation of the Programme of Action
RMAF	Royal Malaysian Air Force
RUF	Revolutionary United Front, Sierra Leone
SADC	Southern African Development Community
SAFICO	Service des Autorisations Financières et Commerciales
SAS	Small Arms Survey

SEESAC	South Eastern and Eastern European Clearinghouse for the Control of Small Arms and Light Weapons
SIPRI	Stockholm International Peace Research Institute
SMEs	Small and Medium Enterprises
TSZ	Temporary Security Zone
UAVs	Unmanned Aerial Vehicles
UNDP	United Nations Development Programme
UNITA	National Union for the Total Independence of Angola
UNMAS	United Nations Mine Action Service
US	United States
USML	United States Munitions List
WA	Wassenaar Arrangement on Export Controls for Conventional Arms and Dual-Use Goods and Technologies
WAANSA	West African Action Network on Small Arms
WFSA	World Forum on the Future of Sport Shooting Activities
WMDs	Weapons of Mass Destruction

1

Introduction to the international arms trade

On 24 July 2007, a French government plane travelling from Tripoli, Libya, carrying five Bulgarian nurses and one Palestinian doctor landed in Sofia, Bulgaria. The healthcare workers had served eight years in a Libyan prison after being sentenced to death, accused and convicted of infecting children with HIV. The release came after a deal was struck between Libya, the European Union (EU) and France, signalling an improvement in Libya's ties with the international community. Although, at the time, France and the EU denied any financial compensation had been given to encourage the prisoners' release, one week later France announced a major conventional weapons sale to Libya, worth a total of $405 million. The arms deal, the first between any western country and Libya since the EU lifted restrictions on arms sales to Libya in 2004, consisted of anti-tank missiles worth $230 million and radio communication equipment worth $175 million. Less than six months later, Libyan leader Moammar Gadhafi visited France – his first trip to the West since he renounced terrorism and nuclear weapons – and announced a $14.7 billion deal for conventional weapons and nuclear reactors. The deal included Rafale fighter aircraft, military and attack helicopters, air defence radars, patrol boats and armoured vehicles.

These arms deals, and their geo-political significance, likely missed the attention of the majority of the world's population. While headlines describing the dire threats of weapons of mass destruction (WMDs) often dominate the front page of daily papers, conventional weapons deals often escape notice. But these weapons cause a far more deadly and current threat – one responsible for hundreds of thousands of deaths a year. Around the globe, people's lives are being irrevocably changed by the effects of guns, tanks and missiles. The international trade in these weapons is a multi-billion-dollar business engaged in by virtually every country around the world.

While countries have participated in the conventional arms trade for decades, attention to, and the effects of, conventional weapons have been more intense since the end of the Cold War. The fall of the Soviet Union and the end of a bi-polar world resulted in the emergence of new kinds of warfare, namely the move from inter-state to intra-state wars. These conflicts often rely solely on conventional weapons. In many cases, small arms and light weapons are the only weapons used by warring parties, including government armies, paramilitaries, rebel forces and terrorists. Since the early 1990s, increased attention has been given to the tools of this violence, not just the violence itself. Although some criticisms have been levied at the conventional arms trade – many of which we discuss in this book – others argue that the international arms trade is a necessary part of many international security frameworks and an important tool that can be used to create and strengthen alliances, influence state behaviour and contribute to economic stability.[1]

Still, the dangers and consequences of the conventional arms trade touch every aspect of society – from political to military and cultural to economic – yet, weapons of mass destruction still pre-occupy the minds of policy makers and the general public. Further complicating matters is the fact that conventional weapons are essential to national security and are tools of national politics, with legitimate military, police and even civilian uses. Thus, controlling conventional weapons is often more difficult than controlling other classes of weapons.

Main findings

This book describes the international conventional arms trade and examines the impact of conventional weapons throughout the world. These are weapons that range from guns to sophisticated fighter aircraft and naval ships – in other words, the conventional weapons of war. The book provides a basic understanding of the myriad aspects of the international arms trade and illustrates why people should be concerned with its details. It also explores how the conventional weapons trade is relevant to any study of war and modern conflict, and describes how the international arms trade affects the lives and deaths of billions of people around the world.

The book provides historical and current perspectives on the arms trade. We highlight the role of the United States, United Kingdom, France, Russia and China – the five largest arms exporters in the world. These five countries are also the five permanent members of the United Nations Security Council, and are responsible for nearly 80 per cent of the entire international arms trade. Thus, their role in the international arms trade is central to any larger discussion of the nature and consequences of the conventional arms trade, as well as efforts to control them. From their export policies, or lack thereof, to the size of their trade, the five largest arms exporters frame our examination of the global arms trade. The largest arms recipients are also examined, as supply alone does not drive the weapons trade. The demand for weapons is driven by a variety of factors and any analysis of international arms transfers must take the wants and needs of importing states and non-state actors into account. Major arms purchasers have seen weapons affect their overall economies, their national and regional stability, and their military and political relationships.

This book provides a historical and conceptual context for the arms trade and draws five main conclusions.

First, the supply of, and demand for, weapons, both legal and illegal, have ebbed and flowed as new international crises emerge and are resolved. Throughout history, the conventional arms trade has been driven by conflicts – both hot and cold – from their conception to their resolution. In fact, significant shifts in the conventional arms trade are marked by major world events, such as World Wars I and II, the Cold War, the 1991 Gulf War, and the War on Terror. Moreover, national and international political and economic issues more generally affect the international trade in arms. Numerous factors, therefore, influence weapons supply and demand.

Second, the control of, and trade in, conventional weapons are more complicated than those of other weapons systems. Unlike weapons of mass destruction, conventional arms are legitimate tools of governments, militaries, police forces and civilians. Indeed, Article 51 of the Charter of the United Nations recognizes the inherent right of all states to individual or collective self-defence and the right to manufacture, import, export, transfer and retain conventional arms toward that end. Thus, regulating and controlling the trade in conventional arms pose additional challenges for states and the international community.

Third, conventional arms are profitable. Conventional arms transfer agreements worldwide were worth approximately $60 billion in 2007.[2] This total only accounts for the legal trade in arms. There is a thriving black market trade in arms, as well as a robust grey market – those sales that fall in the blurry category between the legal and illicit markets. Smaller, however, than the international trade in oil and gas, valued at $1.7 trillion, or agricultural products, valued at $852 billion, the international arms trade is worth only half a percentage of all global trade.[3] Nonetheless, the arms trade has a significant influence on national and global economies.

Fourth, in many cases, national security trumps human security and arms transfers go unchecked. The resulting unrestrained trade of conventional weapons leads to significant consequences. From deaths and injuries, to the undermining of human security, the uncontrolled conventional arms trade has put peacekeepers in danger, diminished national and multinational business opportunities, impeded the ability of humanitarian and relief organizations to conduct their efforts, hampered sustainable development and, overall, negatively affected global peace and security.

Fifth and finally, conventional arms controls are underdeveloped and face significant challenges. One of the most immediate challenges is that some of the primary exporters have not supported or participated in proposed and existing controls. Controlling conventional arms involves multiple solutions with multiple actors in multiple forums. Conventional weapons transfers occur simultaneously at individual, national, regional and global levels and, therefore, require simultaneous responses at various levels.

Content and structure

Each chapter of this book highlights an aspect of the conventional arms trade – from historical changes in the international arms trade to its consequences and control options at a variety of levels.

Chapter 2 examines the arms trade throughout history. Beginning the arms trade narrative at the dawn of western civilization, the chapter links early weapons development, procurement and trade to diplomatic efforts, imperial activities, domestic politics and private business. The chapter also discusses the role of the arms trade in the post-World War II and Cold War eras, which clearly reflected the global stand-off between the United States and the Soviet Union. The end of the Cold War is examined at length, as well as the post-Cold War period, which has led to a dynamic conventional arms market capable of altering itself in response to changing world events. The chapter highlights the increased importance of dual-use technology – and that of the commercial sector and the globalization of the defence industry, including joint ventures and mergers, which have also complicated the relationships between companies and countries. The chapter reminds readers that the post-Cold War world has seen the emergence of intra-state, rather than inter-state wars, which has resulted in increased competition among arms exporters and new markets becoming available to historical rivals. The chapter also examines the 1991 Gulf War, which was a watershed event leading to global efforts to rein in the international arms trade, and yet led to increasing global weapons purchases, particularly in the Middle East. Finally, the chapter describes the economic conditions and international security concerns resulting from the attacks of 11 September 2001, which have created new trends in the international arms market, whereby the major arms importers have shifted away from traditional Middle East customers toward Asian customers, notably India and Pakistan.

Chapter 3 examines the big business of the international arms trade, particularly through the legal supply and transfer of arms, including five short case studies. It focuses on the politics and economics associated with the arms trade and on the actual mechanics of this global trade. The chapter reveals the various issues related to the global transfer of arms, including production of new weapons and stockpiling of weapons (and what happens when those weapons become obsolete), and discusses the impact of some arms transfer trends and technologies. The chapter also examines how market trends influence competition and cooperation between companies, countries and regions, and the symbiotic relationship between technology development and the trade in arms, as exemplified in national procurement strategies. The chapter also focuses on the purchasers of weapons, examining changing trends among arms recipients. The chapter includes a description of the bizarre world of arms shows, explains what makes a sale legal or illicit, and looks at the peculiarities of the legal small arms trade.

After a comprehensive look at the legal trade, chapter 4 focuses on what we can and do know about the illicit arms trade. The chapter highlights the highly profitable illicit trade in arms – both heavy conventional weapons and their spare parts – as well as the significant small arms black market. It examines trends in the illicit trade, and the variety of actors involved. The chapter also describes the multiple ways weapons move from the legal to the illicit market and explores issues related to the supply and demand of weapons, using examples from recent international events. It covers the shadowy world of arms brokers – the individuals or companies that act as intermediaries to facilitate the trade in weapons. Additionally, the chapter surveys the changes in arms brokering since the end of the Cold War and the ways in which arms brokers have had to adapt to the new paradigms of conflict and weapons demand. Finally, the chapter explains how arms brokers are able to manipulate legal networks for illegal purposes and how governments often use the same networks and routes to transport grey market arms.

Chapter 5 turns its attention to the effect these weapons have on countries and societies and unpacks the varied consequences of the arms trade utilizing the human security framework, including the impacts on international peace, security and development. The chapter demonstrates that, although the world remains focused on the threat of weapons of mass destruction, conventional arms are responsible for the majority of deaths and suffering in today's conflicts. Small arms, in particular, have played an important role in the world's bloodiest conflicts. The chapter discusses the direct, indirect and consequential impact of the weapons trade, using examples from every region of the world. The chapter describes how the conventional arms trade – both legal and illicit – has significant negative consequences, and highlights how these weapons are used to kill people in countries experiencing conflict and in countries at peace, and how conventional weapons contribute to cycles of violence, trapping communities in endless fighting and bloodshed. The chapter concludes with an analysis of conventional arms and terrorism.

Chapter 6 examines the various strategies for controlling the arms trade. The chapter highlights the numerous efforts to control the global trade in arms that have emerged over the years. The chapter points out historical arms control efforts, such as the Conventional Forces in Europe (CFE) Treaty, which focused largely on limiting the numbers and types of weapons a state could possess, as well as where they could be deployed. The chapter then describes the evolution of current conventional arms control strategies, which grew out of greater concerns about civil conflict, genocide and other human rights abuses in the post-Cold War era. In this section, the chapter examines a number of instruments that have emerged to control the spread, circulation and misuse of conventional weapons. The chapter describes the various global, regional and national control measures that focus specifically on conventional weaponry, paying particular attention to small arms strategies, such as the UN Conventional Arms Register, the Wassenaar Arrangement, and the UN Programme of Action on Small Arms and Light Weapons. The chapter also highlights the important role of nongovernmental organizations and their efforts to facilitate stronger and more comprehensive measures for the control of the international arms trade.

Finally, chapter 7 concludes the book with a more in-depth discussion of the major findings. We also argue that, although we now know more about the international arms trade, there is still more work to do, more awareness to raise, and more attention to focus on the issue.

Sources

This book draws heavily on news sources, United Nations documents, analyses and data compiled by nongovernmental organizations, author interviews and, when available, primary source government data. However, a significant amount of information on the conventional arms trade is not available to the public in open sources. Governments often prefer to keep information on their arms exports and imports classified, in order to protect their proprietary, political and strategic interests. As a result, analyses of the international arms trade are often limited, particularly in countries without a tradition of transparency and democracy. We have tried to provide a comprehensive and international picture of the arms trade, but ask the reader to take the data limitations into consideration.

2

The international arms trade in historical perspective

From past to present

On 25 July 1969, US President Richard Nixon decided to make a few remarks for reporters while on a refuelling layover in Guam. Those remarks became known as the 'Nixon Doctrine' and ushered in a new era in US foreign policy. Specifically, Nixon's comments suggested that internal security problems in Asia and elsewhere should be handled internally, but the United States would provide military and economic assistance to friendly regimes in order to support them. With this statement, Nixon elevated arms transfers to a prominent foreign policy position, promising to send arms instead of troops as a way to wield force and exert influence in third world countries without assuming the risks and costs associated with intervening directly. Little consideration was given at the time to the fact that once weapons were transferred, the United States would lose all control over how they were used or to whom they would flow next. Although it has been suggested that Nixon did not intend to make such a sweeping announcement on that day in Guam, the new policy was born nonetheless. Soon thereafter, the United States went on a supply spree, sending billions of dollars of weapons around the world, even into the hands of despots and dictators.[1]

Indeed, the history of the global arms trade goes much further back, before 1969 and the Nixon Doctrine. The international arms trade, in fact, has a long and storied past. Politics, power, economics and technology, among other things, have all affected the ways in which, and the extent to which, governments, private enterprises and various actors have engaged in the production and diffusion of weapons. This chapter offers a historical overview of the international arms trade, highlighting the evolution of the trade in armaments over many centuries. Beginning with a discussion of the early arms trade, the chapter then reviews the factors that influenced the modern arms trade system. Several trends evident in the international trade of arms are outlined, and recent (post-Cold War) changes are explored. This chapter serves as a foundation for the remainder of the book as the historical nature of this subject is important for our understanding of the international arms trade today.

The early arms trade

Although we have rather scant information about arms transfers throughout history, we do know that weapons have long been an important commodity. Thucydides wrote in *The Peloponnesian War* about the importance of the trade in arms, supplies, ships and men.[2] Later historical patterns show that fifteenth- and sixteenth-century weapons production and transfers spread from Italy, England and the Netherlands to Sweden, Germany and, later, France, Russia and Spain. The spread of arms production tended to follow the spread of capitalism, generally from Italy and north European states to countries such as France, Russia and Spain, and then to states like Portugal, the Ottoman Empire, Scotland, Hungary, India, Japan, Poland and the Balkans, where manufacturers replicated foreign weapons.[3]

In the early to mid fifteenth century, Italy was the most notable centre of arms production and transfers in the world. Centres of production of secondary importance could be found during this time in Germany and the Low Countries (present-day Benelux countries). Italy was originally able to dominate the arms trade because of its wide trading network, but by the middle of the seventeenth century the Low Countries, Britain and Sweden had taken over as the centres of weapons innovation and production. In 1492, the town of Liège in the Low Countries declared neutrality and disarmed. Because of its vast trading base, this resulted in a boom to the arms industry and Liège supplied vast quantities of arms to the Spanish and Dutch. However, the flow of arms from Liège stopped in 1797 when the town was annexed by the French and a ban was placed on weapons exports.[4]

In the sixteenth century, England transformed from an arms importer to an arms exporter for two reasons. First, a migration of iron workers to England brought knowledge of arms production, and, second, England was under economic pressure to make the transformation. The dominant centre of cast-iron cannon production had moved to Sweden where it stayed until the late eighteenth century after Elizabeth I limited the production of guns to those needed by the realm, resulting in a migration of skilled labour.[5]

In the first half of the seventeenth century, Suhl, Germany was the only large gun manufacturer in central Europe, but political differences and destruction during the Thirty Years' War kept its role in the arms trade minimal.

From 1422 to 1498, the kings of France established Tours as an arms centre and encouraged workers in weapons production to migrate there as a solution to French weapons shortages. France experienced temporary success in arms production during this period, but remained partially dependent on arms imports through the seventeenth century.[6]

The production of arms was well established in Russia by the mid sixteenth century, but the country remained a secondary producer, and had to resort to importing large quantities of arms from the West when arms production technology advanced in the early seventeenth century. Recognizing the problem, Peter the Great pushed for the improvement of Russia's arms production technology and output, and by 1720 Russia had become an exporter of arms, remaining self-sufficient until new technological advances occurred in the nineteenth century.[7]

Spain encouraged the emigration of arms and foundry workers in the 1570s to remedy its near-total dependence on imported artillery. The country experienced some success, but was not able to create a dominant modern armaments industry. The migration of skilled workers and the accompanying diffusion of arms production technology boosted the Swedish, Russian, French, Spanish and Ottoman arms industries. However, only France, Russia and Spain succeeded in developing significant, although far from dominant, production, while Portugal and the Ottoman Empire remained peripheral producers.[8]

The sixteenth to seventeenth centuries saw the spread of weapons to Portugal, Ottoman Turkey, Scotland, Hungary, India, Japan, Poland and the Balkans.[9] During the sixteenth century, Portugal, Scotland and Hungary were peripheral producers, meaning they had some arms production capacity, but mainly imported their weapons. Despite its lack of production, Portugal, with its large trade network, served to bring new weaponry to Asia and Africa. Turkey, India, China and Japan were third-tier producers who were able to imitate the arms developments of European states. By the end of the sixteenth century, cannons were being produced in China, Japan, Korea, India, Java, Burma and Afghanistan. Artillery production developed in India in the late seventeenth century, and Japan was casting its own firearms by the mid sixteenth century.[10]

A primary driver of the arms trade throughout this period, particularly from 1560 to 1660, was the development of modern war-making instruments – firearms, gunpowder and cannon. This 'military revolution' significantly enhanced the international trade in arms. For nearly 200 years following the military revolution, however, the arms trade was relatively stable.[11] The period from the late seventeenth century to the early nineteenth century saw little change in the arms trade after the technological diffusion of arms production during the previous period. The main reason for this stability was the lack of technological innovation in arms production during the period. While weapons continued to be traded, no new centres of production arose from 1650 to 1850. This period was a time of relative peace, and as a result innovation in weapons production slowed, even if the spread of firearms continued.[12] Ultimately, technological advances in armaments progressed rather slowly until the 'industrial revolution' in the mid-1800s.

The advent of the industrial revolution brought metallurgical innovations and the development of steam power, which improved the technological sophistication of weaponry. Moreover, the industrial revolution enhanced the capitalist economic system that dominated international trade. Weapons producers, like any other manufacturer, took advantage of laissez-faire economics and sold weapons to interested customers, no matter who or where they might have been.[13] After the British government began purchasing guns from the private firm of William Armstrong in 1854, other British arms manufacturers began calling for open competition in 1862, which resulted in a crisis that led the government to go back to using state arsenals to supply its arms but left the private arms sector renewed. This resulted in British arms producers vigorously pursuing export sales. Many governments in this period adopted the laissez-faire attitude of the industrial era and entered the international arms market. A French law prohibiting the exportation of weapons was repealed in 1885, allowing the French arms industry, which had doubled in capacity from 1874 to 1885, to export its surplus weapons. The governments in states with first-tier weapons production encouraged the exportation of arms because they thought a greater military advantage could be gained by maintaining their private weapons firms and research development expertise.[14]

Up until World War I, therefore, the international arms trade largely reflected the activities of private enterprise – private weapons manufacturers and merchants. Because of the significant death and destruction resulting from World War I, however, these private actors were eventually labelled 'merchants of death' engaged in a 'bloody business'.[15] Private weapons firms were often accused of inciting war with their irresponsible weapons sales.[16] During the last part of World War I, many members of the public gave some credence to the theory that 'only arms manufacturers could expect to profit by continuance of the struggle and that therefore only arms manufacturers could wish to prolong it'.[17] However, some argue that there was no evidence that arms manufacturers expected to profit from war, as they too were tired of the restriction from foreign markets and the burdensome workload that came with war. In fact, the post-WWI public enquiry into the arms industry in Britain found no evidence of warmongering on the part of arms manufacturers during the war.[18] Studies of conflicts during the past two centuries show that the build-up of arms does not necessarily lead to war, but that almost all wars throughout this period have been preceded by an accumulation of arms by one or more of the parties involved.[19] Nonetheless, some believed that the main cause of World War I was the activities of the private arms manufacturers. As a result, governments began to assert control over the international trade in arms after World War I (see below). Government control, however, did not lead to a reduction in weapons transfers.[20] In fact, the arms trade flourished throughout the twentieth century.

The arms trade in the twentieth century

Early in the twentieth century, some believed that private arms sales were an 'odious form of profiteering likely to cause war'.[21] During the period between World Wars I and II there was public antagonism toward the arms trade and a feeling that the profit from arms sales must be eliminated to preserve the peace. After World War I, preparing for war went 'out of fashion', and standing armies were considered a threat to liberty.[22] Also during this period, a number of pamphlets and books began to appear depicting arms sellers as evil men who only cared for profit, not people. In Britain, this attitude led to calls for an enquiry, both from the readers of these pamphlets and from Members of Parliament.[23]

Once governments assumed control of the arms trade process, however, official and authorized weapons sales were viewed as a 'laudable export achievement . . . necessary to preserve peace'.[24] This shift in controlling actors is the first of four trends evident throughout the modern arms trade period. The second trend is the tremendous growth in the volume of weapons traded in the twentieth century. A third trend demonstrates a shift in the number and type of weapons suppliers, and a fourth trend shows a shift in the location of arms recipients.

From private affair to government authority
The first major trend in the modern arms trade system was the shift from private to government actors as the dominant players. Arms manufacturers were once solely responsible for the promotion of their weapons, but, leading up to World War II, governments became more directly involved in promoting arms exports through government offices, agencies and publications. Governments, for instance, began to increase support for weapons manufacturers by making research and development funds available for new and better weapons designs. Other government support and control came by way of advisory personnel. The United States, United Kingdom, France and even the Soviet Union provided advisors to defence forces in foreign countries to assist in the development of specific weapons systems that would address their individual defensive requirements. This activity led to the development of 'package deals' through which arms buyers could purchase tailored defence systems developed precisely for the country's needs. Ultimately, these package deals allowed arms sellers to make larger sales.[25]

Governments also involved themselves in the international arms trade throughout the twentieth century by offering credit for arms purchases and by offsetting the foreign exchange costs associated with the financial transaction. The Soviet Union, United States and France, in particular, offered credit programmes for arms exports – most often involving large sums of money at little to no interest. Similarly, offsetting the costs of foreign currency exchange allowed governments to significantly enhance the prospect of an arms deal (see chapter 3). Credit and offsets, therefore, were a significant component of government involvement in and control of weapons transfers.[26]

In addition to their direct support of weapons production and arms sales, governments also began to develop and enforce laws and procedures for regulating and licensing the trade in armaments.[27] Such procedures allowed governments to monitor and, ultimately, exert control over where and to whom weapons were exported. Governments and manufacturers, therefore, became collaborators, with governments at the helm, during the twentieth century, to facilitate the international trade in arms. Together they developed, produced and exported arms, under government direction. After all, politics play a key role in the arms trade (see chapter 3). Weapons sales are an important tool of diplomacy and often reflect government desires to ensure sovereignty, express self-determination and enhance state protection, among other rationales (which will be discussed below).[28] Government authority, therefore, continues to be an important aspect of international weapons activities.

Growth in the arms trade
A second trend in the international arms trade that occurred throughout most of the twentieth century, and particularly after World War II, was the tremendous growth in the volume of arms traded worldwide. In 1950, the value of global arms sales totalled around $7 billion. By 1953, the total jumped to a record $20 billion, demonstrating the rapid diffusion of weapons in the early Cold War period. Global weapons sales peaked at $45 billion in 1982. By the end of the Cold War in 1990, global arms sales fell to $30 billion, and continued to decline until later in the post-Cold War period (as discussed in more detail below).[29]

To make sense of the growth in the arms trade, it is important to explore the various reasons why states engage in weapons production and sales. Three motivations are of particular importance – power, security and economy. Pearson refers to these primary factors as 'military ambition', 'threat perception', and 'economic wealth'.[30] Others refer to 'wealth', 'power' and 'war'.[31] Although most analysts suggest that considerations of war and peace – foreign policy and security – matter the most in determining whether, why and when states produce and export weapons,[32] some argue that no one motivation has 'absolute primacy over the others'.[33]

A primary motivation throughout the history of the arms trade is domestic consumption. States encouraged and supported the production of armaments to supply their own military and police forces for the purposes of national defence and internal order. Weapons were exported primarily as an 'afterthought' for many years, but soon arms sales came to be seen as important for enhancing one's power and security – as well as one's economy.[34] The lack of a domestic market, however, also prompted arms exports. Western and central European countries, for example, once sold weapons to Russia, the Ottoman Empire, Romania, Bulgaria, Serbia and Greece, because a small market existed at home. Maintaining production capacity was important for the supply of one's domestic forces, but the domestic market would not always suffice to keep the industry alive.[35] A stark reality for some arms manufacturers was 'export or perhaps die' – and without an arms industry, governments realized they would be dependent on others for their national defence.[36] All of these reasons and more have allowed the international arms trade to thrive.

Power and security are also important factors as weapons have often been exported to support various foreign policy goals. Weapons transfers serve to enhance the military capability of allies and counter the capability of rivals.[37] Arms supplies to foreign forces also work to minimize or avoid a direct military presence.

During the Cold War, the United States and Soviet Union transferred billions of dollars' worth of weapons to their respective
client states to improve their own military and strategic positions.
Exporting arms to increase a government's leverage and influence
over the recipient, or to counteract the capacity of real or potential
enemies, may not, however, always serve to do so.[38] Arms suppliers
cannot always control what recipients do with the weapons – nor
can they control whether and to whom the recipients re-export
the weapons. Suppliers also cannot predict political changes that
may have an impact on weapons deployment, use or transfer. The
United States provided more than half a billion dollars in arms to
Ethiopia over a twenty-year period, before political changes in the
country caused a switch in allegiance from the United States to the
Soviet Union. Similarly, the Soviet Union's client state, Somalia,
experienced a change in regime that led it away from the Soviets
and back to the Americans.[39]

Certainly, recipients of arms transfers have their own power and
security concerns that motivate their weapons purchases. Those
who cannot, or who prefer not to, produce weapons must import
them for national defence and policing purposes.[40] Weapons
importers may or may not share their suppliers' international
political perspectives when it comes to friends and foes or threats
and hazards. In many cases, weapons recipients have their own
agendas and concerns. Nonetheless, experts suggest that arms
transfers are best understood as 'reciprocal, bargaining relations'
rather than 'separate unilateral acts of supplying and receiving'.[41]

Another aspect of power and security is the technological force
motivating weapons transfers. Advanced military equipment is
a symbol not only of power, but also of technological prestige as
there is most often a significant correlation between weapons
production and industrial power. One way in which technology is
transferred is via the arms trade. Krause, for example, describes
how 'first-tier [weapons] suppliers' develop the technological innovations relevant for advanced weaponry, which are then transferred

to 'second-tier suppliers' who develop technological capacities as a result. 'Third-tier suppliers' duplicate the designs of these existing technologies, but do not benefit necessarily from the innovations in the enhancement of technological capacity.[42] State desires for technological capability, as well as desires to transfer and enhance technological capacity, have influenced and facilitated the arms trade as much as more strict concerns with power and security.

Economic motivations for engaging in the arms trade are perhaps more varied. With the growth in technology and enhanced sophistication of weaponry throughout the twentieth century, the costs associated with producing weapons for domestic consumption increased substantially. Due to increased costs in production – and the significantly increased costs of research and development – weapons-producing countries looked to arms exports to offset expenses. The marketability of weapons then became an issue as arms manufacturers found that they could not just develop and produce weapons merely for a domestic market, based on domestic military and other needs, but that they must develop and produce weapons that serve the international market.[43]

In addition to a reduction in costs, there are other economic issues that motivate weapons production and sales. Ownership within the military industrial enterprise may vary from country to country, but whether weapons-producing firms are privately or state owned, arms exports certainly have contributed substantial financial payoffs. Significant profits can be made by manufacturing and selling weapons. The creation of wealth, therefore, has also been a primary motivator for the arms trade. The overall economic benefits are not, however, all that great, and weapons have represented a small amount of overall exports for even the largest exporters. In 1980, for example, arms comprised only 4–5 per cent of the total amount of goods exported from the United States. Nonetheless, domestic employment in the weapons industry has often provided significant motivation for arms exports. Selling weapons abroad, in other words, has sometimes meant keeping jobs at home.[44] Finally, transferring arms to foreign forces may allow for a reduction in domestic defence budgets. It is far more costly to build up, deploy and maintain one's own domestic forces than to rely somewhat on the forces of foreign allies.[45] Exporting arms has, therefore, contributed to reduced costs at home in a number of ways.

Growth in arms suppliers

A third trend in the twentieth-century arms trade was the growth in the number of weapons producers and suppliers. The global sources of weapons multiplied significantly throughout much of the 1900s. A few weapons suppliers have, however, clearly dominated the production of and international trade in arms. The United States and the Soviet Union supplied the bulk of the international arms market throughout the Cold War period, but the UK, France and Germany – and later China – were also major suppliers. From 1950 to 1990, the Soviet Union out-sold the United States by a few billion dollars each year, with the exception of 1963–5 and the early 1990s (see table 2.1).

The United Kingdom ranked third in terms of arms sales with an average of $1 billion to $3 billion throughout 1950–90. China sold a few hundred million dollars' worth of weapons each year until 1971 when it began to sell more than $1 billion to $2 billion a year. By far, however, the Soviet Union and the United States dominated the twentieth-century international arms trade.[46]

Although only two weapons-producing countries cornered the

Table 2.1: US and Soviet Cold War arms sales					
	1950	1960	1970	1980	1990
Soviet Union	$3 billion	$6 billion	$10 billion	$18 billion	$10 billion
United States	$1.6 billion	$6 billion	$8.7 billion	$9.7 billion	$10.5 billion

Source: The SIPRI Arms Transfers Database at http://armstrade.sipri.org, last accessed 31 March 2009.

international arms market, numerous other suppliers emerged throughout the twentieth century, and particularly during the Cold War. Arms sales originating from secondary suppliers, located primarily in the third world, rose steadily until the 1960s and then jumped significantly in the 1970s. In the mid 1960s, third world arms production increased from $6 million to $23 million, from where it grew at a steady pace until another substantial increase in 1972 when third world weapons production rose from $43 million to $129 million. Countries such as India, Israel, South Africa, Brazil, Taiwan, North Korea, Argentina, South Korea and Egypt produced and exported weapons from 1950 to 1984. Although a small part of the worldwide arms trade, such secondary suppliers contributed significantly to the global supply of ammunition, small arms, ships, armoured vehicles, missiles and aircraft.[47] By the end of the Cold War, forty-two countries maintained weapons exports of some variety.[48]

Shift in weapons recipients
A final trend in the twentieth-century international arms trade was the shift in recipients of arms transfers. For nearly seventy years, the major suppliers of weapons sold their weapons primarily to developed countries.[49] Members of the North Atlantic Treaty Organization (NATO), for example, transferred weapons mainly within the alliance.[50] By the 1970s, however, primary recipients shifted to the third world, with the Far East, Indian subcontinent, Middle East, North Africa, Sub-Saharan Africa and Latin America emerging as major recipients of arms produced in the developed and developing worlds.[51] Between 1960 and 1980, third world military spending quadrupled. Third world arms imports swelled from $6.2 billion in 1969 to $15.5 billion in 1978.[52] The Cold War environment facilitated the influx of weapons to the third world as the US–Soviet rivalry allowed arms recipients to play 'one side off against the other'.[53]

The Middle East, in particular, has received the major share of weapons exported since the 1970s, with the United States, Soviet Union, United Kingdom and France providing the overwhelming bulk of arms to the region.[54] As oil prices rose in the 1970s and Britain decided to leave the Persian Gulf region, a 'massive infusion of Western arms to both Iran and oil-rich Arabs' resulted.[55] In 1977, Middle Eastern countries received 39 per cent of global arms exports, with Africa receiving 17 per cent, Asia 11 per cent and Latin America 6 per cent. The Cold War also played out in the Middle East context. By the late 1970s, Iran, Saudi Arabia and Israel were primary recipients of US weapons, while Syria, Iraq, Libya and Egypt received the bulk of Soviet weapons.[56]

The arms trade in a new era

These changing dynamics of the international arms trade throughout the twentieth century laid the foundation for post-Cold War arms trade activities. The supremacy of government authorities came to be challenged by new, non-state actors in the post-Cold War period; the volume of trade continued to ebb and flow; and suppliers and recipients remained in flux. The practices put in place throughout the twentieth century, however, affected how the international arms trade evolved into the twenty-first century.

The end of the Cold War: a new arms trade dynamic

The end of the Cold War marked a significant change in the international arms trade. The days of two superpowers arming their allies in proxy wars around the world came to an abrupt end. Instead, the world witnessed the growing prevalence of intrastate, rather than inter-state wars, which were based on internal struggles for power, rather than battles between Soviet and US ideologies and interests. These new wars resulted in increased competition among arms exporters, as historical rivals could now cater to the same markets. Business could now be dictated by profit, rather than ideology, and the myriad civil wars that took place in the aftermath of the Cold War, along with the numerous countries that began to modernize their outdated Soviet arsenals, meant that the arms trade was an extremely profitable business during the early 1990s. However, by the mid 1990s, several major conflicts were ending and several economic crises were beginning around the world, leading arms sales to decline and causing the defence industry to adjust to new world realities. In addition, traditional major arms suppliers found their supremacy challenged by emerging arms exporters, eager to break into the global market.

Post-Cold War trends

The geo-political changes that occurred at the end of the Cold War spawned several trends in the global arms trade and subsequent control regimes (for more on these control regimes, see chapter 6). In particular, three trends have emerged as most significant for understanding the dynamics of the current international arms trade system. First, global arms sales have fallen dramatically and consistently since the end of the Cold War. According to SIPRI, global arms sales between 1984 and 1988 averaged nearly $42 billion a year. In contrast, global arms sales dipped to approximately $27 billion per year between 1989 and 1993, and continued to fall throughout the 1990s.[57] Between 1994 and 1998, arms sales averaged approximately $22 billion a year.[58] Global arms sales dropped so low that, although arms sales generally increased each year between 2001 and 2005, the average during those years was still only $18.7 billion.[59] Currently, the trend is being reversed. New arms sales agreements reached a new post-Cold War high at nearly $60 billion in 2007, the highest in eight years.[60] However, arms deliveries decreased in 2007 from 2006 levels, due to significantly fewer arms deliveries to China and the United Arab Emirates. However, even with the downturn in the value of arms transferred in 2007, worldwide arms transfer agreements increased over 29 per cent in the 2004–7 period, as compared to 2000–3.[61]

The downturn in global arms sales can be explained by several factors. For the most part, the peaks and valleys in the international arms trade since the end of the Cold War have been tied to global economics and global and regional conflicts, rather than Cold War proxy conflicts supported by the two superpowers. Conflicts such as those in Afghanistan, Angola and throughout Central America had been fuelled by large quantities of arms and, in turn, fuelled global arms sales. With the conflicts' conclusions, the same quantities of arms were no longer regularly and reliably needed.

Furthermore, at the end of the Cold War many countries simply did not need to purchase any more weapons, as their arsenals were already saturated with purchases made during the Cold War.[63] In 1990, for example, the US Congressional Research Service (CRS) reported that many countries continued to absorb the weapons that were purchased in the late 1970s and early 1980s and simply did not need to make large purchases of new conventional weapons systems.[64] The same trend can be observed during the mid 1990s when global arms sales reached a plateau, after most Middle Eastern countries made sufficient arms purchases during the Gulf crisis to meet their security needs for the foreseeable future.

In addition, the economic crises of the late 1990s also lowered the global demand for weapons. For example, in the late 1990s Chile expressed interest in receiving up to twenty-four F-16 fighter jets from the United States. However, in 1998, the cost of copper – one of Chile's most profitable exports – dropped significantly in response to the global economic crisis, and Chile could no longer afford to make such an expensive purchase. The effects of the widespread economic recession in the late 1990s led to the cancellation of potential sales throughout Latin America, the Middle East – where crude oil prices dropped significantly – and Asia, as countries no longer had the resources for new major conventional weapons.

Moreover, at the end of the Cold War, countries began to cut their arms production, due in part to decreases in domestic demand.[64]

In 1995, for example, the Stockholm International Peace Research Institute (SIPRI) reported that Germany cut its arms procurement more than any other European country and that its arms industry cut production by nearly 50 per cent in the previous four years.[65] However, this trend began to reverse itself by the late 1990s and, for many countries, arms production has had a resurgence, particularly since the events of 11 September 2001. (For more on the effects of 11 September, see below.) After a dramatic fall in the early 1990s, Russia has seen its arms production increase since 1998, when it began to increase its arms exports as well as domestic procurement.[66] Russia decided to kick-start its arms production again after realizing that arms exports represented a potentially lucrative avenue for acquiring hard currency.[67]

A second trend that has developed in the international arms market since the end of the Cold War is the rise of the United States as the most dominant arms exporter in the world, despite falling demand for weapons. This pattern marks a shift from a bi-polar arms trade system to a unipolar one.[68] During the Cold War, the United States and Russia were the primary sources for weapons around the world, as they armed their allies and supported proxy wars. With the conclusion of these conflicts, and the dissolution of the Soviet Union, Soviet (and then Russian) arms sales declined dramatically and the United States' share of global arms agreements grew considerably. In 1989, the Russian share of global arms agreements was approximately 35%, while the US share was approximately 22%. By 1991, new Russian agreements were down to nearly 27%, while new US agreements had increased to 39%. This trend was even more dramatic in 1992 and 1993, when Russian sales plummeted to 5% and 7% respectively, while US agreements skyrocketed to 54% and 59% respectively. Russia inherited 71% of the Soviet defence industry at the end of the Cold War, but by the end of 1993 70% of these defence companies were idle.[69] This reduction in capacity was evident in the Russian share of the international arms trade as, by 1994,

Russian weapons made up only 3% of the global arms market.[70] Throughout the 1990s and early to mid 2000s, the United States dominated the international arms market, and by 2003 the United States was responsible for 53% of new arms transfer agreements.

As severe economic problems and political upheaval consumed the Soviet Union and then Russia at the beginning of the 1990s, the United States took advantage of its former foe's weaknesses and began to pursue foreign military sales more deliberately, snapping up the market share once firmly commanded by the Soviet Union. Soviet weapons were also seen as less reliable and believed to be technologically inferior to weapons produced by the United States. In addition, countries worried about the availability of spare parts due to the economic uncertainties at the time.[71] The United States began to help modernize the forces of former Warsaw Pact countries, such as Poland, and could also now arm both sides of a conflict and proceeded to do so, selling arms to rivals such as Egypt and Israel, Turkey and Greece, Armenia and Azerbaijan. The United States took advantage of the numerous regional conflicts that occurred in the 1990s to replenish the depleted arsenals of countries around the world with US weapons. Countries in the market for new weaponry often turned first to the United States, as the quality and cachet of US weapons were unparalleled.

The United States has profitable dealings in every region of the world. The continent with the smallest amount of US arms transfers is Africa, where the largest US weapons recipients in 2006 were Ethiopia, Kenya, South Africa, Uganda and Botswana. These countries totalled only $11 million in new Foreign Military Sales (FMS – government-to-government sales) deliveries. In the Americas, Chile, Canada, Colombia, Brazil and Venezuela rounded out the major recipients of US FMS, receiving $606 million in arms deliveries in 2006, including weapons specifically designated for counter-narcotics programmes. The main European recipients in 2006 were the Netherlands, Poland, Greece, the United Kingdom and Italy with approximately $2.54

billion in arms deliveries, while in Asia, Australia, Taiwan, South Korea, Japan and Singapore were the primary US trading partners, receiving $4.21 billion in new arms deliveries.[72]

Although the totals to the rest of the world are impressive, the Middle East remains the United States' largest arms trading partner. Since the 1991 Gulf War, the United States has made billions of dollars' worth of arms deals with the Middle East every year. The top recipients in 2006, for example – Israel, Egypt, Saudi Arabia, Kuwait and Oman – received $4.29 billion in new weapons deliveries. Since 1999, Saudi Arabia alone has received over $15 billion in US weapons. In July 2007, the Bush Administration announced that members of the Gulf Cooperation Council – Saudi Arabia, the United Arab Emirates, Kuwait, Qatar, Bahrain and Oman – would receive approximately $20 billion worth of new US weapons deals. Details of the sales have yet to be finalized, including the type and amount of weapons, the timeframe for their delivery, and the exact recipients of which specific systems.[73]

The United States sees even greater opportunity for increased arms sales in the years to come. FMS agreements in 2006 were $20.9 billion – nearly twice the 2005 total of $10.6 billion.[74] New arms deals with Pakistan, India and the Gulf States will only cement these higher totals for years to come. Iraq has also stimulated the US defence industry with significant heavy conventional weapons purchases from the United States. In addition, as the United States and other countries around the world worry in earnest about the strategic threats of Iran and North Korea, worldwide arms sales will also increase in the near future.

Although in some regions the United States was not the world's largest exporter, its forays into several different regions give it a solid base around the world. The diversity of customers, coupled with the perceived unreliability of Russian weapons, have ensured US dominance in the global arms trade in the post-Cold War era. Still, it is worth noting that many experts see Russia's return as an arms trade leader and that its success in gaining new arms orders, particularly from the developing world, and from countries that had traditionally been western customers, reflects a re-emergence of Russia's position in the global arms trade.[75]

A third post-Cold War trend in the international arms market has been the elevation of economic considerations in arms export decisions. In some cases, global economic recessions and the disappearance of Cold War conflicts created tensions between business and diplomatic interests. Regardless of how the international supply and demand for weapons have ebbed and flowed, the defence industry has been anxious to keep supply lines open and has encouraged governments to keep up arms production, national procurement and exports.

The United States Office of Technology Assessment highlighted this trend in 1991 in a report for the Senate Committee on Armed Services and the House Committee on Government Operations:

> the end of the Cold War and the accompanying decline in defense spending have weakened the political foundation for continuing arms transfers and enhanced the economic motivations for international arms sales. Worldwide, the defense industries face deep recession (and probably permanent adjustment to much lower levels of production) brought on by a general erosion of demand and continued strong overcapacity of production.[76]

As the deciding factor for choosing a weapons supplier switched from ideology to cost, traditional allies and former recipients of weapons could not necessarily be counted on to be reliable long-term customers. Likewise, in pursuit of profit, countries began to sell weapons to traditional allies as well as the potential enemies of these allies. In desperate need of hard currency with the sudden disappearance of economic support from the Soviet Union, many former Soviet republics and satellites began to sell previously restricted weapons to countries outside the former Soviet bloc. Russia sold its stockpiles to anyone willing to pay the price, exporting MiG-29 fighter jets to China, Syria and Malaysia in the early

1990s[77] and also selling significant quantities of weapons to Iran, even though, throughout the 1980s, Iraq had been a significant ally and customer. As described above, the United States began to sell to former Soviet states, while other countries found that economic considerations trumped national security issues. For example, Israel sold weapons to China, even though China had previously re-transferred Israeli technology to Arab countries.[78] Although many countries remained loyal customers of traditional suppliers, and others still refused to sell weapons to stalwart enemies, for the most part the end of the Cold War has seen more competition between countries motivated by price, not political ideology.

National governments have also had to react to the pressures on the defence industry since the end of the Cold War and to manipulate their foreign policies accordingly. While France, for example, has consistently used profits from arms exports to fund domestic weapons development and procurement,[79] the United States and Russia have had to learn to use arms exports to their economic benefit. The two superpowers historically focused on domestic arms production and procurement, using foreign arms sales primarily to achieve diplomatic ends. Only since the end of the Cold War have they viewed arms sales as a means to generate income.

In 1990, the Congressional Research Service revealed that 'United States weapons systems have been built primarily for the American armed services, with only secondary consideration being given to foreign sales'.[80] In 1995, however, US President Bill Clinton released his Administration's Conventional Arms Transfer Policy, delivered through Presidential Decision Directive (PDD) 34. For the most part, PDD 34 reiterated overarching criteria for arms transfers that had been a part of US policy and practice for decades.[81] However, PDD 34 also stated that 'the impact on U.S. industry and the defence industrial base whether the sale is approved or not' would also be taken into account when the US government considered a potential arms transfer.[82] This guideline, which had not been spelled out in previous US arms transfer policy, reflected the new perception of the arms trade as a money-making industry in the post-Cold War economy.

Russian arms exports plummeted at the end of the Cold War, but, as the country began to see the potential for arms sales to contribute to the rebuilding of the economy, Russia stepped up arms production in the late 1990s, and began to reach out to new and nontraditional purchasers. Russian arms exports have steadily increased from $2 billion in sales in 1994 to $8 billion in 2006.[83] Moreover, by 2005 Russia ranked second only to the United States in weapons supplies to third world countries[84] and indeed ranked first in arms transfers to the developing world in the 2004–7 period.[85] Russia has repeatedly expanded into markets in the Middle East, Asia and Africa, challenging the United States in many regional arms markets.

The 1991 Gulf War: a watershed event for global arms exports

The three trends that developed at the end of Cold War created drastically new parameters for the international arms trade; however, the global arms market continued to evolve. The 1991 Gulf War was a watershed event from which two important new patterns emerged. The first (which will be discussed in chapter 6) was the emergence of global efforts to rein in and better control the international arms trade. Years of arms trading in secret had allowed Saddam Hussein to build up his military by making weapons purchases from many different countries. Without an international transparency regime, the extent of these sales had gone unnoticed and the size of Saddam's arsenal was an unpleasant surprise to an unsuspecting international community. The second, which will be discussed here, was a reinvigoration of global arms sales, particularly to the Middle East. The Gulf War highlighted an interesting tension presented by the new shape of the international arms trade, namely the problem of creating an international control regime that prevents future Saddams from amassing huge arsenals unbeknown to the rest of the international community, while still allowing for countries to arm their allies as quickly and effectively as possible in the case of conflict.

An ample supply of heavy conventional weapons acquired by Saddam Hussein in the years and months prior to the August 1990 invasion of Kuwait, combined with the significant amount of weaponry that remained in Iraq's arsenals after the Iran–Iraq war, allowed Saddam to instigate the conflict with confidence. Between 1987 and 1990, Iraq purchased approximately $10 billion of arms.[86] Of this $10 billion in weaponry, $4 billion was from the Soviet Union, $2.7 billion was from western Europe (including France, the United Kingdom, Germany and Italy), and $615 million was from China.[87] In addition, between 1985 and 1990, the United States licensed $1.5 billion in military technology for export to Iraq. Iraq had already received half of this amount when the United States imposed sanctions on it in 1990.[88] No major arms exporter can escape blame for Saddam's well-stocked military.

In the immediate aftermath of the Gulf War, arms exporters scrambled to help arm the Middle East. Despite the fact that the region had just emerged from a deadly conflict which had been facilitated by a secretive military build-up, many Middle Eastern states still saw Saddam as a threat and were interested in acquiring weapons to defend themselves against possible future aggression from Iraq. In addition, the United States and its partners were interested in both gaining allies in the Middle East, and making them formidable opponents, by arming them sufficiently. These increased arms sales were in part a form of military diplomacy. These purchases by Middle Eastern states also reversed a decline in arms transfers to developing countries that had begun at the end of the Cold War.

The tension between restraining arms transfers in order to avoid future Gulf wars, and the desire to arm allies in order to defend national interests in the event of future Gulf wars, was most apparent in the US sale of advanced weaponry to Saudi Arabia. In 1990 President Bush announced a $20 billion arms deal to Saudi Arabia but, only a year later, fallout from the Gulf War gave some US policy makers pause over authorizing such a large arms transfer, and the sale was broken into several smaller sales, with transfers of some of the more expensive weaponry reorganized or postponed indefinitely.[89] Still, Washington power players supported increased sales of arms to the Middle East and then Undersecretary of Defence Paul Wolfowitz was a strong advocate of ensuring that the United States' Middle Eastern allies received the weaponry that they requested.[90] Indeed, the United States was the primary supplier of arms to the Middle East throughout the 1990s, making large sales to Bahrain, Egypt, Israel, Kuwait, Oman, Saudi Arabia and the United Arab Emirates. Bill Hartung reveals that 'in the nine weeks from September 1992 until election day, the Bush Administration announced over $20 million in new overseas arms deals. In just two months, George Bush rushed through the equivalent of a year's worth of weapons exports.'[91] Russia, China and western Europe (France, Germany, Italy and the United Kingdom) also maintained clients in the Middle East during the same period, although to a much smaller extent.

Conflicts fuelled arms exports throughout the 1990s. Although Africa was plagued by several inter-state and intra-state conflicts during the decade, these conflicts were mainly fought with cheaper small arms and light weapons and, as a result, had little overall effect on the global arms market. Although nearly $6.5 billion in military equipment was exported to Africa during the 1990s,[92] Africa made the lowest value of arms purchases in the world, compared to all other regions. After the massive, post-Gulf War military build-up, international arms exports began to decline again, with global arms sales hitting a post-Cold War record low of $18.3 billion in 1997. However, another major turn of events would again reinvigorate and reshape the international arms market.

The aftermath of 11 September 2001

The events of 11 September 2001 proved to be another defining moment for the global arms trade because of the subsequent drastic changes in economic conditions and the international security landscape. Much like the 1991 Gulf War, 11 September 2001 led to a resumption of major international arms sales. As explained above, global arms sales tapered off during the late 1990s as the last orders generated by the 1991 Gulf War were filled, and Asia and Latin America experienced major economic crises. Total arms sales reached new lows, with only $23.6 billion in new arms agreements in 1997.[93] However, the international security crisis spawned by 11 September 2001 gave governments and defence industries an impetus for new sales, and introduced new trading partners. Since 11 September, countries such as India and Pakistan have become lucrative arms purchasers, in some cases overshadowing purchases by the Middle East. New arms sales agreements reached $48.7 billion in 2005, the largest amount of new arms sales since 1992. In 2006, global arms agreements rose again to nearly $55 billion and global arms deliveries increased from nearly $32 billion in 2005 to over $34 billion in 2006.[94]

The United States has led the post-11 September arms extravaganza, increasing its exports dramatically, as well as adjusting its existing arms trade policy to fit what it considers to be a new security environment. Traditional US arms export policy, based on US legislation and regulations, executive orders and Administration policy statements, states that US arms exports should not undermine long-term security and stability, weaken democratic movements, support military coups, escalate arms races, exacerbate ongoing conflicts, cause arms build-ups in unstable regions, or be used to commit human rights abuses. The United States, however, has put these tenets on the back-burner in order to give highest priority to countries which are supporting US efforts in Afghanistan or Iraq and which assist in the eradication of international terrorist networks. In some cases, this new effort stands in stark contrast to previous arms export decisions.

An analysis of twenty-five countries[95] that play strategic roles in the United States' global anti-terror operations finds that the events of 11 September 2001 have dramatically increased US arms sales to countries that have been repeatedly criticized by the US State Department for human rights violations, lack of democracy and even support of terrorism and that, in some cases, are weak and failing states. Analysis of US government data on arms sales to these twenty-five countries reveals that, in the first five years following 11 September 2001, total US arms sales (Foreign Military Sales and Direct Commercial Sales) were worth four times more than those concluded in the five years prior to 11 September 2001. Moreover, these same countries received eighteen times more total US military assistance (Foreign Military Financing and International Military Education and Training) after 11 September than they had before. Perhaps even more striking, 72 per cent of the twenty-five countries received more military assistance and 64 per cent conducted more arms sales with the United States during the five years after 11 September than during the entire period between the end of the Cold War and 11 September 2001 (fiscal years (FY) 90–01).[96]

However, even as US military assistance to these countries is on the rise, already poor human rights situations in some of them have not improved, and have, in some cases, deteriorated still further. In 2006, the US State Department reported that 'serious', 'grave,' or 'significant' abuses were committed by the government or state security forces in more than half of these twenty-five countries. For example, in the years since 11 September 2001, Uzbekistan received nearly ten times the amount of military assistance that it received prior to 11 September despite the fact that the State Department has described the human rights situation in Uzbekistan as 'very poor' every year from 1993 until 2004, and in 2005 and 2006 reported that the situation 'continued to worsen'. Several countries now receiving increased quantities of US military assistance have also undergone serious political changes since 2001, and are in some cases quite unstable. In 2006 alone, Chad, Nepal and Thailand, all of which have enjoyed increased US military assistance, experienced widespread political upheaval and internal violence.

Countries besides the United States are also reaping the rewards of the upturn in global arms sales since 2001. In 2006, Russia increased its total arms agreements to $14.3 billion, from $7.3 billion in 2005. Although Russian arms sales fell to $10.4 billion in 2007, Russia continues to demonstrate a resurgent arms trade industry. Russia relies on China and India to purchase the bulk of the weapons that it exports each year, though it is making inroads into North Africa, the Middle East, Southeast Asia and Latin America.[97] Western European arms suppliers have seen their arms sales totals rise and fall based on large sales from single purchasers. For example, the United Kingdom had a major military procurement deal with Saudi Arabia, Germany enjoyed a large submarine sale to Brazil, and France saw a significant jump in its arms sales in 2005 – total sales increased to $8.4 billion (from $2.2 billion in 2004), in part due to a $3.5 billion attack submarine deal with India.[98]

A changing international arms trade environment

The international arms market has had to adjust to the changing international system. Major arms exporters and importers shift with changes in the geo-political landscape. Although the countries of the Middle East continue to present lucrative opportunities for arms sales, countries in South Asia – particularly India and Pakistan – have now become leading arms importers. In the developing world between 2002 and 2005, for example, Asia was the largest recipient of new arms agreements,[99] and India concluded nearly 18 per cent of all new arms transfer agreements and was the largest recipient of new arms agreements between 1998 and

2005.[100] Pakistan claimed the top spot for new arms agreements in 2006, concluding $5.1 billion in new arms purchases.[101] In 2007, Pakistan ranked third in new agreements in the developing world with another $4.2 billion.[102] Part of Asia's dominance can also be attributed to China. China has stepped up its role not only as a major arms exporter, but also as an importer. Although China primarily provides missiles and small arms to countries around the globe, it was the third-largest developing-world recipient of weapons between 2000 and 2007, behind only India and Saudi Arabia.[103]

Although Asia is playing an increasingly important role in global arms purchases, during the period of 2003–6 the Near East reclaimed its spot as the top arms-recipient region in the developing world, accounting for $46.7 billion in new arms agreements.[104] The United States is the largest supplier to this region and, in 2006, made new arms agreements with Israel for $1.2 billion, Saudi Arabia for $1.1 billion, Iraq for $920 million, Kuwait for $390 million, and Egypt for $280 million, among others.[105]

As the international system has grown more interconnected, the defence industry has had to adjust to the new market dynamics presented by globalization. More joint ventures and mergers have complicated the relationships between companies and countries. When global arms sales dropped after the end of the Cold War, the defence industry worldwide needed to consolidate to survive. The 1990s saw a significant number of mergers and acquisitions. In 1998, for example, the United States was left with only four major arms contractors – Boeing, Lockheed Martin, Northrop Grumman and Raytheon.[106] The consolidation of the defence industry is particularly remarkable since World War II. According to the US Government Accountability Office, the number of companies producing aircraft fell from twenty-six to seven between the end of the war and 1994, missile contractors from twenty-two to nine, and tank producers from sixteen to two.[107] During this unprecedented consolidation, governments

faced the new question of whether or not to allow foreign partners in the mergers and acquisitions taking place.[108] Because the
defence industry is owned or supported by the government to
varying degrees, depending on the country, the degree to which
foreign companies were integrated into the domestic defence
industry varied from country to country. However, by the late
1990s, joint ventures had become the name of the game as close
allies saw the benefit of developing and using the same military
hardware, including lower research and development costs for
each individual company and country, as well as increased interoperability. One prominent example of these new joint ventures
is the F-35 Lightning II, known as the Joint Strike Fighter, a joint
venture that was first conceived in 1993.[109] Nine countries are currently involved in the development, production, testing, training
and operation phases of the fighter jet.[110]

In addition to the fluctuation of importers and exporters and
consolidation of the defence industry, the international arms
trade in the post-11 September era is also marked by the rise in
importance of dual-use (those items with both military and commercial applications) and commercial technologies to the global
defence industry. A part of this turn toward dual-use technologies
has been rooted in the new global economy. Indeed, some saw the
military industrial complex as an impediment to economic vitality,
and believed that investment in dual-use items could spur greater
economic benefits for both the commercial and military sectors.[111]
Dunne and Surry found this trend to be crucial to explaining
recent changes in the global defence industry:

> Many areas of technology that were once the preserve of the
> military and security services, such as cryptography, now have
> primarily commercial applications. In addition, the use of
> standard commercial components is an increasing feature
> of the arms industry: many components of major weapon
> systems are commercial off-the-shelf-products, produced by
> manufacturers that would not consider themselves part of the

arms industry. The major contractors have become increasingly systems integrators, retaining the characteristics of defense specialized firms.[112]

Although technology developed by the military was the most cutting-edge between World War II and the 1980s, since the end of the Cold War technology developed in the commercial sector has become essential to weapons development. After the Cold War, the military suffered, with its technology quickly becoming obsolete and overshadowed by civilian advances.[113] Advances in military technology since the end of the Cold War have led to the development of many high-technology weapons, but these new weapons have come at a cost to older weapons systems. Many weapons have become obsolete and production lines have closed. In addition, the post-Cold War reliance on small arms and light weapons in the majority of conflicts around the world has meant that even the most advanced technology is not always necessary to fight wars.

Conclusion

To put the global arms trade in perspective, the international trade in oil and gas is valued at $1.7 trillion and the global trade in agricultural products is valued at $852 billion.[114] SIPRI puts the value of the global arms trade at only 0.4 per cent of total world trade.[115] Still, as will be discussed in chapter 3, the arms trade influences national and global economies and arms transfer decisions. By 2007, conventional arms transfer agreements worldwide amounted to nearly $60 billion. The international arms trade is clearly big business and continues to reflect new security challenges. However, it is important to keep in mind that this total only accounts for the legal trade in arms. The black market trade in arms is robust, as is the grey market – those sales that fall in the blurry category between the legal and illicit markets. Arms are also transferred in the shadows, on the edge of these various categories, through covert sales and operations. Details of these markets, the types of sales that occur there, and the effects of these sales on the international arms trade will be discussed further in chapter 4.

3

The legal supply and transfer of arms

In May 2007, representatives of the Royal Malaysian Air Force (RMAF) travelled to the Irkutsk Aviation plant in Siberia for a first glimpse of the Su-30MKM fighter aircraft they had ordered in 2003. Until the Su-30 purchase (and with the exception of a few, ageing Russian MiG-29s in its fleet), the RMAF had primarily been a client of western arms suppliers. But, although several manufacturers – including the United States – competed for the chance to upgrade the RMAF's fleet of combat aircraft, the RMAF signed a contract for eighteen Russian-produced jets during an August 2003 visit to Malaysia by Russian President Vladimir Putin.[1]

Why did the Malaysian Air Force choose the Russian aircraft after years of purchasing from other suppliers? The answer reflects the complexities of the global legal arms trade. In this particular instance, factors in play included the success that neighbouring India had experienced with the same aircraft, a competitive price, Malaysia's interest in diversifying its defence suppliers, and a Russian promise to train a Malaysian astronaut and send him to the International Space Station. Like many arms sales, the Malaysian Su-30 sale was a result of a variety of economic and political considerations, which are explored in this chapter.

The international arms trade is big business, worth nearly $60 billion a year in new arms sales agreements and $31 billion in arms deliveries in 2007 alone.[2] This chapter explores the legal arms trade – those sales that conform to international law and the national laws of the countries involved in the transfer, including transshipment countries – by profiling major suppliers and recipients, sources of legally traded arms, and emerging trends. In particular, the chapter examines how market trends influence competition and cooperation between companies, countries and regions, and the symbiotic relationship between technology development and the trade in arms. The mechanics of the arms trade – how weapons move from point of production or storage to the end-user – is also discussed. Finally, the chapter highlights and discusses the peculiarities of the small arms trade, a small but pertinent sub-category of the conventional weapons trade, valued at approximately $4 billion a year.

Why seek arms?

To understand fully the dynamics of the legal arms market, we must first examine why countries, groups or individuals seek arms, and why countries choose to sell them. Even though arms sales have increased since 11 September 2001, the arrival of a Democratic majority in the US Congress in January 2007 sparked fears within the defence industry that Congress would pursue a so-called 'peace dividend', which would channel funds away from defence priorities and into other, non-defence-related initiatives. Indeed, in May 2007, the head of the Boeing Company's defence unit went so far as to tell investors that pursuing a decrease in defence spending 'would be clearly the wrong thing to do with the aging equipment we [the US military] have and also the different threats that are out there that weren't out there the last time a peace dividend was achieved'.[3]

But Boeing need not worry just yet. No matter what the situation, there is always an opportunity to buy and sell weapons, the constant dissatisfaction of the defence industry notwithstanding. The Ferengi, a commerce-driven race inhabiting the fictional Star Trek universe, has two rules – 'war is good for business' and 'peace is good for business' – which accurately sum up the realities of the global arms market.⁴ Since the beginning of time, countries have sought weapons innovation to improve their military capacity. Arms are sought by countries preparing for conflict, replenishing supplies during conflict, rebuilding their armed forces after conflict and for self-defence. Countries also continually look to upgrade their existing systems or to modernize obsolete systems. Militaries can always find some new weapon they cannot live without, and governments are loath to admit their militaries are not the best-equipped with the latest technology.

Arms are sought for all of these reasons, as well as for more abstract ones, and thus the constant demand for weapons translates to a global arms production and export industry. With very few exceptions, countries need to make foreign purchases in order to fill all of their needs. While nearly all industrialized countries produce some conventional weapons, the most desired commodities, such as high-tech fighter jets, sophisticated counter-insurgency equipment and state-of-the-art warships, are produced by relatively few countries. As mentioned in chapter 2, the United States has dominated international arms exports since the end of the Cold War, though Russia is re-emerging as a dominant player. France, the United Kingdom and China, as well as Germany and Italy, round out the top tier of arms exporters and are responsible for the majority of global arms sales.

So how do countries decide from which country they want to purchase their foreign military equipment? Decisions as to what supplier will be chosen to provide weapons usually depend on two main factors: economics and politics.

Economics of the arms trade

Economic considerations encompass everything from the cost of weapons to the influences of globalization. France finds – as do many other exporters – that arms exports help the French economy in three distinct and important ways: 'competitiveness of defence industries, reducing equipment unit cost, and on the foreign trade balance'.[5] Yet, the global arms market does not operate under traditional market economics. Speers and Baker describe the post-Cold War arms market as 'oligopolistic', meaning that many defence companies have cosy relationships with foreign governments, making it exceptionally hard for new companies to break into the market and true competition impossible. Moreover, because governments are the major clients of the defence industry, they play an enormous role in determining what weapons are available to all customers, as well as the price of particular weapon systems. Furthermore, as weapons exports are tightly controlled by most governments, the defence industry is subject to the political priorities of the host government, and therefore does not have total control over business transactions.[6]

Even though the global arms market does not act like markets for other goods, cost and other economic indicators do still vary to a certain degree. The cost of a particular weapons system can readily fluctuate based on a variety of factors, including currency values, the modernity of the weapon purchased and offsets.

Changes in currency values can change the price of weapons overnight. In June 2007, Rosoboronexport, the Russian state-owned company responsible for the import and export of all defence equipment, announced that it proposed negotiating all defence contracts in euros, as opposed to rubles. Russian defence manufacturers were keen to make the switch because the relative instability of the Russian ruble vis-à-vis other world currencies meant that it was no longer profitable for them to do business. Moreover, many in the Russian defence industry favoured the switch, as it had an added political bonus for Russian defence companies. Avoiding American banks allowed Russian industry to keep their transactions and incentives for arms suppliers secret from US intelligence agencies.[7] The switch was proposed for two major sales to India – 230 Su-30 MKI fighter jets worth over $4 billion, and a Vikramaditya aircraft carrier worth over $1.5 billion.

When the deal was originally made in 2000, neither the Russians nor the Indians expected such a fast appreciation for the ruble. Without the switch to the euro, Russia would have to increase the annual price indexation to make the sale profitable for the Russian industry. In addition to the India sale, a Russian arms expert said that unfavourable currency exchange rates had also frozen a Russian sale to China for transport planes.[8]

Economic considerations for arms sales can also be based on prices of other goods in the global market. If a country suddenly loses cash on hand due to fluctuations in the prices of other exports, weapons purchases may be postponed or cancelled. In 1997, then President Bill Clinton lifted a twenty-year-old prohibition on high-tech arms transfers to Latin America, and decided that arms sales to the region would be considered on a case-by-case basis. Although many thought this decision would yield a flood of arms sales to Latin America, a global economic crisis derailed many potential deals. For example, when the price of copper fell in the late 1990s, Chile had to postpone a purchase of F-16s until 2003.[9] Under Chile's Reserved Copper Law, 10 per cent of copper revenues are split equally by the three branches of the armed forces to purchase equipment, meaning that, when the price of copper falls, the military has less money with which to procure defence equipment, and vice versa.[10] Thus, when the price of copper rose to a sixteen-year high in 2005, Chile went on a buying spree and, in addition to buying new fighter jets, signed letters of intent with the United Kingdom for three Type 23 frigates.[11]

Similarly, oil prices have historically influenced the arms-purchasing habits of countries in the Middle East. When oil prices fell in the late 1990s, many countries, most notably Saudi Arabia, went into debt in order to cover the costs of outstanding weapons contracts made in the boon after the end of the 1991 Gulf War. When oil prices rose again in the early 2000s, many Middle Eastern countries were much more hesitant to enter into new contracts.[12] However, arms sales did in fact increase. When oil revenues rose, beginning in 1998 (from a low of $12 per barrel to a high of over $50 per barrel in March 2005), Russian arms sales increased to the region, particularly to Algeria, Iran, the United Arab Emirates (UAE) and Yemen.[13] In 2007, as oil neared $60 a barrel, analysts anticipated that the UAE would spend up to 20 per cent of a potential $100 billion oil windfall on defence modernization.[14]

Offsets

Another economic factor in a country's decision to choose a certain country and/or company as an arms supplier are offsets, or 'industrial compensation required by a foreign government as a condition of purchase of . . . defence articles and services'.[15] Offsets can take the form of an item directly tied to the weapon, or goods and services completely unrelated to the purchase. A 2003 *New York Times* article revealed that, in exchange for weapons exports, the US defence industry did everything from building shipyards for foreign countries, to allowing foreign-made engines to be installed in US helicopters, to purchasing Danish Christmas hams for employees.[16]

In 2005, the US Department of Commerce's Bureau of Commerce and Industry issued a report on offsets that found offset demands are increasing around the world. Moreover, countries often choose a weapons manufacturer based on the value and utility of the offset package. In some cases, offset values can equal 100 per cent of the item that was actually sold, and some reports place the value of offsets at up to 300 per cent of the original defence article.[17] For example, in 2005, the Swedish Company Gripen approved an offset to Hungary valued at 110 per cent of the cost of the fourteen Gripen fighters purchased by the Hungarian Air Force. The offsets were exports of Hungarian products and investment in Hungarian industry, particularly by the Swedish companies Electrolux, Ericsson and Semecs.[18] In Europe, the European Defence Industry is attempting to rein in offsets in order to liberalize defence procurement to make sales more competitive. However, until there is a global effort to minimize offset agreements, they will continue to be attractive bonuses, if not required additions, to any foreign weapons purchase.

Politics of the arms trade

Just as economic considerations fluctuate, political considerations also play a major role in legal arms sales. Shifting political alliances can quickly open and close doors between potential customers and suppliers. During the 1970s, the United States sold F-14 Tomcat fighter jets to Iran, but immediately ceased all sales to Iran when the Shah was deposed by Islamic militants in 1979. The legacy of those arms transfers continues as those planes remain in the Iranian Air Force. Nearly thirty years later, in June 2007, the United States Congress banned all sales of F-14 spare parts, to avoid continued diversion of the parts to Iran. When the United States and the West cut off arms sales to Iran, Russia stepped in and discovered a lucrative and regular transfer partner. Similarly, Russia benefited from a $325 million arms deal with Kuwait when the United States refused to sell Kuwait the Stinger missile launchers that it had requested.[19]

Arms sales are often used as tools of foreign policy. During the Cold War, the United States and Soviet Union each filled the defence needs of their allies. The Soviet Union was so eager to cement favourable military relationships with its allies and fill their arsenals with Soviet defence equipment that some analysts estimate up to two-thirds of all Soviet arms exports were provided either free or on credit.[20] In addition to the Warsaw Pact countries, the Soviet Union sold millions of dollars' worth of arms to Central American countries, many of which were involved in proxy civil wars. For instance, before cutting off military exports at the end of the 1980s, the Soviet Union supplied the Sandinistas in Nicaragua with numerous helicopters and other arms to use against the US-backed Contra rebels. By the first half of the decade, Soviet arms exports to Nicaragua already totalled half a billion dollars.[21]

The end of the Cold War presented the opportunity for many countries to expand their lists of traditional arms trading partners and build new military and defence relationships. As former Warsaw Pact members sought to join the European Union and the North Atlantic Treaty Organization, they needed to replace their outdated and crumbling Soviet fleets with western-manufactured defence equipment. Several former Warsaw Pact countries have updated their military hardware, after finally raising the cash needed and making necessary political changes. In February 2007, Romania announced that it was looking to acquire four dozen new fighter jets and was considering replacing its Russian MiGs with US, Swedish or British aircraft. Poland also updated its fleet of fighter jets with four dozen US-made F-16s, and the Czech Republic turned to an Austrian subsidiary of US defence giant General Dynamics for an order of armoured personnel carriers.[22] All three of these countries had previously relied almost exclusively on Soviet weapons systems.

According to a former senior US Department of State official, the end of the Cold War has created new opportunities for arms exporters. The Middle East has been particularly fluid in its loyalties to arms producers. Prior to the 1991 Gulf War, Qatar bought solely French weapons. However, after the war, Qatar switched to US weaponry and is now a reliable US customer.[23] Similarly, the UAE, which bought billions of dollars of US weaponry after the 1991 Gulf War, is now one of the top three importers of Russian arms in the Middle East.[24]

As detailed in chapter 2, in the initial aftermath of the 1991 Gulf War a glut of weapons were sent to the Middle East, as countries rebuilt their militaries in the wake of Saddam Hussein's aggression. Following this binge, the region limited its arms purchases for the next decade. Since 2007, however, the threat from Iran has caused countries in the region to reassess their military power, and purchases are likely to increase.[25] Indeed, in May 2006, US Air Force Lt General Jeffrey Kohler, who is in charge of US government arms sales, told a Reuter's interviewer that all of Iran's neighbours were 'talking to the United States about ways to bolster their defences'. Although Kohler admitted that France and other countries might compete with the United States for these arms sales, he believed the United States was well positioned to win the sales, and that 'most of the countries realize that a partnership with the U.S. is critical' for dealing with the threats in the region.[26] In fact, according to Lockheed Martin, many Middle Eastern countries, in addition to Japan, have expressed increased interest in the Patriot Advanced Capability-3 (PAC-3) missile because of perceived threats from Iran and North Korea.[27]

Interoperability

Another political justification for arms sales has been interoperability. The US Department of Defense (DOD) defines interoperability as: 'the ability to operate in synergy in the execution of assigned tasks'.[28] Countries often seek to sell arms to countries they are fighting alongside in order to ensure that everyone is familiar with or using the same technology. While this sounds good in theory, in practice interoperability is difficult to achieve even within a single country's armed forces, let alone multinational forces and operations. Even when countries are using the same hardware, differences in measurement systems can cause tremendous difficulties. For example, during the 1991 Gulf War, US and British ammunition for the same weapon – the M109 155mm howitzer machine gun – could not be interchanged between US and British guns, as the propellant was measured in different metrics and created a different firing table solution.[29]

Building relationships post-9/11

Throughout history, arms sales have been used to influence state behaviour, and that trend readily continues today. Military diplomacy – the practice of trading arms for influence over another nation's foreign and domestic policies – is a popular tool in many

countries' foreign policy toolboxes. Craft highlights four elements
that are crucial for understanding when arms sales garner influence in a foreign country. First, the recipient must be dependent
on arms imports; second, the supplier must be either the sole supplier, or one of very few, to the country in question (influence is
inversely related to the number of current or potential suppliers);
third, gifts and grants allow more influence than cash purchases;
and, fourth, arms sales are more likely to affect foreign policy
instead of domestic policy, and inter-state conflicts rather than
internal conflicts.[30]

However, the reality is that using arms sales to encourage a
particular behaviour only works in very specific circumstances
and is otherwise very unlikely. For example, despite the billions
of dollars of military assistance it sends to Israel each year, the
United States does not have enough influence to control where
or how Israel uses US-provided weapons. For example, under US
export agreements, Israel is not permitted to use US-origin cluster
munitions in heavily populated civilian areas. However, in August
2006, the State Department began an investigation into the Israeli
Army's use of US-produced cluster bombs in Lebanon during the
summer 2006 Israel–Hezbollah war. The preliminary results of
the State Department investigation reveal that Israel used cluster
munitions in populated civilian areas, which may constitute a
violation of the terms of the sale.[31]

Even though military diplomacy is difficult to achieve, the
United States continues to use arms sales as a way to try to exert
influence, most recently as an incentive for countries to lend their
support to the US 'war on terror'. As mentioned in chapter 2, the
global arms market was significantly altered after 11 September,
and the United States, in particular, has profited from the new
economic and security landscapes and has used support for the
US 'global war on terrorism' as a primary focus for new and growing arms sales.

A former senior State Department official claims that convincing

Pakistani President Pervez Musharraf to switch his allegiance from the Taliban to the United States during the week after 11 September 2001 was the single most important post-11 September event for the United States, and essential to US prosecution of the war in Afghanistan. Although the United States had secured basing rights with Uzbekistan, military commanders said the war in Afghanistan would not have been possible without Pakistan's help and land rights. The official maintains that, for these reasons, Pakistan deserves to be rewarded with arms sales.[32]

The United States has readily obliged with increased military assistance and weapons sales, not only to Pakistan but to many other countries as well. In May 2007, the independent Center for Public Integrity reported that the United States had increased its total military aid by 50 per cent since 11 September 2001. In addition to Pakistan, billions of dollars of US military aid, often with lax or little oversight, has gone to countries that have upped their lobbying efforts and seek to be rewarded for their political and strategic alliance – such as Ethiopia, Indonesia and the Philippines.[33] Although it is too soon to tell if any of these post-11 September arms sales will have long-term effects on the policies of current US allies, the official we spoke to believes that courting these military relationships is crucial to success of the US effort in Iraq and Afghanistan, and globally.

Other countries have used the continuing war in Iraq as an opportunity to develop or cement military relationships with arms transfers. To demonstrate its support for US operations in Iraq and to supplement its participation in the US-led coalition, Hungary donated seventy-seven surplus tanks and millions of rounds of ammunition to the fledgeling Iraqi Army.[34] The transfer curried favour with both the United States and Iraq and paved the way for further arms sales to both countries.

Russia has also taken advantage of the post-11 September landscape, increasing its defence sales to countries shunned by the West as supporters of terrorism. Russia's continued arms transfers to Iran have infuriated the West, but Russia sees Iran as an important and 'untapped' market for Russian arms exports and has thus far been unwilling to halt weapons sales to the country.[35] To date, Russia has suffered few political or economic penalties for maintaining its defence relationship with Iran. And, as long as Iran remains isolated from the West, Russia has a virtual monopoly on sales to the alienated country.[36]

The mechanics of the legal arms trade

Political and economic factors clearly influence decisions to transfer arms, yet, once the decision has been made, how do weapons move from country to country through legal channels? The answers vary as each state has its own export and import policies and systems. Because there are no international arms trade controls (see chapter 6), the technical aspects of the arms trade differ depending on the countries involved in the trade. Examining different aspects of the arms trade from the five largest arms exporters – the United States, Russia, the United Kingdom, France and China – we can get a snapshot of the many ways in which the international arms trade works.

The United States: maintaining a comprehensive and multifaceted arms export system

As the world's largest arms exporter, the United States maintains one of the most complex and comprehensive arms export systems in the world to deal with the volume and size of its arms sales.[37] Although US arms are exported through a variety of channels, historically there are five main mechanisms – maintained by both the DOD and the US Department of State – through which the majority of US arms are transferred to other countries. Most arms are transferred through two main programmes: US FMS or Direct Commercial Sales (DCS), which are sales between US companies and foreign recipients. Leases of military equipment, the transfer of excess defence items and emergency drawdowns of DOD stocks are other traditional avenues for US arms to end up in the hands of foreign buyers.

A vast array of legislation, regulations and presidential directives govern US arms export policy and sales. Executive Order 11958 delegates presidential authority for arms exports to the DOD, Department of Commerce and Department of the Treasury, but the President also has the prerogative to change arms export policy through presidential directives. For example, during his term, President Bill Clinton released PDD) 34, which enunciated his conventional arms export policy, and most notably added commercial concerns ('[t]he impact on U.S. industry and the defence industrial base') to the list of criteria used to guide decision making about arms exports.[38] President George W. Bush used his term to waive sanctions on numerous countries, most notably India and Pakistan,[39] which has legitimated billions of dollars in arms sales to both countries. President Bush's Administration also undertook comprehensive reviews of US arms export policy and signed Defense Trade Cooperation treaties with the United Kingdom and Australia.

Decisions for most US arms sales follow the Regulations outlined in the 1976 Arms Export Control Act (AECA) and the 1961 Foreign Assistance Act.[40] The AECA delineates the President's arms sales authorities by creating limitations and restrictions concerning the use of defence articles, prohibiting arms exports to particular recipients, requiring the development of arms export controls, and setting out mandatory Congressional reporting requirements, such as advance notification to Congress for any major arms sale.[41] The Foreign Assistance Act (particularly sections 502, 503, 506 and 516) establishes the specific processes and procedures through which the United States provides foreign aid, including military assistance.

With a complex network of legislation, US arms transfers also require specific regulations to implement the various standards and laws. Thus, the International Traffic in Arms Regulations (ITAR) regulates US transfers of defence items and services, as identified in the US Munitions List (USML). The ITAR contains rules and regulations for arms manufacturers and brokers, establishes penalties for violations of rules and requirements, and explains the conditions that prohibit recipients from receiving US defence items and services. The State Department, with input from the DOD, determines what items should be on the USML. Dual-use items are under the jurisdiction of the Department of Commerce[40] and Commerce Control List (CCL). With a very few exceptions (namely, defence articles sold to Canada) all commercial sales of items on the USML require an export licence issued by the State Department. Small arms exports are handled in the same way as other conventional arms. However, small arms exports that fall under USML Category I and are over $1 million also go through a Congressional notification process. In addition, the State Department summarizes commercial sales of semi-automatic weapons in the annual Congressional Budget Justification for Foreign Operations.

By Presidential decree, various government agencies have a role to play in the US arms trade. The State Department's Directorate of Defense Trade Controls (DDTC), within the Political–Military Affairs Bureau, has primary responsibility for the administration and regulation of US arms exports. The DDTC is in charge of the registration of licensed arms manufacturers, brokers and exporters and reviews licence application requests, which totalled more than 80,000 in FY 2007.[43] The DDTC utilizes D-Trade, an Internet-based licence application procedure, to handle the majority of its licence requests. The DDTC also manages the State Department's end-use monitoring programme, known as Blue Lantern, which includes both pre-licence checks and post-shipment verifications. In FY 2007, the Blue Lantern programme initiated 705 end-use checks, which marked a 15 per cent increase over FY 2006 totals. Of the 634 Blue Lantern cases which concluded in FY 2007, 143, representing 23 per cent of all checks, received 'unfavorable' determinations.[44]

The DOD also has a key role in US arms exports. The DOD's largest role is to manage the US FMS programme. Through the FMS programme, governments and international institutions purchase US defence items and services directly from the US government – from existing DOD stocks or through DOD-awarded contracts. FMS requests are also reviewed by the appropriate State Department offices and other agencies. Additionally, Congress must be notified of prospective FMS agreements. Golden Sentry is the DOD's end-use monitoring programme, which conducts pre-sale, in-transit and post-transfer checks on sales and transfers.

The Commerce Department's Bureau of Industry and Security (BIS) is also responsible for the licensing and export of dual-use items and technology at the same time that it emphasizes US exports and international leadership in technology. With a seemingly contradictory mission, BIS is responsible for controls over satellites and other systems with both civil and military applications. Far fewer arms exports originate under BIS's purview than from the FMS or DCS programmes. In FY 2007, 19,512 export licence applications worth an estimated $52.6 billion passed through BIS's licensing officers – a 3 per cent increase in applications from the previous year, and the largest number of applications in over ten years. The BIS also has an investigatory role and in FY 2007 achieved sixteen individual and business convictions and levied over $25.3 million in criminal fines for export violations.[45]

US intelligence agencies collect information on diversions or illegal transfers, and the Department of Justice and US Attorneys handle court cases against violators of US arms export laws. The shipment of US defence articles is monitored by the Department of Homeland Security (DHS) Immigration and Customs Enforcement agency (ICE), the agency's largest investigative unit. In FY 2007, the agency made 188 arrests and achieved

127 convictions.[46] ICE investigations have successfully uncovered plots to ship illegal weapons to China, Indonesia, Iran and Sri Lanka, among many others, and have resulted in the successful prosecution of companies and individuals that have violated the AECA. Overall, ICE seeks 'to prevent terrorist groups and hostile nations from illegally obtaining US military products and sensitive technology, including weapons of mass destruction (WMD) components'.[47] The CPI unit is specifically focused on preventing and stopping arms export violations through inspection and interdiction, investigations and outreach and international cooperation. A unique way in which ICE operates is through 'Project Shield America', a programme that works directly with US defence companies and manufacturers. The programme is both a preventive measure to teach companies about US export control policies and help identify ways in which criminals or terrorists would try to acquire US defence products and a way to ask for their assistance in preventing illegal exports of their products. ICE has held more than 16,000 industry outreach visits since 2001.[48]

Under US law, particularly the AECA, Congress develops arms export legislation and oversees arms exports. Section 36 of the AECA requires Congressional notification of potential arms sales above a specified dollar value – depending on the type of weapon and recipient of the sale, the threshold can range from $1 million to $50 million. Then, the relevant Congressional Committees, in both the House of Representatives and Senate, review the sale to ensure it is in the US interest. Under the AECA, Congress can formally oppose or block a sale through joint and veto-proof resolutions of disapproval. Because this process is rife with bureaucracy, Congress's real power and authority on arms sales come in the form of legislation and accountability, whereby Congress can impose conditions on a sale or pass legislation on arms sales processes. Congress can also call members of the Administration to testify in hearings and to defend publicly certain arms trade policy decisions and explain specific arms sales. An informal notification process is also generally respected with the Administration and Congress, whereby members are given the opportunity to review the sale consultations and inquire about specific sale details.

Overall, this arrangement has worked well to prevent Congress from protesting a sale, causing embarrassment to the Administration. However, in December 2006, the Bush Administration waived the informal process with Congress concerning a $1 billion arms package for Pakistan, raising the ire of many members of Congress. The House International Relations Committee held a hearing in response and publicly rebuked the Bush Administration's decision to ignore the informal precedent. Assistant Secretary of State for Political–Military Affairs, John Hillen, admitted the intentional absence of the informal discussions and said Congress was powerless to stop the sale, causing tension between the Administration and Congress.

Since 2000, the United States has undertaken several attempts to modify its arms export control system. In May 2000, the Clinton Administration launched seventeen proposals under the Defense Trade Security Initiative (DTSI). These proposals were intended to streamline the arms export licensing process and expedite exports to close US allies, particularly Australia, Japan and NATO countries, as well as Sweden. Advocates of the proposals hoped that the DTSI would enhance joint and cooperative defence projects and allow US defence companies to work more easily with their foreign counterparts. While some DTSI proposals have been implemented, others have not and reform advocates have pushed to achieve greater changes. The Bush Administration has sought waivers from existing legislation to allow licence-free exports to Australia and the United Kingdom. Such attempts were blocked by Congress, and, in the summer of 2007, the United States announced it had reached defence cooperation treaties with both countries that essentially side-stepped Congressional opposition. The treaties have been met with scepticism from the Senate, which is responsible for ratifying them. Although a hearing was held on the British treaty in May 2008, the Bush Administration has yet to answer satisfactorily Senate concerns on treaty enforcement and implementation, and, thus, the treaties have not yet been ratified.

The Bush Administration also attempted overhauls of the US export control system, and reorganized the State Department's Office of Defense Trade Controls – making it a directorate with more licensing officers, more resources and updated technology. The Bush Administration also conducted a review of US defence controls in National Security Policy Directive 19 (NSPD-19). The classified review met strong opposition from Republicans in Congress and attempts were shelved in 2004. In spring 2007, the arms-industry-based Coalition for Security and Competitiveness introduced their new proposals for arms export reform. The industry's key argument is that process and procedural changes are imperative in order to help the United States and its allies more effectively fight the 'War on Terror'. Their proposals repackage the traditional mantra of 'higher fences around fewer items' – which advocated removing items from the USML – and instead suggest 'modernization', 'efficiency', 'predictability' and 'transparency' changes for the US arms export system. These groups advocate licence-free transfers and fast-tracking exports to close allies – all proposals that have been blocked by Congress in the past.

As mentioned in chapter 2, one of the most significant changes to US arms sales since 11 September 2001 has been the export of US weapons to countries that have patterns of human rights abuses and weakened democracy, and have supported terrorism. Now, the United States is also undermining traditional arms export programmes, which are funded out of the Foreign Operations budget and under State Department purview, in favour of newly created programmes that avoid such restrictions. The US government has created new counter-terrorism programmes that are funded by the Pentagon and under the DOD's oversight. Two such programmes are the Regional Defense Counterterrorism

Fellowship Programme (CTFP) and the 'train and equip' authority in Section 1206 of the defence authorization bill. At its inception in FY 2002, CTFP was to provide non-lethal anti-terrorism training to US allies. In FY 2004, the CTFP was changed to include lethal training. Although similar to the State Department's International Military Education and Training programme, CTFP does not contain the same prohibitions on training of human rights abusers. Training often precedes larger weapons deals and allows countries to get their foot in the door of US defence companies, paving the way for future collaboration. In 2006, the US government established 'train and equip' authority, which allows the DOD to train foreign militaries for counter-terrorism operations by using $200 million to $300 million of its Operation and Maintenance funds. This programme is not bound by legal restrictions on training and weapons recipients. These programmes are becoming increasingly popular among new allies in the US 'war on terror'. Although legislators have been cautious about these new programmes, the Pentagon is eager to expand such programmes and make them permanent.

Russia and an arms trade resurgence

While the United States arms trade system is quite developed and complex, the Russian arms export control system is far less so. When the Cold War ended and Russia inherited the Soviet legacy of arms production and sales, the new government was faced not only with maintaining or sustaining defence enterprises and competing in an international arms market, but with creating policies and procedures that would control the country's trade in international armaments. Although Russian arms sales initially and substantially declined following the end of the Cold War, Russia has re-emerged as a significant player in the international arms trade. Now, nearly twenty years later, Russia has developed conventional arms control capacities, but, according to the United States and other western countries, the Russian government continues to sell arms on the global market to questionable or undesirable end-users such as Iran, Syria, Venezuela and China.

Control over arms export decisions in Russia has changed hands frequently since the breakdown of the Soviet Union. First, the government allowed the arms industry to control, coordinate and manage arms exports while the government controlled export licensing. That arrangement changed to state control of weapons exports in 1997 when Presidential Decree #907 created the state arms company Rosvooruzhenie.[49] This organization too underwent reorganization in 2000 with the issuing of Presidential Decree #1834 establishing Rosoboronexport. Today, Rosoboronexport is the most significant player in the Russian arms trade as it is the only state-owned-and-operated agency that is allowed to import and export military items, dual-use products, technologies and services. In January 2007 the agency was made the sole exporter of Russian arms by government statute. Debates about the role and organization of Rosoboronexport have continued to rage, however, as other industrial agencies have argued for a restructured arms exporting process.[50]

Russia has established various legal instruments in an effort to control the arms trade process. In 1998, the Russian government adopted the Federal Law of the Russian Federation on Military–Technical Cooperation of the Russian Federation with Foreign States, which outlines legal arms exporting procedures. In December 2000, a presidential decree established the Committee for Military–Technical Cooperation with Foreign States, which became the primary arms export licensing authority. The Ministry of Foreign Affairs, Ministry of Defence, Ministry of Finance, Ministry of Economics, State Customs Service, Foreign Intelligence Service and Federal Security Service are also involved in the export licensing process. According to the Russian government, the Federal Law applies to all relevant actors and any activity involving export and import of military products, with the state-owned trading company, Rosoboronexport, mediating military cooperation and transfers.[51] Moreover, Russia is a member of international organizations that seek to control the unrestrained spread of conventional weaponry, such as the *Wassenaar Arrangement on Export Controls for Conventional Arms and Dual-Use Goods and Technologies*, and the Organisation of Security and Cooperation in Europe, both of which have established criteria for and principles on conventional weapons exports.[52]

Although Russia has expanded its arms export control system, the country continues to export weapons to countries with questionable records. For example, Russia has historically supplied major weapons systems to Iran, including tanks, air-to-air missiles and combat aircraft. In 2005 and 2006, numerous weapons deals were arranged between the two governments, whereby Russia would transfer to Iran surface-to-air missile defence systems and upgrades to tanks and aircraft, in addition to numerous small arms and light weapons. Reportedly, some of these small arms have been re-exported from Iran to Hamas and Hezbollah.[53] Moreover, in 2005 Russia sold $238 million of spare parts for fighter jets to China, and authorized China to re-export 150 jets, worth $2.3 billion, to Pakistan.[54] In May 2007, Russia was working on a contract to sell $2.2 billion of air defence weapons to Libya – a country that has not purchased Russian weapons for over fifteen years. As part of the deal, Russia plans to cancel Libyan debt in exchange for cooperation in the areas of fuel, energy and nuclear technology.[55]

Russia is also interested in expanding its arms exports to Latin America. The Russian government plans to open a helicopter maintenance and training centre in Venezuela, which has already purchased large quantities of helicopters from Russia. In August 2006, Russia sold twenty-four fighter aircraft to Venezuela and plans to modernize aircraft previously delivered to the country. The 2006 deal also included 100,000 Kalashnikov rifles.[56] Although Putin has refused to supply Syria with short-range ballistic missiles, Russia did cancel 73 per cent of Syria's debt in 2005 and authorized the transfer of air defence missile systems. Syria has provided Hezbollah with Russian-made weapons in the past, leading Russia to announce in February 2007 that it will supervise Syrian storage facilities to prevent the leakage of arms to terrorists. There are unconfirmed rumours, however, that Russia is planning to sell modern anti-aircraft systems, MiG-29 fighter jets, and surface-to-air missiles to Syria through Belarus.[57] Ultimately, Russian arms sales to Iran, Venezuela and Syria prompted the United States to issue sanctions prohibiting Russian defence contractors from doing business in the United States or working with US companies.[58]

Although Russia does not perceive a problem with what they consider to be legal and legitimate arms sales to countries such as Iran, Venezuela, China and others, the United States and its allies often do consider Russian weapons exports problematic. In response to US sanctions on Rosoboronexport, President Putin stated that Russia will not allow anyone to limit its arms sales. He argued that 'Russia has always adhered, does adhere and will adhere to all international obligations in the sphere of military cooperation, including the current regime of export control.'[59] Furthermore, Putin stated that 'Any attempts to bind us with other limits based on unilateral or political evaluations cannot and will not be accepted by us.'[60] Recent Russian arms exports have increased tensions with the United States, as the two largest arms exporters often compete directly for major weapons contracts – and neither may necessarily agree with the other regarding the security implications of particular arms deals.

Ultimately, Russia has made substantial progress in developing an arms trade mechanism that governs the country's legal weapons exports and, ideally, prevents illicit transfers. A legal basis and relevant institutions exist. The system is largely centralized, involving primarily one state-owned and sanctioned arms exporter. Russian authorities are more aware than ever before about arms control requirements, although most export control activity in Russia has focused almost exclusively on preventing the spread of weapons of mass destruction rather than on conventional arms.[61]

The United Kingdom: responding to arms trade scandal

Since 1997, the United Kingdom has revamped its arms export control system. Under the leadership of the Labour party, the United Kingdom has developed new domestic policies governing arms exports, as well as led international efforts to control the arms trade. However, a 2006 arms trade scandal and a 2007 report on British arms exports to human rights abusers has resulted in a review of the UK's current system and calls for major reform.

In the United Kingdom, arms exports are governed by the Consolidated Criteria, which are based on the EU Code of Conduct (see Appendix). The criteria describe the circumstances under which arms exports are determined. UK arms exports are also subject to a number of EU Regulations, notably the EC Dual-Use Regulation, the EC Regulations on Products used for Capital Punishment & Torture, and the Common Position on Brokering.[62] However, critics maintain that the system is weighted towards favourable licence decisions, including advising defence companies of the likelihood of a licence, and permitting exports unless a persuasive reason not to is provided.[63] In 2002, the UK government passed the Export Control Act (ECA), which developed a licensing process for arms trafficking and brokering. To facilitate increasing arms exports, in September 2007, the Export Control Organization (ECO) unveiled an electronic system for licence applications for arms exports, known as SPIRE.[64]

UK export licences for strategic goods are granted by the ECO in the Europe and World Trade Directorate of the Department for Business, Enterprise and Regulatory Reform (BERR). The Secretary of State for BERR, through ECO, relies on the Foreign and Commonwealth Office, the Ministry of Defence and, in certain circumstances, the Department for International Development for advice on determining arms exports.[65] Her Majesty's Revenue & Customs (HMRC) enforces the body of UK export control legislation and undertakes enforcement actions and investigations in order to prosecute appropriate cases.[66] The Quadripartite Select Committee (QSC), which is composed of members of the Defence, Foreign Affairs, International Development and Trade & Industry Committees, examines the UK government's expenditure on, administration of and policy for the licensing of arms and holds the government accountable for its decisions.[67]

The Export Control Act 2002 came into force on 1 May 2004. Prior to the ECA, UK arms exports were governed by the Import, Export, and Custom Powers (Defence) Act of 1939, which had been amended as the Import and Control Act 1990. The ECA outlines the UK government's controls over the arms trade, including establishing licensing procedures, requiring greater transparency on arms exports for Parliament and developing punitive measures for transfer violations. The ECA also clearly enunciates the criteria used to determine whether to grant arms exports.[68] Under the ECA, there are two types of licences – standard and open. Open licences have less publicly available information, for example with regards to value, than the standard licence, making it difficult to get a complete picture of the British arms trade.[69] The United Kingdom also regulates dual-use items through the European Union's EC Dual-Use Regulation, first published in 2000.

Britain's arms exports totalled $3.3 billion in deliveries and $3.1 billion in new agreements in 2006.[70] However, many of those transfers have been shrouded in controversy. Although Britain maintains a list of embargoed countries – primarily those that are embargoed under UN or EU guidelines – Britain has supplied arms to countries its own government has described as 'countries of major concern'. These transfers have occurred during the same period the United Kingdom is pushing an international Arms Trade Treaty (see chapter 6). A 2006 investigation revealed that Britain had exported weapons to nineteen of the twenty countries listed as 'countries of major concern' in the Foreign Office's annual human rights report. Only North Korea was denied arms transfers, among a group of countries that includes Burma, Uzbekistan, Indonesia and Sudan.[68] Some of these countries are under UN or EU arms embargoes; others are 'zones of major armed conflict' or what the Red Cross defines as 'hot spots'. Critics of the transfers point to the lack of strong British brokering laws, which have allowed weapons to be dumped around the world with impunity.[72]

Many critics have blamed the Defence Export Services Organization (DESO) for the contradiction in British arms exports and international control efforts. DESO, which was created in 1966 as the Defence Sales Organization, worked to market and push UK arms exports abroad.[73] DESO was part of the Ministry of Defence, yet the staff was made up of civil servants and it was led by a defence industry executive. Indeed, taxpayers funded the organization, but the chief's salary was supplemented by defence companies.[74] While DESO had been seen as instrumental in expanding Britain's role in the international arms market, it was also criticized for letting profit trump foreign policy considerations. With a focus purely on selling arms, DESO's staff of 450 worked to ensure that British arms were chosen over other countries' wares. For years, nongovernmental organizations repeatedly called for the shut-down of DESO, and the Labour government announced it was looking into cutting DESO as part of its overhaul of arms export policy and cost-cutting measures.

The debate over DESO intensified in December 2006 when the UK's Serious Fraud Office announced it was dropping an investigation concerning corruption regarding a British arms deal to Saudi Arabia. The investigation centred on BAE Systems – Britain's largest defence company and the fourth-largest arms producer in the world (see table 3.1). BAE was alleged to have created a slush fund for Saudi royal family members in order to cement an arms deal in the 1980s, an arms deal pushed by DESO and the government of Margaret Thatcher. Although the bribery investigation had been ongoing for two years, Prime Minister Tony Blair announced the probe was dropped because of possible harm to national security, claiming that Saudi Arabia would withdraw cooperation and intelligence sharing in the war on terror. The Saudis had threatened to cancel an order for seventy-two BAE Eurofighter Typhoon jets worth £10 billion if the investigation was not closed within ten days. Further, the Defence Industry Council – composed of six British defence companies – urged the probe's end due to the potential loss of jobs that could come from the concellation of the Eurofighter deal.

The Blair decision prompted worldwide criticism and action. In the United States, Justice Department officials met with British officials to discuss the case and a possible US probe, and offered to help tighten British law. Moreover, the European Commission announced plans to conduct its own investigation of the British handling of the inquiry, and the Organization for Economic Cooperation and Development's (OECD) Working Group on Bribery in International Business Transactions announced plans to continue the investigation as it potentially violated an article of the OECD Convention, of which Britain is a signatory.[75] In

Table 3.1: Top 10 largest arms-producing companies 2004[76]
1.   Boeing (US)
2.   Lockheed Martin (US)
3.   Northrop Grumman (US)
4.   BAE Systems (UK)
5.   Raytheon (US)
6.   General Dynamics (US)
7.   EADS (Europe)
8.   Thales (France)
9.   United Technologies (UTC) (US)
10.   L-3 Communications (US)

July 2007, Prime Minister Gordon Brown announced DESO's closure. UK Trade and Investment, a government entity that promotes British exports, took over the promotion of British arm sales.[77]

France: modernizing an antiquated arms export system

France's arms export regime is governed by Article 13 of a legislative decree from 18 April 1939, which was outlined in the Code of Defence. The decree prohibits all arms exports unless authorized by the French government. The arms export control system in France requires 'prior authorization to negotiate, authorization to conclude a sales operation, and authorization to export equipment'.[78] The 'Export/Import Decree' of 30 January 1967 establishes the conditions necessary for authorization. Implementation and enforcement of the sum of the French arms export decrees fall under Article 38 of the French Customs Code.[79]

Although under the authority and oversight of the Prime Minister, arms exports are also determined by the Commission for the Study of Military Equipment Exports (CIEEMG) and bound by the European Code of Conduct. The CIEEMG has administrative authority over French arms exports. Decree 55–965 of 16 July 1955 reorganized the CIEEMG, which is made up of three permanent members – the Ministries of Foreign and European Affairs, Defence and Finance – which all get one vote, as well as other relevant agencies depending on the topic. The CIEEMG looks at each export as a separate case and provides a determination to advise the Prime Minister, who makes the final decision to grant arms exports.[80] The arms export process, including licensing, is coordinated by the Section des autorisations financières et controle de la destination finale, Service des Autorisations Financières et Commerciales (SAFICO) in the Ministry of Finance's Customs and Excise Department. Once an arms export has received CIEEMG approval, the transfer requires SAFICO authorization to proceed. Enforcement of export control policies is left to the National Direction of Customs Research and Investigations (Direction Nationale des Recherches et Enquêtes Douanières), except for cases of espionage which are under the jurisdiction of the Ministry of the Interior's Direction de la Surveillance du Territoire.[81]

France controls its arms exports based on commodity and destination. Control lists, which inform exporters what items require a licence for export, are updated and published in the *Journal Officiel*. The French government periodically updates national control lists under a formal notice in relation to technology exports. Licensing determinations are then based on the destination of the export, organized into three groups of countries:

> Group One includes former CoCom members; Group Two includes Austria, Finland, Hong Kong, Ireland, Singapore, Sweden, Switzerland and Yugoslavia; Group Three includes all other countries. In general, exporters to Group One nations may be able to obtain preferential licenses. On the other hand, exporters to Group Three nations are subject to much stricter licensing requirements, requiring both an individual export license and a letter of intent by the co-signee declaring that it will not retransfer the exported items.[82]

France began to control its exports of dual-use goods in 1994. Since 1995, France controls its dual-use exports in accordance with European rules, which have been most recently amended as EU Regulation 1334/2000 of 22 June. All EU member states utilize the same lists of controlled goods and technologies.[83]

Since the end of the Cold War, France has consistently been the world's third-largest arms exporter. Yet, in recent years, France's market share has decreased. France opposes the EU arms embargo to China and calls for its lifting, and in 2007 the country lost several major sales due to a lack of competitiveness and coordination within the French government system. Thus, when French Defence Minister Hervé Morin undertook his current position, he prioritized modernizing the French export control process.[84] In December 2007, Morin announced a new strategic direction, based on two main principles – control of, and support for, the French system. Morin unveiled the new plan for boosting arms exports, which focuses on 'three major initiatives intended to: develop a national strategic plan to support defence exports; modernize ways of coordinating support measures; and reorganize procedures for the sale and disposal of surplus and second-hand equipment'.[85] According to Morin, the new plan will help France 'reduce processing times for export applications; simplify and reduce procedures of industry; align France's list of military equipment with European norms; reinforce dialogue with industry, with a special emphasis in favour of Small and Medium Enterprises (SMEs); and facilitate changes with European partners and allies'.[86]

Among the changes proposed have been: to develop a new inter-ministerial computer system known as SIEX to handle all licensing approvals; to use the online ENODIOS system to handle industry export requests; to reduce the applications that are tabled and provide a 'yes' or 'no' decision on export requests as quickly as possible; to take advantage of an accelerated decision process to handle decisions regularly, rather than making decisions only at the monthly CIEEMG meetings; to utilize global approvals for licences to European and allied partners, rather than requiring a licence for each export; and to adopt the European Union's export-controlled equipment list.[87]

France seems to be taking guidance and suggestions from the US export control system. Indeed, Morin admitted that France is 'considering adopting the Pentagon's Foreign Military Sales procedure to allow government-to-government contracts in addition to normal commercial deals'.[88] In the meantime, under Morin's new plan, France will 'computerize requests for export licenses, cut delays in handling applications, and ease restrictions on products and personnel moving within the European Union'.[89]

Chinese arms sales, restraints and secrets

In response to criticism regarding arms sales to Iraq, Iran and Pakistan, China began to develop a system of conventional arms controls in the early 1990s.[90] In 1992 the government created the Military Exports Leading Small Group to oversee and approve all sensitive military exports. An arms trade office was established within the People's Liberation Army to administer the Small Group's work, and the Ministry of Foreign Affairs (MFA) became involved in considering the foreign policy consequences of China's arms exports. This process was in place for five years, but in 1997 China issued more detailed regulations regarding military sales – the Regulations on Export Control of Military Products. These regulations specifically outlined the arms export licensing process, but loopholes, such as the lack of a list of controlled military items, led to the exploitation of the rules. The regulations were, therefore, updated and improved in 2002 and serve as the basis for arms export procedures today.[91]

Regarding export procedures, only authorized weapons companies may export arms from China – and only a handful of defence enterprises have such authority. Before exporting arms, these companies must first submit a proposal for examination to the Commission on Science, Technology, and Industry for National Defence (COSTIND) – a commission established in 1982 as the primary agency overseeing all of China's defence enterprises.[92] COSTIND reviews proposals and either approves or rejects the applications, sometimes in consultation with high-level offices in the State Council and the Central Military Commission. When foreign policy issues must be considered, the MFA is also consulted. When a proposal for an arms deal is approved, the company may sign a contract with the recipient, but it must then submit another application with the contract to COSTIND for further review. Relevant documents such as end-use and end-user certificates from the recipient country must also be provided. COSTIND may then issue an export licence on the basis of the proposal approval, contract and valid documents. Chinese Customs must then examine the licence and clear the export for delivery. Finally, COSTIND issues internal notices of the approved export informing other government agencies and local government officials that the arms transfer may proceed.[93]

Because of this legal arms trade process, Chinese officials have refuted international criticism and suggest that the government abides by Chinese law and adheres to national and international standards regarding weapons exports.[94] Officials have, in fact, argued that their arms exports are guided by three principles: (1) arms exports should help enhance the self-defence capability of import countries; (2) exports should not impair regional and global peace, security and stability; and (3) exports should not be used to interfere with the internal affairs of recipient countries.[95] Analysts report that China is committed to arms control because of the negative consequences for China's international reputation, the need to enhance Sino-US relations, and the recognition that weapons proliferation endangers China's long-term interests.[96] Moreover, China has publicly announced its concerns about the illicit trade in small arms and light weapons, suggesting that China 'has formulated strict laws and administrative regulations in this regard'.[97] China is even said to be working with African nations, after the signing of the Beijing Declaration at the Forum of China–Africa Cooperation Ministerial Conference in 2000, to strengthen efforts focused on illegal weapons production, circulation and trafficking.[98]

Although China has not contributed to the international arms market at the same level as the United States, Russia, the United Kingdom and France,[99] the Chinese, like the Russians, have been criticized for their weapons sales to countries of concern. Unlike the Russians, however, China is not integrated into international arms control mechanisms such as the Wassenaar Arrangement. Moreover, China rarely offers information about its arms exports to the UN Conventional Arms Registry[100] and, according to some, the government regularly flouts international norms regarding appropriate and legal weapons transfers.[101] Transfers of aircraft, arms and ammunition to Sudan in the mid-2000s, for example, caused significant international outcry.[102] Some even suggested that the 2008 Summer Olympics in Beijing be branded the 'genocide Olympics' to bring attention to China's supply of weapons to a country where genocide is taking place in the Darfur region.[103]

Other Chinese arms deals have also raised concerns. Weapons transfers to Iran and Iraq in the 1980s increased global awareness of China's role as a major exporter of military items. In particular, the sale of Silkworm missiles to Iran in the 1980s and ballistic missiles to Pakistan in the 1990s heightened concern about Chinese arms sales in the United States and elsewhere in the international community.[104] China sold Ethiopia and its neighbour Eritrea hundreds of millions of dollars' worth of weapons before and during their border war from 1998 and 2000. Other African and Asian countries – such as Burundi, Tanzania, Zimbabwe, Nigeria, Angola, Burma, North Korea and Thailand – are also major recipients of Chinese arms, many of which have been used to fuel insurgencies and violent conflict.[105]

Despite the legal process in place for licensing weapons exports and Chinese government insistence that their country abides by national law and international principles regarding conventional arms transfers, Chinese experts suggest that government authorities in China are much more interested in, and focus most of their energy on, preventing transfers of WMDs. In fact, the primary international agreements to which China has become a party focus on WMDs – the Nuclear Non-proliferation Treaty, the Chemical Weapons Convention, and the Comprehensive Test Ban Treaty.[106] Chinese officials are, according to weapons proliferation experts in China, far less concerned with conventional weapons proliferation. Experts suggest that it took nearly two decades for the Chinese government to accept norms and ideas regarding the spread of WMDs and that it will take just as long, if not longer, to internalize similar ideas regarding conventional arms.[107]

Who buys weapons?

Although analysts, policy makers and the media often focus primarily on the countries that supply weapons, an equally important aspect is which countries are purchasing these billions of dollars of weapons every year. As legal suppliers of weapons become more diverse and globalized, so too do the recipients. Recipients of arms transfers have been affected by geo-political events – those based on political upheaval and economic turmoil. During the Cold War, the Soviet Union and United States supplied their proxies without interference. Now, the arms market is much more open, with Russia and the United States arming former enemies. For example, Russia has made several lucrative deals with Venezuela (a former US recipient) for both heavy conventional weapons and small arms, while the United States is a major supplier for former Soviet states, including Georgia, which entered into a conflict with Russia in the fall of 2008. Similarly, economic booms and busts can influence whether a country purchases weapons or waits for better economic circumstances, as described above. For example, although the price of oil skyrocketed in 2008, generating huge profits that could be used by oil-supplying states for new weapons acquisitions, some oil-consuming states faced budget shortfalls and had to halt or reduce their weapons purchases.[108]

As mentioned in chapter 2, today the Middle East is the world's largest arms-importing region. However, Asia and Europe also buy weapons in increasing numbers. For example, in 2006, Australia was the largest recipient of weapons from the United States with $1.7 billion in new deliveries. Although Israel, Egypt and Saudi Arabia were the second-, third- and fourth-largest weapons importers from the United States in 2006, respectively, Asia also had an additional three countries in the top ten – Taiwan (fifth), South Korea (eighth) and Japan (ninth). Europe also had three countries in the top ten recipients of US weapons – the Netherlands (sixth), Poland (seventh) and Greece (tenth).[109] In addition, as Russia looks to continue its new partnership with Venezuela, Brazil and Chile will also seek to acquire new weapons, potentially renewing an arms race in South America.

China: not just an arms exporter

On 1 April 2001, an American EP-3E surveillance plane collided with a Chinese F-8 fighter, forcing the American pilots to land on the Chinese island of Hainan.[110] Before landing, the EP-3E was able to photograph the Chinese fighter jet and noted that under the wings were Israeli-made Python 3 missiles. This finding seemed to confirm continued Chinese arms imports and indicated that US allies are infusing China with significant military capability, in direct contravention of US wishes. Although the United States has been somewhat successful in blocking many military sales to China – preventing, for example, the Israeli government from transferring the Phalcon airborne radar – it has been unable to thwart all arms sales to the country. In general, China's weapons exports in the 1990s to governments such as Iran and Iraq are seemingly related to previous Chinese weapons imports from countries like Israel.[111]

China's role as a recipient has often been overlooked. On occasion, re-exports of these Chinese military imports to other countries have raised concerns. The value of Chinese arms imports has grown from approximately $5 million in 1980 to nearly $4 billion in 2006.[112] Occasional spikes in weapons imports have been evident throughout that time period, but, beginning in 1992, China has consistently received billions of dollars' worth of armaments from numerous suppliers. Russia transfers the overwhelming bulk of Chinese weapons imports.[113] Indeed, approximately 45 per cent of Russia's total arms exports are trans-ferred to China. Since 1992, Russia has sold $26 billion in arms to China.[114] Europe also supplies weapons to China, despite an EU arms embargo that was placed on China after the 1989 crackdown on democracy protestors in Tiananmen Square.[115] France leads European military exports to China, with $1.2 billion in arms since the 1980s. Germany exported $339 million in arms to China, and the UK $242 million, during the same period.[116] Moreover, the UK has been training Chinese military officers at the Royal Military Academy Sandhurst.[117]

In an effort to modernize the country's military, China has significantly increased its military spending in recent years, pur-chasing primarily naval destroyers, submarines and fighter jets. However, Chinese arms imports have recently declined, and China is instead increasing its import of 'cutting-edge Western technology'.[118] Arms deals with Russia, for example, were cut in half in 2007 as far fewer weapons deals were made.[119] Instead of focusing on weapons systems, China is actively purchasing information technology, aerospace equipment, microelectronics and other high-tech commercial items. Although many coun-tries are concerned about the security risks of some technology transfers to China, the risks are often outweighed by the eco-nomic benefits to the exporter. Although the United States, for example, has criticized European arms sales to China, and has actively opposed the lifting of the EU arms embargo, the United States has nearly doubled its high-tech exports to China, valued at approximately $18 billion in 2007. Many agree that 'China is the poster child for the double-edged nature of globalization and technology'.[120] China's military imports – both conventional weapons and sensitive technology – are concerning to many gov-ernments, as they struggle to understand whether the Chinese government intends to abide by international regulations and standards of behaviour regarding the use and re-export of these deadly items.[121]

From where do weapons come?

Looking for a bargain: the bizarre world of arms shows

With so many potential suppliers, once a country decides that it is in the market for a new weapons system, the best way to go shopping for one is to attend an arms show. Arms shows are more than a venue for countries and companies to showcase their wares and entice governments to purchase particular technologies – they also include major social events for governments and industry to schmooze over cocktails as they discuss the relative efficiency of weapons systems. Bill Hartung describes the 1991 Paris Air Show:

> Temporary money exchanges, refreshment stands, and even a haircutting salon were being set up to accommodate the tens of thousands of visitors expected to attend the daily sessions. A small army of caterers and florists ferried provisions to the long rows of corporate entertainment 'chalets' that were being built specially for the occasion to wine and dine potential clients. Invitations had already gone out for the dizzying round of luncheons, receptions, and parties in and around Paris that had become an integral part of the air show experience.[122]

Companies are also careful to euphemize the exact nature of their business, referring to missiles and battleships in vague terms such as, '"battlefield management systems" and "mission packages"'.[123] These shows are incredibly successful for defence companies. At the 2005 Idex exhibition in the United Arab Emirates, $2 billion of weapons deals were completed during the show's five days.[124]

Even if a customer wants to buy a weapons system they see at an arms show, there are no guarantees that an export licence will be granted to sell them that particular system. However, getting potential customers to an arms show is the first step toward making a sale. And even countries with poor human rights records are allowed to attend international arms shows. At the 2005 Defence Systems & Equipment International (DSEI), the British government listed sixty countries invited to the show to shop for weapons from 300 companies. To the consternation of many, the list included Saudi Arabia, Vietnam, Colombia, Algeria, Jordan, Indonesia, Libya and Iraq, all countries that had been singled out by the British Foreign Office for poor human rights records.[125]

Although such shows are traditionally left to first- and second-tier arms suppliers, developing countries are now getting into the arms show game. These third-tier suppliers are not only increasing their share of arms imports, but pitching their wares as well. Amnesty International's study of arms shows revealed that, at the Eurosatory 1992 exhibition in Paris, only two Middle East companies represented non-European exhibitors. By Eurosatory 2006, fifty-two companies from the Middle East and ten Asian-Pacific companies participated. Similarly, at the annual United Arab Emirates arms show, Idex, companies from the Asia Pacific region more than doubled in number and Southeast Asian companies increased their participation threefold, between 1999 and 2006.[126]

Once a country decides on a specific weapons system and identifies the country of origin for that purchase, the actual sale begins. This can be a complex or simple process, depending on the countries involved.[127] Once the details of the sale – price, quantity, method of payment – are hammered out, the weapons have to be delivered. These weapons can come from one of two places: new production or existing stockpiles.

Arms production

Most industrialized countries have the capacity to produce at least some kind of conventional weapons systems. Throughout history, states have worked to develop their own arms in order to assert power and engage in military operations, or for self-defence. Krause organizes arms producers into tiers in order to illustrate the various levels of capacity to produce weapons possessed by various countries. In Krause's framework, the United States and the former Soviet Union are first-tier producers, European countries fall into the second tier, and the third tier is reserved for countries that are more limited in their arms production capabilities, such as Brazil, Argentina, Egypt, India, Iran and South Africa.[128]

Krause's analysis was published in 1992, but his findings hold true. Although Russia faced a temporary slump in production after the Cold War, the same countries that dominated the arms production landscape during the Cold War continue to do so today. According to SIPRI, seven of the ten largest arms-producing companies in 2004 were US companies (the remaining three were European).[129] Only eighteen countries are represented in SIPRI's list of the top 100 arms-producing companies.[130] Although many countries are involved in arms production in some capacity, the top tier of production continues to be dominated by very few of them.

National Procurement

National procurement is another reason to produce arms, yet is also relevant to arms exports as well. Countries produce weapons for their own use, yet they may decide to export the same item, or a stripped-down version, in order to lower the unit cost of production. However, as Speers and Baker point out, this practice essentially amounts to a 'taxpayer subsidy on the initial [R&D] investment that companies use to drive export profits'.[131] The end of the Cold War has resulted in falling rates of national procurement, without a commensurate drop in production rates of defence manufacturers,[132] and with costs associated with R&D for new weapons systems continuing to rise,[133] arms exports must make up this difference and offset weapons research and development costs to a greater extent than during the Cold War.

National procurement is also used to replace obsolete and outdated systems. In January 2007, Boeing Defence Unit Chief James Albaugh told an audience of investors that more military spending was crucial as 'much of this equipment [has not been replaced] since the 1980s and 1990s, and of course the obsolescence is being accelerated by all the use it is seeing over in Iraq and Afghanistan'.[134] When wars last for several years, countries are often forced to replenish dwindling supplies of weapons and munitions. Thus, defence companies and governments are eager to increase exports at the same time, in order to cut down on production costs and increase potential industry revenue.

Globalization of the defence industry

As mentioned in chapter 2, the globalization of the arms industry and the resulting mergers and acquisitions have changed the arms export landscape. The defence industry saw significant consolidation in the 1990s – particularly between 1993 and 1998 – and most major mergers and acquisitions took place due to political and economic disruption that occurred during that period: fewer threats meant fewer weapons were required, and a global economic crisis meant less money to buy weapons. Now, the defence industry is experiencing lower levels of consolidation, but current consolidation is motivated by altering needs of militaries due to the changing nature of conflict.

Consolidation of the defence industry in recent years has been primarily driven by companies' desire to move into new sectors of the defence industry and acquire capabilities that fill emerging technology gaps. But rather than major companies joining forces, larger companies are tending to acquire smaller companies that focus on the new technologies. Globalization has effected where companies manufacture and compete for business – BAE working in the United States, for example – but also how companies and countries do business – Russia switching their arms prices to euros, for example. In addition, some consolidation has occurred as foreign companies attempt to acquire US companies for a piece of the lucrative US arms market. The wars in Afghanistan and Iraq have benefited US defence companies, and foreign companies are eager to cash in on the opportunity. BAE's acquisition of United Defense is one example of this effort. The $4.192 billion sale marks the largest purchase of a US defence contractor by a foreign company and makes BAE the sixth-largest contractor for the DOD.[135]

However, a former senior US Department of State official rightly notes that 'there are no defence industries without borders'.[136] Companies, no matter where they operate, will be subject to government oversight of their activities; thus globalization of the defence industry can only occur to a certain extent. For example, BAE North America buying a Swedish company as one of its subsidiaries expands the goods produced by BAE, but, in the end, it does not affect US arms sales or the way the USA does business. The United States will still produce its complement of products, will still compete for arms sales with other countries and companies, and will still hold to its standard of arms exporters. BAE's acquisition will only change the name of the competitor for the United States, not the quality of its product or its sales strategy.

New technologies

Globalization has also affected the battlefield, and new kinds of weapons systems and weapons technologies are being sought by militaries around the world. This military transformation focuses on what is called 'network-centric warfare', where militaries are focused on real-time information and connecting the variety of forces it has in the field. A former State Department official believes the availability of new technologies will continue to be the major trend in global arms sales. According to the official, night vision equipment and Unmanned Aerial Vehicles (UAVs) are the 'next big things' for global arms sales. He claims that these kinds of technological advance allow small units to have fantastic situational awareness over large areas. And the official believes that, if industry could develop effective technology to counter improvised explosive devices (IEDs), that would be even better and make a lot of money for the companies.[137]

While the US official is correct about how these new technologies are affecting the global arms market, US struggles in Iraq and Afghanistan have allowed some critics to encourage more of a focus on traditional weapons systems as a better use of defence spending, and, thus, low-technology systems continue to be pursued.

Weapons stockpiles

Weapons can also be purchased or transferred from existing stockpiles of weapons (for a discussion of illicit transfers from existing stockpiles, see chapter 4). These weapons, which often sit idle in warehouses, can be lucrative sources of income to revive struggling economies or for countries that use military exports to support production lines used for their own national military procurement.

The end of the Cold War created a weapons bonanza, and many weapons that flooded the market were used to fuel conflicts and create arms races in various regions of the globe. The fall of the Soviet Union left storage facilities throughout the former Soviet states and satellite countries full of weapons accumulated during the Cold War build-up. These weapons quickly became obsolete as new geo-political alliances were formed and former Warsaw Pact members, eager to join NATO, upgraded their militaries in order to comply with NATO standards.

Moreover, without the threat of a world war looming overhead, many countries felt as though they could downsize their armed forces and state arsenals. Many countries profited, both legally and illicitly, from sales of these weapons. Human Rights Watch has documented and reported particularly troubling arms sales that took place during the 1990s, prompted by overflowing weapons stockpiles and the transition from a bi-polar world. Included among the numerous examples brought to light by Human Rights Watch were Bulgarian tanks sold to Ethiopia and Uganda, German combat vehicles and artillery systems sold to Turkey,

Russian ammunition and armoured vehicles sold to Burundi, and Ukrainian arms that made it into the hands of Rwandan exile forces in Zaire.[138]

The United States has created an entire programme dedicated to exporting stockpiled weapons it has no need for. The US Excess Defense Articles (EDA) Program has been referred to as a flea market or yard sale for US weapons, and is a programme that either sells surplus and obsolete weaponry at drastically reduced prices or gives weapons away for free to invited governments. The programme has grown in recent years. In 2006, the equipment available for acquisition through the EDA programme was originally worth $1.56 billion, twice the value of the defence articles available in 2005. Managers of the programme expect further growth in the coming years as the US Coast Guard is slated to receive new ships, helicopters and planes, rendering their current equipment surplus. According to a *New York Times* exposé on the programme:

> Between 2000 and 2005, the Pentagon offered up wares origi-nally valued at $8 billion: helicopters, torpedoes, airplanes, a wind tunnel, utility landing craft, cargo trucks, high-power radars, missiles, ammunition, uniforms and tenders, harbor craft and other vessels. Around $2 billion of this merchandise was given away to countries deemed needy enough to qualify. Another $800 million worth of defense equipment was sold at drastically reduced prices – even as low as 5 cents on the dollar.[139]

These giveaways are used as enticements to develop defence relationships and encourage future sales of US defence equip-ment to countries already familiar with the products. The *New York Times* report points to the delivery of two used F-16s to Pakistan, which are described as 'a sign of appreciation for its help to the United States when it invaded Afghanistan after 9/11' – as part of the EDA programme. The 1980s-era planes were still worth approximately $6.5 million, but Pakistan received them at no cost. Soon after, Pakistan ordered a fleet of sixteen more advanced F-16s, at a cost of $5 billion.[140]

The legal small arms trade

In any analysis of the arms trade, a discussion of small arms and light weapons – an important sub-category of conventional weapons, hereafter referred to primarily as 'small arms' – must be included. Although part of the larger conventional weapons category, small arms are usually dealt with separately from their heavier counterparts. According to the widely accepted United Nations definition, small arms include revolvers and self-loading pistols, rifles and carbines, assault rifles, sub-machine guns and light machine guns; and light weapons include heavy machine guns, hand-held under-barrel and mounted grenade launchers, portable anti-tank and anti-aircraft guns, recoilless rifles, portable launchers of anti-tank and anti-aircraft missile systems and mortars of less than 100mm calibre.[141] In other words, small arms are any weapon that can be carried by one or two people, mounted on a vehicle or carried by a pack animal.

In the intra-state conflicts of the post-Cold War world, the majority of fighting has been done with small arms. These weapons are used by both governments and non-state actors fighting in conflicts around the world. In fact, small arms have been the primary, and in most cases only, weapons of war in all but a handful of conflicts fought since the early 1990s. While the costs and consequences of weapons proliferation will be further discussed in chapter 5, it is worth noting that hundreds of thousands of people are killed every year by these weapons in conflicts, and an additional 200,000 people are killed in countries at peace. Many of these deaths are attributed to legal small arms purchases and transfers.

Small arms have such a large impact for two primary reasons: they are easy to use and they are abundantly available. According to the Small Arms Survey (SAS), nearly 875 million small arms are in circulation around the world.[142] The SAS breaks down this total figure into approximately 241.6 million military firearms, 22 million shoulder-fired rocket launchers and 781,000 mortars.[143] In addition, 75 per cent of the global supply of weapons (approximately 650 million weapons) is thought to be held by civilians, rather than national militaries, armed groups or police.[144]

Where do small arms come from?

Just like heavy conventional weapons, small arms are available for purchase on legal markets from increasing numbers of suppliers. Purchasers have even more potential sources since the end of the Cold War.[145] When the Cold War ended, many small arms stockpiles became obsolete due to upgrades, or superfluous to the security needs of a given country due to the changing political environment. Many of the Cold War-era weapons were sold, both legally and illicitly, at the end of the Cold War by countries eager to bring money in quickly.

Ukraine is a clear example of a country that had an abundance of weapons and took advantage of many opportunities to acquire cash through the sales of both heavy conventional weapons and small arms and light weapons. In 1998, a Ukrainian Parliamentary Commission estimated that, at its independence in 1992, Ukraine's military stocks were worth $89 billion. During the following six years, countries around the world reported at least $11 million in imports from Ukraine of small arms and light weapons,[146] and Ukraine reported the export of 319 battle tanks, 186 armoured combat vehicles, 29 combat aircraft, 7 attack helicopters and 351 missiles and missile launchers to the UN Register of Conventional Arms. However, the Commission found that, over these six years, weapons from Ukrainian stocks totalling approximately $32 billion were stolen and re-sold abroad. This investigation was the only one to examine the illegal arms flows and no action was taken on the findings of the Commission.[147] More recently, the NATO Maintenance and Supply Agency estimated that 7 million small arms and 2 million tons of ammunition remain stored insecurely in more than 80 depots across Ukraine.[148]

Existing weapons stockpiles are only one source of weapons. New supplies of small arms are produced every year and added to their global circulation. The SAS reports that more than 1,200 companies in over ninety countries produce 8 million new small arms annually.[149] While the small arms trade has nowhere near the value of the heavy conventional weapons trade, it still brings in an estimated $5 billion each year – approximately $4 billion in legal sales and $1 billion in illegal sales.[150]

The accuracy and reliability of small arms transfer data are difficult to determine. Unlike the heavy conventional arms trade, there are few national transparency mechanisms, and no international ones at all, to help determine the sources, quantity and value of the legal small arms trade (for more on control efforts, see chapter 6). Instead, analysts use a variety of sources to try to piece together an accurate picture of the global small arms trade. For example, according to one report, the US small arms manufacturing industry's 2006 revenue totalled approximately $2.15 billion, based on the 178 companies that manufactured individual firearms.[151] Although specific information on every country is difficult to ascertain, we can still discern several distinct patterns in small arms production and transfer. The majority of small arms producers are in the global north – 80 per cent of producers are located either in Europe and the former Soviet Union, or in North and Central America. Moreover, just as with heavy conventional weapons, the P-5 (the five permanent members of the Security Council – China, France, Russia, the United States and the United Kingdom) are significant arms producers and exporters. Along with Germany and Italy, the P-5 exported more than 1 billion dollars' worth of small arms in 2003.[152]

Small arms production also takes place in the global south, although few of these producers are globally significant. For instance, the SAS reports that there are at least thirty-eight small-arms-producing companies in Sub-Saharan Africa, but South African arms companies are the only significant exporters in the region.[153] Likewise, Brazil is by far the only significant small arms producer in Latin America, with nearly ten times the volume of small arms exports of Argentina, its closest competitor.[154]

Small arms are also procured by national governments for their own militaries. Procurement can replenish depleted supplies, prepare for upcoming military operations or, in some cases, modernize or upgrade government forces. According to an analysis of 151 militaries conducted by the SAS, approximately 1 million small arms and light weapons are procured by government militaries every year, though this total is not necessarily all made up of newly produced weapons.[155]

Although Africa is often believed to be a major destination for small arms transfers, the continent's legal sales totalled only $25 million in 2005.[156] The five largest small arms recipients in 2003 were the United States, Cyprus, Germany, Spain and France, but no African countries. Even African producers export outside the region. Of the $6 million in small arms South Africa exported in 2005, the majority went to recipients outside of Africa.[157]

Small arms ammunition

Small arms ammunition is often dealt with separately in small arms initiatives – including production, control and destruction. Yet, just as with the weapons, it is difficult to get an accurate picture of global ammunition production. The SAS reports that at least seventy-six countries produce small arms and light weapons ammunition. Just as with the weapons, the majority of ammunition producers are in the global north; 70 per cent of producers are located either in Europe and the former Soviet Union, or in North and Central America.[158] Only 7 per cent of ammunition producers are in Africa. The largest capacity for ammunition production in Africa is at the F. N. Herstal-built Kenya Ordnance Factory at Eldoret. Although many specifics about the Eldoret plant are unknown, the factory is believed to produce 20,000 to 60,000 rounds every day. The factory provides 2 million rounds per year for local consumption.

Although the purpose of the plant is reportedly to help train the Kenyan Army and provide sales to neighbouring countries – and not to produce ammunition for conflict zones – no information about the types and amounts of, or buyers for, the ammunition have been released.[159]

Obviously, more rounds of ammunition are needed than actual weapons, so finding supply lines for ammunition is crucial to waging and preparing for conflicts. The ammunition trade differs slightly from the trade in weapons. Ammunition can be transferred either with the weapons or in separate transfers. In general, ammunition follows similar trade patterns to the weapons themselves, utilizes the legal, black, grey and covert markets, and uses the same networks and brokers. However, there are two distinct differences in the global ammunition trade. The first is the ant trade – small-scale cross-border smuggling – which is the common way ammunition moves from one country to another. In West Africa, for example, the SAS reports that the border between Benin and Nigeria is a particularly popular trafficking route.[160] The second is that craft and indigenous production can be more widespread and a greater source of ammunition if other supplies dry up. Anders and Weidacher report that, when South Africa's ammunition supply dried up due to arms embargoes between the 1960s and 1990s, the country used reverse engineering to produce adequate ammunition supplies.[161]

According to the SAS, between 1999 and 2003 the value of the global ammunition trade was estimated to be at least $700 million, but was likely much higher, due to lack of accurate data and under-reporting. The top exporters of ammunition during this period were the United States, Italy, Brazil, Belgium, the United Kingdom, Russia and Germany, and the top importers were the United States and Saudi Arabia.[162] Although often considered secondary to weapons transfer, ammunition transfers can often impact the dynamics of ongoing violence to a greater extent than transfers of weapons themselves. Philip Alpers reported that, when Australia and New Zealand reduced their transfers of ammunition to Papua New Guinea in the early 2000s, in light of ongoing armed violence and crime, the cost of ammunition doubled in the Southern Highlands region of the country. The higher prices indicated a shrinking supply of ammunition, which made it harder for individuals to acquire bullets.[163] However, legal ammunition transfers are just one piece of the ammunition trade, and thus halting legal transfers may not halt all flows of ammunition to war zones and other areas plagued by gun violence. The black market and other illicit transfers of both weapons and ammunition are discussed in chapter 4.

Whereas heavy conventional arms transfers are prompted by constant upgrades, development of new technology and required maintenance, small arms transfers rely primarily on simple demand. Small arms transfers are less driven by technology advancements than by a need to acquire weaponry to wage war, for self-defence or to supply infantries with standard-issue weapons. Indeed, the most ubiquitous small arm in the world is a weapon developed at the end of World War II – the AK-47. In the sixty years since the weapon's design, between 70 million and 100 million AK-47s or its variants have been produced, compared to only 7 million M-16 and M-4 rifles.

Small arms in Iraq

The situation in Iraq provides an excellent backdrop for understanding small arms proliferation and transfer issues. Small arms proliferation in Iraq has perpetuated violence and instability and limited reconstruction throughout the country. The Iraqi people have suffered tremendously from both the threat and use of these weapons, and the proliferation of these weapons presents significant difficulties for the US and coalition forces attempting to maintain law and order.

Prior to the 2003 invasion, citizens collected guns and ammunition to prepare for the impending conflict. In the immediate chaos caused by the quick defeat of the Baathist regime, US troops neglected to secure the numerous weapons stockpiles littering Iraq. These weapons made attractive targets for fleeing Iraqi soldiers and citizens who often took weapons for self-protection, and for criminals and insurgents to use for illegal purposes.

The continued conflict in Iraq has created a lucrative legal arms market there for the United States, and more than $2 billion in Foreign Military Sales alone were proposed in 2006 and 2007. Two Defense Security Cooperation Agency (DSCA) notifications in September 2006 outlined proposed sales of defence articles to Iraq totalling $750 million and including over 100,000 new small arms and light weapons, as well as helicopters and armoured personnel carriers. This request was followed by a 7 December 2006 memo providing notification of a possible sale of nearly $500 million worth of major defence equipment (as well as non-defence equipment), and a May 2007 notice requesting sales of up to $500 million in small arms ammunition and explosives.[164]

Originally, the United States decided to allow Iraqi soldiers to keep the AK-47s that had been used during Saddam's reign. However, in September 2006, the United States announced that Iraq would be purchasing M-16s and M-4s (as well as other weapons) through the FMS programme. Over 10,000 9mm Glock pistols and 3,400 sniper rifles were also requested in the sale.[165] Colt Manufacturing produces the M-16, and some media reports reveal they will receive $50 million for the deal. The announcement of the switch to M-16s was surprising as Iraq had initially requested that the Army keep the AK-47 as a standard-issue weapon. The United States had even gone so far as to purchase new stocks of German-made AKs from Jordan (despite the massive stockpiles of weaponry already in Iraq) before announcing the switch.[166]

Iraqi soldiers believe the AK-47 is more accurate, durable and powerful than the M-16, and the relative merits of the M-16 are a continuing debate within the United States. In a throwback to the Vietnam War, many US soldiers are using AKs in Iraq, even though it flies in the face of official policy. Although it is more accurate and lighter in weight than the AK-47, the M-16 requires more cleaning and is less reliable.[167]

The new transfers of small arms to Iraq highlight a challenge with legal small arms sales. Even if a supplier knows exactly what weapons are delivered, it is difficult to keep track of these small, portable and easily concealable weapons once they have arrived. The United States has had a difficult time keeping track of the small arms it has already provided to the Iraqis. The November 2006 release of the audit of the Special Inspector General for Iraq Reconstruction revealed that the United States purchased 370,000 weapons at a total cost of $133 million, and ranging from pistols and assault rifles to heavy machine guns and rocket launchers.[168] According to the Inspector General's report, of more than half a million US weapons legally transferred to Iraq, the serial numbers of only 2 per cent were recorded, resulting in 'major discrepancies' in records of the weapons' whereabouts.[169] Although the United States does not know where a majority of these weapons are, what is obvious is that these weapons, in conjunction with the millions that were already in the country prior to the US invasion, are regularly falling into the hands of insurgents. In addition, the US government reports that looted munitions are being used to make the IEDs plaguing the country and causing 65 per cent of all US troop deaths in May 2007, up from 0 per cent in May 2003, 26 per cent in May 2004, 41 per cent in May 2005, and 52 per cent in May 2006.[170]

Conclusion

The changing global environment is leading to continuing transformations in the international legal arms trade. In some cases, these changes have come in the form of loosening export controls; in others, countries are working together to develop standard arms export procedures. The events of 11 September 2001 have also shaped the future of the international arms trade, in promoting faster arms exports to those involved in the 'war on terrorism'. Even with what some see as the loosening of export controls by the world's largest arms exporter, some customers still have difficulty purchasing arms on the legal market. Thus, they turn to a thriving illicit market to meet their needs.

4

The illicit arms trade

In November 2003, 'the Devil' got his due. After a nine-month investigation, the United States, working with authorities in the Philippines, arrested Victor Infante, also known as 'the Devil', on weapons and drug-trafficking charges. The arrest closed down a methamphetamine and firearms organization that shipped illegal drugs and guns within the United States and to the Philippines. Infante, who was born in the Philippines but is a naturalized US citizen, was also known to have supplied weapons to the Abu Sayyaf terrorist organization in the Philippines.[1] This one case of illegal weapons dealing reflects various themes present in the discussion of the illicit arms trade in this chapter. First, unscrupulous individuals often contribute to the global trade in illegal arms. Second, weapons trafficking is often connected with the trafficking of other substances such as illegal drugs. Third, the illicit arms market often helps to arm dangerous actors such as terrorist organizations. And fourth, holding individuals, groups and governments accountable for such illegal dealings often requires international collaboration and cooperation.

Ultimately, news of illegal weapons deals is not hard to find – but intercepting, or better yet preventing, illicit arms transfers is far more difficult. Illegal weapons sales run the spectrum from government authorities arranging for and implementing arms deals that flout international law (such as arms embargoes), to corrupt officials engaging in illegal weapons sales for personal profit and gain, to gun runners who operate on the margins of the law shuttling weapons and ammunition around the world with impunity. Examples are plentiful. The Serbian government was found in 2002 to have transferred 210 tons of small arms, light weapons and ammunition to Liberian rebels in clear violation of the UN arms embargo set in place in 1992.[2] Ukrainian officials have been accused of being directly involved, or looking the other way, while billions of dollars of Ukrainian arms were illegally sold to embargoed locations such as Sierra Leone, Croatia, Iraq and Afghanistan.[3] Moreover, individual middle-men, such as the infamous Victor Bout, maintain illegal gun channels around the world, become the subject of Hollywood films and take on mythical proportions.[4]

Despite all the shocking stories and made-for-television drama, the illegal weapons trade is a relatively small part of the overall global trade in arms. The illicit trade in arms, however, is believed to be among the causes of instability and violent conflict.[5] Thus, most regional and international efforts to address the weapons trade have largely focused on illegal transactions – leaving the issue of the legal trade in arms nearly untouched. Without a doubt, it is the illegal arms trade and its various actors, agents, causes and consequences that capture our attention and motivate our action. But to what effect? What can and do we really know about the illegal weapons trade – and how can we really effect any change and stem the flow of illegal weapons worldwide?

This chapter focuses on what we do and can know about the illicit arms trade. Because the illegal trade in arms operates on the margins of the law, it is difficult to gather data and publish specifics in a systematic way. The study of the illicit trade in arms relies largely on anecdotal and case-specific information. Nonetheless, we can draw some conclusions about the illicit arms trade that frame our larger understanding of the international arms trade in general. After a brief outline of what we know about the volume and value of illegal weapons traded around the world, the chapter discusses the demand for and supply of illegal weapons. Specifically, the chapter outlines the methods by which arms are illicitly traded via the black and grey markets, as well as the ways in which legal weapons move to the illegal market. The chapter then offers an overview of illegal arms channels with a specific discussion of arms dealers. The discussion then moves to the connections between illegal arms trafficking and other forms of trafficking (drug, human and other smuggling). In conclusion, the chapter discusses possible measures to combat the illegal trade.

Defining the illicit arms trade: grey and black markets

The illicit trade in weapons is difficult to define and even more difficult to identify, prosecute, punish or prevent. The 2001 Small Arms Survey defines illegal black market transfers as those 'in clear violation of national and/or international laws and without official government consent or control'.[6] Although these illegal transfers are not authorized by government authorities, they may involve corrupt government agents who are seeking to gain personally from the transaction. The illegal arms trade is not as simple as black and white – there are many shades of grey, which complicates the illegal trade in arms significantly. Illicit grey market transfers typically involve 'governments, their agents, or individuals exploiting loopholes or intentionally circumvent-ing national and/or international laws or policies'.[7] This would suggest that covert arms transfers are not necessarily illegal, but travel a fine line between legal and illicit. Grey market or covert sales may actually be semi-legal activities that violate international norms or policies, but not laws, whereas black market sales are those that are wholly illegal and are conducted with full knowl-edge that national and international laws are being violated.[8] Covert arms deals themselves add another level of analysis, with some suggesting that an arms deal authorized covertly is 'legally-questionable'.[9] Despite the difficulty in clearly and precisely defining and, therefore, pinpointing the meaning of the illicit arms trade, it is important to study and understand what we can and do know about the illegal weapons trade in order to address better and hopefully prevent such illicit transactions in the future.

What we can and do know about the illicit trade in arms

Studying the legal trade in conventional arms is quite difficult, given the lack of transparency in the legal arms trade. Institutions such as the UN Arms Register attempt to enhance information sharing and data gathering on the transfer of large conventional weaponry, but not all states provide information to the Register as submissions are purely voluntary. States are encouraged to provide arms trade data that will inform the world's governments about arms sales and acquisitions, including national procurement. For many years, no such agreement, voluntary or otherwise, existed regarding small arms and light weapons. In 2006, however, the UN added an additional voluntary category for the sharing of information on small arms exports.[10] Still, states rarely share information about their legal small arms transfers. Even what we can and do know about the legal trade in arms, therefore, is limited,[11] and what we can and do know about the illicit arms trade is even more constrained. And yet it is the illicit trafficking of small arms and light weapons that compounds the effects of weapons proliferation and significantly affects our ability to address the problem.[12]

Experts estimate that the illicit small arms trade accounts for more than $1 billion every year.[13] Estimates, often based on weapons seizures and confiscations, are admittedly conservative. The actual value of illegal arms sales may be considerably higher – especially when you consider grey market and covert sales. Knowledge of the true value of such weapons deals, however, is very difficult, if not impossible, to develop.

Although most illegal weapons transactions involve small arms and ammunition, as these are the easiest to conceal, transport and smuggle due to their small size, heavier weapons and especially spare parts are more and more often being funnelled through black market channels.[14] Spare parts for fighter jets, for example, are a significant problem. For example, a US private contractor, Government Liquidation, has been selling military surplus, including F-14 spare parts, since 2001. The Government Accounting Office reported in 2006 that it was far too easy to acquire F-14 and other spare parts via organizations such as Government Liquidation and highlighted the concern that Iran, a country very dependent on imported spare parts for their F-14 fighter jets purchased from the United States in the 1970s, could gain access to the parts they need.[15] Today, US law prohibits the shipment of F-14 components to Iran, but, despite US Defense Department efforts to control the legal sale of restricted material, mistakes have allowed vast quantities of US weapons and necessary components to be sold on the international black market. In 2005, US defence investigators found a cache of F-14 spare parts headed for Iran, which turned out to be the same parts previously intercepted in an investigation two years earlier.[16] On 30 January 2007, the US Pentagon declared that it would suspend selling F-14 spare parts, to prevent their acquisition by buyers in Iran or elsewhere. Meanwhile, Congress debated a bill to 'permanently end all Pentagon sales of surplus F-14 parts'.[17] In fact, the Pentagon has begun 'shredding' retired F-14s to keep their parts from being purchased by unauthorized buyers like Iran, after the Associated Press reported that spare parts had leaked into Iran and China through 'gaps in surplus-sale security'.[18]

The demand that fuels the illicit arms trade

The Iranian desire for F-14 spare parts that must be acquired illegally is but one example of weapons demand that fuels the illicit arms trade. To be sure, there are many reasons why states, sub-state actors and individuals seek to acquire weapons – and many reasons why states, sub-state actors and individuals funnel weapons to interested parties. Each instance of illegal weapons acquisition may indeed be unique – shaped by specific political, social, economic and/or cultural circumstances. Primarily, however, demand for weapons may reflect concerns for personal security, demonstrations of power, interests in acquiring territory or resources, desires for independence or separation, attempts to prevent independence or separation, or other foreign policy, individual autonomy or security reasons. For many of the same reasons that states, sub-state actors or individuals acquire weapons legally, many more actors may be driven to seek weapons via illicit channels. The success with which actors gain access to illegally traded weapons often depends on 'preference, price, and availability'.[19]

Certainly, the demand for weapons can also be affected by the supply. The same events that can create a flood of available weapons – regime collapse, violent conflict or economic crisis – can also create the motivations and the means to acquire weapons.[20] Instability, in general, creates a demand for weapons as it breeds insecurity, which, for states, sub-state groups or individuals, creates a perceived need for protection or defensive capabilities.[21] Moreover, weapons demand may be fuelled by social, psychological or cultural factors. In Brazil, for example, pro-gun groups have successfully tied weapons possession to honour, masculinity or virility and status. The wealthy find the police inadequate, so there is a demand for firearms in order to secure wealth privately. Among *favela* residents, drug factions demand firearms, and individuals demand guns to show their membership of a faction, as well as to demonstrate power and wealth. On 23 October 2005, 64 per cent of Brazilians voted against a referendum to ban firearms, suggesting that they feel the private ownership of firearms is necessary for security.[22] Many of these individuals must turn to the illicit market to acquire such weapons.

Civil conflict, terrorist activity and other illicit activities, such as drug trafficking, may also fuel the demand for weapons. In Colombia, the forty-year-long conflict among the army, irregular paramilitary forces and the two left-wing guerrilla groups (Revolutionary Armed Forces of Columbia FARC – and the National Liberation Army ELN) has fuelled the demand for firearms and subsequent violence. The criminal industry of drug trafficking also stimulates the demand for illicit arms as the Colombian government only allows a small number of firearms to be owned legally. Because of the large weapons supply in Colombia, the price for illicit arms is relatively cheap, and the successful prosecution of violent crimes is rare, leaving criminal demand for firearms unhampered by the fear of police action.[23]

Specific historical circumstances may also affect the demand for weapons. In South Africa, the demand for weapons is based on the state's history of militarization and armed conflict, and small arms and light weapons, in particular, were necessary in the maintenance of apartheid oppression. However, the weapons used by the liberation armies – primarily the AK-47 – became symbolic of freedom. Illicit firearms are available in large supply in South Africa, contributing to the creation of a 'gun culture'.[24] In addition to their symbolic importance, firearms are in demand for reasons of political identity, status and personal security. Firearms are equated with masculinity and virility, as well as 'full citizenship'. In South Africa, women are also starting to demand firearms, as part of the feminist movement or for self-protection. This demand is also fuelled by the perception that the police are not a competent source of security.[25]

Local violence and a lack of personal security significantly influence the demand for weapons. In Papua New Guinea, gang violence has created a large demand for arms, including automatic and semi-automatic rifles and pistols, home-made firearms, and hand grenades. Stolen police and defence force weapons supply the illicit arms market in the country. Firearms are even used by politicians to influence elections. Demand for firearms is growing because of police incompetence and corruption, fighting among tribal clans, the status and personal security associated with firearm ownership and drug use. However, means to own firearms are scarce, and prices are relatively high. Thus, there is a high demand for craft-produced or home-made firearms.[26]

Governments and militaries also demand weapons, parts and technology to which they cannot easily gain access. The United States alone has investigated, documented and interdicted numerous illegal weapons deals involving countries such as China, Iran, Pakistan and Libya. Weapons ranging from sensitive military technology, such as satellite, radar and night-vision capability, to tanks, fighter jet parts, missile and artillery components, communications equipment and small arms and light weapons are in demand for many governments and military forces around the world. Many of these items are illegally transferred via individuals, companies and groups working outside the law, but governments may also engage in covert trades (to be discussed in more detail below). No matter what the method of transfer, however, numerous players (individuals, terrorists, organizations, governments and militaries) often seek weapons for a multitude of reasons.

Although various factors may contribute to the demand for weapons, and motivations are diverse, some common trends are evident. First, demand is socially and historically determined. Second, structural factors of governance, such as police capacity, often determine the intensity of demand. Third, the availability of arms affects demand. And fourth, demand is different for individuals and groups.[27] It is often argued that a 'culture of weapons' leads to a 'culture of violence', which increases the demand for weapons. States that cannot or will not guarantee the security of their citizens, or that cannot or will not control the illicit spread of weapons, perpetuate this cycle of weapons supply and demand and should be mindful of how supply and demand issues affect the illegal weapons trade.[28]

Illicit arms trade channels: the global supply of illegal guns

As discussed above, black and grey market weapons sales are difficult to define and often more difficult to detect. Numerous methods are used to funnel weapons via both black and grey markets – methods such as concealed and smuggled shipments, use of fake shipping documents, mislabelled goods, and secret financial transactions that hide funds used for or resulting from illegal sales.[29] Moreover, a lack of governmental oversight and loose regulation of military and police stockpiles may result in the loss, theft and illegal diversion of weapons that end up on the black market. The unreported theft and loss of civilian weapons also fuel the illegal supply of guns.[30] Finally, covert sales authorized by governments contribute to the global supply of illegal weapons. Weapons legally traded reach the black market, and grey market sales are used to channel weapons illicitly for foreign policy and other purposes.

Legal transactions to the illicit market

Experts have identified several ways in which legal gun markets fuel the illicit trade.[31] Specifically, weapons shift from legal to illegal in the following ways.

1. Corrupt or negligent government officials may sell weapons for personal gain. In Ukraine, for example, corrupt officials are believed to have sold billions of dollars of weapons to various conflict hotspots around the world.[32] Numerous other examples of such activities exist as well, for example in Bosnia, Serbia and other East European countries.[33] Corrupt officials may also accept bribes to overlook weapons documentation and allow illegal shipments to proceed without scrutiny.[34]
2. Government arsenals and weapons stockpiles may be looted. Stolen weapons may then be diverted to the black market and

traded illegally. This is a concern especially during internal government crises. The Albanian government, for example, disintegrated in 1997 after a pyramid scheme collapsed and bankrupted thousands of Albanian citizens. The outraged population stormed and looted more than 1,000 official stock-piles, and more than 600,000 weapons and 1 billion rounds of ammunition, in addition to thousands of tons of explosives, were stolen and diffused throughout the country and the Western Balkan region.[35] Even in the absence of significant crisis, government stockpiles may suffer from small-scale loss and theft – as well as illegal sales via soldiers or stockpile security guards who are often underpaid and prime targets for bribery.[36]

3. Privately owned weapons among the civilian population are also a significant source of illicit weapons, as personal stock-piles that have been purchased legally may be stolen or lost and then sold on the black market. Moreover, primary sales of legal guns to individual civilians are often regulated, but secondary sales to other individuals are not.[37] Legal loopholes, for example, allow someone with a clean, legal background to buy weapons and then sell them to people who are unable to purchase guns legally. Such 'straw purchasing' is a significant way in which legal guns become illicit ones.[38]

4. Weak national legislation and regulations governing the trans-fer, acquisition and ownership of weapons may lead to the diversion of arms to the black market.[39] The lack of strong domestic laws that are implemented and enforced is a sig-nificant concern, particularly in countries that possess many weapons and few resources to control their transfer. In south-eastern Europe, for example, international organizations have concentrated efforts on trying to enhance legislative capabilities and the rule of law in an effort to prevent the illegal spread of weapons into, from, and through these highly militarized countries.[40]

5. Legal gun manufacturers may also illegally produce weapons and sell them on the black market.[41] Weapons producers that once manufactured guns under a licence may continue to produce the weapons once their licences have expired. Russia, for example, has sued companies in Eastern Europe for illicitly producing AK-47s after their legal licences, which were granted during the Cold War, expired.[42]

6. Gun shows are also a significant source of legal weapons that may enter the black market. In fact, gun shows are an important venue for 'straw purchasing' as mentioned above.[43] Small arms, however, are not the only weapons that can be found at weapons shows. Large, international arms shows may also lead to illegal sales of advanced civilian weapons or even weapons of mass destruction. At an arms show in Karachi, Pakistan in November 2000, for example, a company associated with the now infamous nuclear weapons dealer, A. Q. Khan, was distributing brochures stating they were selling dual-use materials necessary for producing nuclear devices.[44]

7. Finally, the legal collection of weapons at the behest of governments, international organizations and nongovernmental organizations may further fuel the black market. Through weapons buy-back programmes, some weapons holders will buy weapons from the black market and sell them back for double their price to the buy-back agency, then buy more illegal weapons with the money earned.[45]

Covert sales and the perpetuation of the grey market

Secret weapons transfers have long been used as a tool of foreign policy in an effort to support insurgent or revolutionary forces fighting against enemy governments, or to arm governments attempting to stave off enemy insurgents or rebel fighters. The Cold War period was particularly characterized by numerous illicit weapons transfers as the United States and Soviet Union armed their client states in Africa, Asia and Latin America. Moreover, grey market transfers to governments and non-state actors have been important sources of subsequent black market transactions. The two markets are, therefore, intricately intertwined.[46] States may transfer arms illegally to other states, or directly to non-state actors themselves. Front companies and legitimate businesses may also be used to funnel weapons, or may themselves engage in the transfer of military-relevant items or dual-use goods outside of government authority. Regardless of the specific method, weapons large and small, as well as dual-use items, are the subject of grey market transfers – and examples abound. Several types of grey market transfers are discussed below to demonstrate the extent to which covert weapons deals characterize the illicit arms trade.

State-to-state covert sales
States involved in conflict are often placed under international arms embargoes, but this does not always stop the flow of weapons.[47] Many states continue to flout the prohibitions and clandestinely ship weapons to embargoed destinations. Most often, these illicitly traded weapons are paid for with hard currency as financial transactions are easy to hide. Indeed, profits sometimes provide funding for an underground treasury to finance future political or military operations. There are some cases, however, where a commercial trade takes place instead of a financial exchange. For example, during the Iran–Iraq war, when South Africa was under an oil embargo, it traded arms to both countries in exchange for oil. In a commercial exchange between states involving covert weapons, brokers are normally not used. On the other hand, gun-selling states that would like to 'maintain deniability' might work through intermediaries, such as in a deal between a private supplier and a sub-state buyer, in an effort to obscure the activity further.[48]

Many governments use financial calculations as the ultimate determinant of whether and to what extent they will sell their weaponry to state forces under an embargo, or to countries that are engaging in questionable human rights practices, or are otherwise unstable. This was the case after the end of the Cold War and during the early years of NATO expansion when several former Soviet-Bloc nations in Eastern Europe found that they had numerous military items, both large and small, that could bring a quick profit to ailing economies. Bulgaria, for example, calculated that it could get $30,000 for each intact excess tank, whereas those scrapped and sold for parts would only garner $2,000 each. In December 1998, therefore, Bulgaria sold 140 surplus tanks to Ethiopia and Uganda, both involved in violent conflicts.[49]

Some illegal arms shipments, however, have been stopped and weapons confiscated. In violation of the UN arms embargo against the former Yugoslavia, a plane destined for Croatia, carrying 11 tons of arms from the Chilean military, including rifles, mortars and bazookas, was forced down in Budapest in November 1991. In September 1992, an aircraft from Iran destined for Bosnia carrying 4,000 guns and 7 million rounds of ammunition was intercepted in Zagreb.[50]

Not all illegal weapons shipments and seizures, however, are that straightforward or uncomplicated. For example, in March 1993, a ship called the *Malo*, carrying Serbian small arms and ammunition in transit to Somalia, was stopped by Seychelles authorities and the weapons were placed in their government-controlled stockpiles. On 4 June 1994, a former South African official, Wilhelm Tertius Ehlers, and a senior Rwandan official in the Hutu government, Colonel Theoneste Bagosora, negotiated the purchase of the arms in the Seychelles. During the nights of 16 and 18 June 1994, an Air Zaire aircraft flew two loads of the weapons to the Goma airport. The weapons, which included anti-tank and fragmentation grenades and high-calibre ammunition, were then transferred to the ex-FAR (ex-Armed Forces of Rwanda) in Gisenyi inside Rwanda.[51] The Seychelles government, which had seized the weapons because they were originally destined for Somalia – a country under a UN arms embargo – had planned to dispose of the arms, but changed their minds when Ehlers, posing as the director of a company called Delta Aero, said the government of Zaire wanted to purchase them. He and Bagosora purchased all of the weapons with an end-user certificate apparently issued by the Zairian Ministry of Defence. After realizing the fraud, the Seychelles government cancelled a third scheduled shipment of arms. The arms were purchased with two separate payments of $179,965 and $149,982.50 from the Federal Reserve Bank in New York to the Central Bank of Seychelles, which had been transferred out of Ehlers' Swiss bank account at Union Bancaire Privée, funds that had originated in Paris and Kigali.[52]

State covert transfers to insurgents or non-state actors
During the Cold War, a large contributor to the international spread of arms was covert trafficking from governments to foreign insurgents.[53] In 1980, the US Congress appropriated $30 million in covert programmes to aid the *mujahideen* in Afghanistan. The United States arranged covert arms shipments to the anti-Soviet rebels in Afghanistan through Pakistan. Between 1979 and 1989, the CIA channelled $2 billion in aid for weapons to the *mujahideen* – about 80 per cent of its covert aid budget. The legacy of this trade in Afghanistan was the contribution to 'an ongoing humanitarian crisis and to state and regional instability', as well as the strengthening of anti-American terrorist organizations.[54] In the United States, covert arms transfers to insurgent groups reached their height during President Reagan's second term, when he and his associates sent large quantities of covert aid to rebel groups in Afghanistan, Angola, Chad, Cambodia, Libya and Nicaragua. The high-profile Iran-Contra case is but one important example of US covert arms deals during the Reagan Administration – and is an example of how difficult it is to hold

officials accountable for illicit weapons transfers.[55] As a result, however, many of these underground arms supply channels were shut down by 1990.[56]

Nonetheless, covert arms transfers to rebel or insurgent groups continued throughout the post-Cold War period, and do so even today. Two notorious examples of covert shipments in the post-Cold War period are the pre-1999 supply of arms and training by some NATO member states to the Kosovo Liberation Army, and the supply of weapons to ninety anti-Saddam Hussein groups in Iraq by the United States, starting in 1994.[57] One continuous problem with restricting covert arms sales such as these between states and non-state actors is that some states view the activity as illegal under the UN Charter, whereas others do not. In fact, some states continue their efforts at the global level to preserve the right of states to sell arms to non-state actors, opposing any attempt to restrict such weapons transfers. Despite the opposition, however, it remains clear that these types of covert transfers have contributed in a large way to the proliferation of weapons around the world. Weapons covertly delivered in the 1970s and 1980s using brokering networks throughout South Asia, Southern Africa and Central America have since been recycled into the hands of terrorists or combatants in other conflicts and continue to wreak havoc in conflict-prone regions today.[58]

State and commercial covert sales of military and dual-use items
Some covert arms deals are considered 'hybrid cases where private firms sell dual-use equipment to pariah states', expecting their own government will overlook the risk of the deal for the sake of its foreign policy objectives.[59] During the Nixon era, for example, US firms sold military hardware to South Africa in the belief that the State Department tacitly approved.[60] Between 1978 and 1989, James H. Guerin, the then former owner of the Philadelphia-based electronics firm International Signal and Control Group, smuggled $30 million of munitions and electronic equipment to

South Africa. From there, some of it was transferred to Iraqi forces during the 1991 Gulf War.[61]

States may also sell military equipment and dual-use goods to front companies run by another government, who then use such sensitive items to develop major weapons systems or weapons of mass destruction.[62] Many cases of companies exporting arms or dual-use goods without government approval or due to government confusion also exist. For example, Yueqiang 'Bill' Chen of Data Physics Corporation in San Jose is accused of lying on US export declarations and shipping $1.3 million of equipment to a cruise missile laboratory in China. Exports of dual-use goods from the United States to China are only legal if they are sent to a non-military facility. However, US government officials claim that many shipments allegedly destined for non-military customers are transferred to weapons factories. Legal experts claim that it will be hard for either side to prove where the dual-use technology ended up. Another Chinese businessman, Philip Chen, pleaded guilty to illegally supplying night-vision cameras to the Chinese military. In addition, Supermicro Computer Inc. in San Jose paid $275,000 in criminal and civil fines in 2006 for illicitly selling large amounts of controlled computer equipment to Iran via Dubai.[63] Companies, as well as governments, therefore, have their hand in the illicit arms trade, and some, although not many, are held accountable for their illegal weapons activities. Arms brokers, in particular, tend to conduct their illegal transactions with impunity.

Sourcing the guns: the role of arms dealers

Arms dealers, intermediaries or brokers are those individuals who negotiate and arrange weapons transfers, purchases or sales, in exchange for a return on the transaction or some kind of fee.[64] Dealers do not necessarily engage in illegal activities, as some weapons agents may be licensed by their governments to participate in the arms trade. Many arms brokers and their respective companies, however, operate on the margins of or outside the law as they import, export, buy, sell, transfer, supply or deliver weapons to, from and between parties that may not otherwise be able to sell or acquire arms legally. Illicit weapons transactions facilitated by these 'gun-runners' or 'merchants of death' have been the subject of much concern and discussion in the international community, as weapons brokers and brokering activities significantly affect the availability and circulation of weapons worldwide.[65]

Although gun brokering is not a new phenomenon, the post-Cold War period witnessed a tremendous growth in the practice as numerous conflicts erupted or spiralled further into violence. In addition, highly militarized regions of the world, especially the former Soviet bloc, became prime targets for weapons dealers looking to turn a profit on weapons systems big and small, as Soviet satellites looked to modernize and upgrade and quickly get rid of obsolete and surplus stocks. Many well-connected individuals who ran guns for either the United States or the Soviet Union, or both, during the Cold War, maintained their connections after the Cold War and found that illegal gun dealings were quite lucrative. For example, Adnan Khashoggi, a broker for Lockheed working in the Middle East in the 1970s, remained active in the weapons trade after Northrop and Lockheed bribery scandals, and after participating in the Iran-Contra deal.[66] Victor Bout (discussed in more detail below) and other high-profile arms dealers also began their business during the Cold War and continued to arrange and direct illicit weapons transfers thereafter.[67]

Arms brokers carry out their illegal activities using various methods for skirting the legal system and flouting the law. Brokers forge documents to make the shipment appear as though legitimate items are being transported.[68] They divert shipments from one place to the next, often using multiple shipments and transfers to confuse the process. For example, the United Kingdom company Mil-Tec Corporation Ltd supplied $6.5 million of weapons to the Hutu regime in Rwanda. The weapons were transferred in seven air shipments between April and July 1994, from Tirana, Albania to Tel Aviv, Israel and then on to Goma and Kinshasa to forces committing genocide.[69] The diversions often include stops in countries that have lax controls and are not capable of identifying and intercepting illegal activities.[70]

Brokers also set up multiple fake, and sometimes even legitimate, companies in several different countries to avoid connections between enterprises and arms transfers. Brokers particularly like to set up freight-forwarding and transport services that provide the aircraft, boats and other transportation methods to move concealed weapons between sellers and buyers. Dealers operating out of South Africa, for example, worked through companies they set up in Germany, Belgium and Italy to funnel weapons to Congo-Brazzaville during periods of intense fighting in the late 1990s.[71] Ultimately, arms brokers are involved in every angle of an illicit arms deal, and may even finance the transactions, playing banker as well as broker by organizing payments through front companies and secret offshore bank accounts.[72]

While there are some well-known gun dealers who broker arms around the world, few are as infamous as Victor Bout. Victor Bout 'specialized in breaking international weapons embargoes' and 'quickly delivered entire, customized weapons systems to his clients, something none of his competitors could do'.[73] In the late 1990s, Bout provided weapons to several areas under international arms embargoes, including the Democratic Republic of Congo, Angola and Sierra Leone. Between July 1997 and October 1998, the UN documented that Bout made thirty-seven arms deliveries from Bulgaria to Lomé, Togo to supply the National Union for the Total Independence of Angola (UNITA) rebels in Angola, which included 15 million rounds of ammunition, 20,000 82mm mortars, 100 anti-aircraft missiles, 20 missile launchers and 6,300 anti-tank rockets. Bout used forged end-user certificates from Togo through a company called KAS Engineering to facilitate his transfer. In 2000, Bout began trading with Liberia's Charles

Taylor, who wanted helicopters to fight the Liberians United for Reconciliation and Democracy (LURD) army. Bout arranged for his business partner, Sanjivan Ruprah, to buy Mi-2 and Mi-17 attack-capable helicopters, along with spare parts and other weapons (anti-tank and anti-aircraft systems, missiles, armoured cars, machine guns and 1 million rounds of ammunition) from the former Soviet bloc, which arrived in Monrovia on Bout's aircraft. From there, the weapons were transferred to Liberia under the cover of a ghost company, Abidjan Freight, set up by Ruprah, and another Gambian front company, New Millennium, to hide the fact that arms were entering Liberia on Bout's aircraft in violation of the UN arms embargo. In return, Bout was paid for the weapons with diamonds, which he then easily sold.[74]

Victor Bout has been accused of numerous illegal weapons deals, but has also been involved in legal arms transfers as well. He is known to have assisted governments of countries such as the United States and the United Kingdom in transporting goods and personnel. Bout's aircraft companies received multi-million-dollar contracts to assist companies like FedEx, and Kellogg, Brown and Root, in hauling military supplies and construction equipment.[75] Bout's many activities came to an abrupt halt when he was arrested on 6 March 2008 in Bangkok, Thailand, accused of attempting to procure and deliver $5 million of weapons for the FARC, a rebel group in Colombia that is on the US list of terrorist organizations.[76] US authorities were deeply involved in the arrest and are seeking Bout's extradition to the United States in order to try him in US courts.

Other high-profile gun runners include Leonid Menin who in 1999 delivered 68 tons of weapons, including surface-to-air missiles and anti-tank weapons, to Chucky Taylor, Charles Taylor's son, for use by the Revolutionary United Front (RUF) in Liberia. Menin bought a forged end-user certificate from Burkina Faso and used his private plane to make the delivery. Menin also used forged documents in mid-2000 to authorize the transfer of 113 tons of weapons to Liberia, which included 5 million rounds of AK-47 ammunition, 50 M-93 30mm grenade launchers, 10,000 launcher munitions and 20 night-vision binoculars. Like Victor Bout, Menin traded his arms for diamonds.[77]

Despite the global activities of arms brokers, few countries around the world have developed laws regulating arms brokers and brokering activities.[78] Even fewer countries have developed what are called 'extra-territorial' regulations that claim jurisdiction over their citizens' brokering activities no matter where they occur. The United States, for example, not only regulates arms brokers and brokering in the United States, but extends its jurisdiction to cover the brokering activities of US citizens operating abroad.[79] Global efforts to control arms dealers and prevent gun running have been, for many, frustratingly slow. Nongovernmental organizations have been at the forefront of this issue, creating a 'Model Convention on the Registration of Arms Brokers and the Suppression of Unlicensed Arms Brokering'.[80] The Convention, however, has yet to be adopted at the international level and few states seem motivated to take on the issue of arms brokering directly.

The United Nations *Programme of Action to Prevent, Combat and Eradicate the Illicit Trade in Small Arms and Light Weapons in All Its Aspects* specifically encourages states to develop national legislation governing arms brokers and their activities, as well as suggesting that states should 'develop common understandings' about the definitions of brokers and brokering at the global level.[81] In fact, a Group of Governmental Experts to address the prevention and eradication of illicit brokering of small arms and light weapons concluded its work in December 2007 with a report that urges nations to develop and implement national laws focused on arms brokering, engage with others in the international community to stop brokering activities, offer more assistance to those countries who struggle with arms brokers, share more information on brokers and brokering activities and do more to implement UN arms embargoes and sanctions.[82] Significant problems with the implementation of the *Programme of Action* and other brokering agreements remain, however, as many states have not accomplished much regarding suggested activities.[83] Ultimately, as long as states do not develop comprehensive national control measures appropriate for the regulation of arms brokers and their activities, gun dealers will continue to exploit gaps in the legal infrastructure and facilitate and perpetuate illegal weapons transfers well into the future.

The illicit connection: illegal weapons and other illicit goods and activities

The illicit trade in arms is rarely an isolated activity. Illegal arms transfers often follow trade routes and employ smuggling practices that are relevant for other illicit activities. Drug-trafficking and human-trafficking routes, for example, are also used for arms trafficking – and vice versa.[84] Arms brokers who smuggle weapons around the world often engage in other illegal activities and smuggle drugs, humans and other contraband. Moreover, arms dealers engaging in the illicit arms trade may even engage in legitimate, legal trade in other items as well. Victor Bout, for example, has also traded cut flowers and frozen fish and provided transportation services to US personnel working in Iraq.[85] Gun runners in Turkey boast of illegally transporting weapons throughout their region and into Africa, but also highlight legal activities such as their trade in textiles and shoes.[86]

Arms are both the currency and the commodity of various illicit markets. This is particularly the case in Western, Central and Southern Africa. Diamonds, gems, minerals and timber are often traded for weapons and other contraband in countries such as Sierra Leone, Angola and the Congo.[87] Cotton, coffee and even seafood have also served as payment for arms shipments. Embargoes on such natural resources, and campaigns focusing on ending the trade in 'conflict' or 'blood' diamonds, for example, attempt to heighten our awareness of the connections between natural resources and illicit trafficking of all kinds, but particularly the trafficking of weapons that leads to significant violence, death and destruction around the world.[88] Addressing the illicit trade in arms requires more comprehensive action that focuses on illegal trafficking and organized criminal activities more generally.

Combating the illicit trade in arms

Many measures have been identified to stem the trade in illicit arms.[89] Quite clearly, no one actor alone can address the illegal flow of weapons. Comprehensive and compatible procedures, laws and regulations are required for all states and relevant actors at all levels to fight the illicit trade in arms effectively. Efforts to combat the illicit arms trade must address both the demand for and supply of illegal weapons – as well as address the legal trade in arms to prevent legal guns from becoming illegal ones. The few international efforts that do address the global trade in weapons, however, focus almost exclusively on illicit weapons trafficking. The illicit trade is a recognized problem about which nearly all governments agree, but disagreements remain regarding the control of arms transfers to non-state actors and the impact of the legal trade on the illicit market. Major weapons suppliers do not wish to limit the legal trade in weapons, and often refuse to acknowledge the connection between legal arms sales and the illicit arms market.[90] Moreover, few governments will seek to limit covert sales. Governments do, however, have several tools to limit the international illicit arms trade.

The focus on supply

To limit the illicit supply of arms worldwide, governments around the world can develop laws, policies and procedures that are compatible and comprehensive concerning all aspects of the illegal supply chain. Legal loopholes can be closed so that countries with lax controls cannot be exploited and used as points of transit or transshipment. National laws can incorporate controls on arms brokers and their brokering activities by requiring gun traders to register and submit their arms activities for government registration and approval like any other weapons-producing or trading company. End-use and end-user certificates can be used universally to heighten information and awareness about weapons transactions. Moreover, these certificates can be standardized across countries and measures should be taken to prevent the fraudulent production of the documents. Governments can work to enhance their customs and border controls and require that all arms shipments that flow into, out of and through their countries be checked for authenticity and legitimacy. In addition, weapons shipments can be verified after delivery and importers required to seek approval from the original source before re-exporting guns to another destination. Governments can require gun manufacturers to mark their weapons and ammunition at the time of production so it can be traced in the event it is diverted to the illicit market, and appropriate criminal and civil penalties can be established and levied when anyone along the arms supply chain breaches the law and engages in illicit arms transfers. Individual gun dealers, weapons-producing and exporting companies or irresponsible state actors currently operate with impunity. Physical security of official weapons storage and stockpile facilities, therefore, can be enhanced to prevent loss and theft, and individuals who do not report the loss or theft of their weapons can be subject to penalties. Finally, surplus weapons that are no longer of use or needed for appropriate defence forces can be collected and destroyed. All of these legal and procedural actions, if taken, will serve not only to identify illegal or questionable weapons transactions so that appropriate action can be taken, but also to prevent and limit the overall supply available to the illicit arms market. Yet, state capacity must also be improved concurrently to ensure that these procedures can be implemented.

The focus on demand

Attempts to combat the illicit arms trade will be incomplete with a strict focus only on weapons supply. An equal, and perhaps more challenging, requirement is to address the demand for illicit weapons. As discussed above, many demand factors are relevant in terms of fuelling the illicit arms trade. A few important factors, however, can be identified for specific action. First, in territories that have experienced armed conflict, post-conflict reconstruction can occur in order to prevent a resumption of the conflict and a return to arms. Specifically, former combatants can be demobilized, disarmed and reintegrated into society as the entire area seeks to recover from their conflict experience. Leaving former combatants armed, mobilized and on the fringes of society increases the risks of future violent conflict. Second, the global community can seek to address and minimize instability and crises of all kinds – whether those crises involve social, political, economic and/or cultural circumstances. Where they occur, problems such as oppression, ethnic tension and concerns for personal security increase the likelihood that illegal weapons will be acquired and used, further undermining chances for a stable and secure environment. Related to these circumstances are the gun and violence cultures that can be minimized to avoid personal weapons misuse and larger-scale violence. Finally, addressing and minimizing organized criminal activity and other trafficking activities will also limit the demand for illegal arms, as the illicit trade in arms is significantly linked with other forms of criminal action.

Ultimately, the prescriptions for treating the illicit arms trade are many and include a complex array of activities across a spectrum of actors. No one easy solution exists and no one actor will succeed alone. A collective and concerted approach is required.

Conclusion

Studying the illicit arms trade is very tricky indeed. We know weapons are traded illegally. We know that illegal weapons are used to commit crimes and abuses and to perpetuate violence, death and destruction. But we do not and most likely cannot know the true value, nature and extent of the illicit trade in arms. Although the illicit arms trade is a relatively small part of the overall global trade in weapons, it is the greatest concern in terms of causing violent conflict and instability. Indeed, both the legal and illicit arms trades contribute in a variety of ways to serious human security crises and human suffering.

5

The consequences of the international arms trade

In November 2002, al Qaeda-linked terrorists attempted to shoot down an Israeli 757 jet as it took off from the airport in Mombasa, Kenya. However, the lives of hundreds of passengers were spared when the attackers' weapons – two SA-7 Grail shoulder-fired surface-to-air missiles – failed to detonate. As international agencies strategize ways to ensure that dirty bombs and nuclear devices stay out of the hands of terrorists, in reality conventional weapons are the first choice for many terrorists and terrorist groups. On a daily basis, conventional arms are responsible for the majority of deaths and suffering in conflicts around the world. Small arms in particular have played an important role in the world's bloodiest conflicts and are responsible for hundreds of thousands of conflict deaths every year and 200,000 deaths in countries at peace. These weapons contribute to cycles of violence, trapping communities in endless fighting and bloodshed.

Around the world, the conventional arms trade – through both legal and illicit channels – has put peacekeepers in danger, diminished national and multinational business opportunities, impeded the ability of humanitarian and relief organizations to conduct their efforts and hampered sustainable development. This chapter describes the human security consequences of the international arms trade, including its impact on international peace and security and development. It starts with a description of the human security framework and examines how the conventional arms trade impacts many aspects of human security. It also examines cases from every world region that demonstrate how the current uncontrolled state of the arms trade fuels regional arms races and causes countries to prioritize military spending over all other investments.

From national security to human security

As Cold War battle lines faded at the beginning of the 1990s, new conflicts arose – primarily intra-state conflicts that wrought massive devastation on communities. Policy makers quickly realized that the traditional framework of national security would not work to address these new realities, and the state-centric concerns of the Cold War eventually gave way to a new focus for governments and the United Nations. The conflicts of the 1990s demonstrated that securing the borders of a nation state from external threats does not necessarily secure the people within those states. Out of this realization a new concept was developed: human security. According to the Human Security Report: 'The traditional goal of "national security" has been the defense of the state from external threats. The focus of human security, by contrast, is the protection of individuals . . . . Human Security and national security should be – and often are – mutually reinforcing. But secure states do not automatically mean secure peoples.'[1]

Human security focuses on the protection of individuals and their communities. As the United Nations Commission on Human Security puts it, 'human security complements state security, furthers human development and enhances human rights'.[2] From protecting people from death and injury during conflicts to ensuring their economic security, human security approaches reflect the widespread and diverse needs of individuals and communities. Although this may seem an obvious approach in the post-Cold War world, the links between development and security are a relatively new concept. Only in the past two decades have organizations such as the World Bank and publications such as the Human

Development Report acknowledged and addressed the ways in which security, or the lack thereof, affects development.

What does this shift in frameworks mean for the study of conventional arms? The human security consequences of a nuclear, chemical or biological device are obvious – massive human deaths and suffering. But the human security consequences of conventional arms, both large and small, are perhaps more difficult to assess. They can range from direct effects, such as death and injury, to indirect effects, such as the inability to return home from refugee camps. Human security consequences may also vary depending on whether a population is concerned with small arms or heavy conventional weapons.[3]

Human security and the arms trade

Let us examine these human security consequences – which will differ in affected countries and conflicts depending on the weapons used – one by one. In many cases, it is difficult to separate the effects of the weapons from the effects of the conflict, but we do know that the misuse and proliferation of weapons can affect individuals as well as entire communities. Heavy conventional weapons, which cause widespread and impersonal devastation, may impact a society in different ways from small arms, whose effects can be more localized and personal. Regardless of the category of weapon used, the consequences of all conventional arms may either reveal themselves immediately – as with death and injury – or take years to be fully felt, such as unfulfilled development and economic objectives. Although we tend to think first of deaths and injuries, which are the most obvious consequences of these weapons, non-fatal consequences can be just as devastating to populations. For example, the strain weapons injuries place on the medical system, the thwarting of educational opportunities, the denial of humanitarian aid, the increase in refugees and populations of internally displaced people (IDPs), the development of cultures of violence, the use of child soldiers, the threats to humanitarian workers and peacekeepers, and the slowing of economic development are just some of the human security consequences of the proliferation and use of conventional arms.

Death, injury and trauma

The direct impacts of weapons proliferation are measurable and include deaths, injuries and psycho-social trauma. Hundreds of thousands of civilians die every year in conflict zones. And, each year, at least 200,000 more people die as a result of small arms-inflicted suicides and homicides in countries at peace.[4] Researchers estimate that these weapons are also responsible for three times as many injuries worldwide. Although much of the data on deaths and injuries focuses on small arms and light weapons, heavy conventional weapons can do enormous damage as well. From aerial bombings in Iraq and Afghanistan, to cross-border fighting between Lebanon and Israel, conventional wars and weapons still cause tremendous human suffering. The border dispute between Ethiopia and Eritrea in the late 1990s and early 2000s is believed to have cost 70,000 to 120,000 lives of soldiers and civilians. Unlike many wars in Africa, the conflict in the Horn of Africa involved heavy conventional weapons to a significant extent.[5] In Brazil, gun violence is the number one cause of death for young men aged fifteen to twenty-four.[6] Many of these young men are killed by armed gangs in the country's poorest regions. Even if these vulnerable groups escape death and injury, as witnesses to the carnage around them they suffer from the psycho-social trauma of continued violence and fear.

Human rights abuses

Human rights abusers use conventional weapons to carry out horrific practices, such as extra-judicial executions, forced disappearances and torture. Vulnerable populations, particularly women, children and the elderly, are often specifically targeted by gun-toting assailants. In the Democratic Republic of the Congo (DRC), women and girls endure rape, assault and torture by young men armed with guns and seeking power and resources. The United Nations reported at least 12,000 rapes in the first half of 2006 alone – many of which took place at the barrel of a gun – a likely underestimation due to lack of reporting and a number of victims who were also killed.[7] In addition to their physical wounds, these survivors must also live with the psychological scars of their attacks.

Refugees and Internally Displaced People (IDPs)

Millions of people are forced from their homes every year in conflicts fuelled by conventional weapons. The United Nations High Commissioner for Refugees estimates that, as of 1 January 2005, there were 9.2 million refugees worldwide.[8] In addition, as of December 2006, conflicts in twenty-three countries around the world had resulted in 24.5 million conflict-related IDPs, 70–80 per cent of whom are believed to be women and children. Although IDPs are traditionally people displaced within their own country, IDPs fleeing conflict in these twenty-three different countries actually affect at least fifty-two countries in total. According to the Internal Displacement Monitoring Centre, almost half of the world's IDP population – 11.8 million people – is in Africa, and half of all African IDPs – 5.4 million – are in Sudan.[9] Even when conflicts conclude, these weapons continue to affect refugee and IDP populations, who are often afraid to return home due to explosive remnants of war or unexploded ordnance or weapons in the hands of criminals, insurgents and soldiers in their communities or along their travel routes. However, refugee camps do not provide much solace, as they often experience rising crime and violence rates and are lucrative sources for child recruitment and the illegal arms trade.[10]

Conventional weapons proliferation and misuse also have many indirect consequences as well. Most of these are non-fatal consequences that affect the fabric and operation of society. Some of these indirect effects are personal and individual in nature and impact individual families or local communities, while others have more widespread impacts and affect society as a whole.

Weakened social structures

Traditional family and societal structures are weakened and disrupted by weapons proliferation and misuse when families and societies experience the death of parents, the separation of children from their families and the undermining of community elders by those with guns. Weapons can affect traditional patterns of warfare or ways of doing business. Just as the Karamajong in Uganda have seen weapons infiltrate their society, changing the dynamics of tribal warfare with an increase in deaths and injuries, other areas of Africa have seen weapons alter traditional society as well. The Nuer of southern Sudan, a traditionally semi-nomadic agro-pastoral group, have seen weapons alter their economies, societal structures and culture. Once introduced into society, guns were exchanged in bridewealth negotiations and became crucial indicators of wealth, power and masculinity. Guns have become part of rituals and ceremonies in Nuer society, and traditional purification regimens for inter-Nuer homicides were cast aside as the impersonality of using guns replaced the personal nature of fighting with spears. Nuer elders have also complained that youths with guns no longer listen to their parents or community leaders, and crime, violence and fear plague Nuer communities.[11]

Other regions of Africa have experienced similar situations, where guns have become part of the societal fabric. In a presentation at the United Nations Conference on the Illicit Trade of Small Arms and Light Weapons in all its Aspects, the former Interim President of Liberia, Dr Amos Sawyer, told the assembled delegates how small arms have changed the way of life in Liberia. He

explained how 'once the introductory [sic] of weapons takes place
in any local community, it changes the social order and the value
system is undermined. For example, in Liberia, after our war,
there was a new system and sayings: Oh, you have your MA, I have
my M-16, you have your BA, and I have my AK.' [12]

Pressure on healthcare systems
In many conflicts, arms-related violence puts increased pressure
on health systems by overwhelming hospitals with injuries, or
disrupting the delivery of life-saving and disease-preventing vac-
cinations and medicines. Healthy citizens may be unable to access
preventive care for treatable conditions or communicable diseases,
as resources may be diverted from vaccination programmes to
dealing with gun injuries or increased security. Furthermore,
health centres may be destroyed by bombings and other violence
and simply cannot operate. During the civil war in Mozambique,
experts believe that 34 per cent of the medical system there was
affected, through the destruction of nearly 200 health centres
as well as the damaging of nearly 300 more that were forced to
close.[13]

Malnutrition
Large numbers of conflict refugees and IDPs face additional hardships from weapons proliferation. Often, much-needed food aid
is unable to get to needy populations due to continued armed
violence. In some cases, the resulting lack of food contributes
to malnutrition, which affects the most vulnerable members of
a population, particularly children. In Liberia, for example, the
United Nations Food and Agriculture Organization (FAO) found
that, once the conflict began in December 1989, malnutrition
levels ranged from 10–50 per cent, as compared with 1.6 per cent
prior to the conflict. According to the FAO, 'the increases in malnutrition followed periodic upsurges in the scale of conflict and
displacement of segments of the population'.[14]

Lost educational opportunities

Educational opportunities and systems are also undermined by weapons proliferation and related conflicts. In some cases, schools may be destroyed or bombed during conflicts, which makes them unusable. During the civil war in Mozambique, the Mozambican government reported that an estimated 68 per cent of primary schools were closed or destroyed between 1981 and 1987, and one-third of the teaching staff was lost due to the ongoing conflict.[15] In other cases, schools become recruitment and abduction centres for armed groups, government forces or insurgents, putting children and teachers at even greater risk. As these threats escalate, teachers become unwilling or unable to return to schools. In countries such as Afghanistan, Colombia, Mozambique, Nicaragua, Sierra Leone, Sudan and Uganda, researchers have found that school enrolment in primary, secondary and night schools declined during armed conflicts, and only began to increase once the conflict or violence had ended.[16]

Interference with humanitarian assistance

The delivery of humanitarian assistance is often obstructed and delayed by the proliferation and threat of conventional arms. Although aid workers provide life-saving assistance, they are often themselves targets of violence, extortion, theft, rape and other criminal threats by armed perpetrators. As a result, some aid agencies remove staff from particularly dangerous communities when their safety cannot be guaranteed, leaving especially desperate populations with no means of outside help. When they do remain in conflict zones, aid agencies are often forced to spend increased resources on security, which diverts money from direct services. A comprehensive study by the Geneva-based Centre for Humanitarian Dialogue and the Small Arms Survey found that, of more than 2,000 humanitarian and development workers in ninety countries surveyed, 33 per cent reported that armed conflict had caused them to suspend operations or projects during the six months prior to the survey, and 26 per cent reported that suspensions in their work were due to armed crime and banditry.[17]

Hindered peacekeeping and peace-building

Excessive and destabilizing accumulations of weapons may also hinder peacekeeping and peace-building by multinational or national forces. African Union (AU) peacekeepers in Sudan have been prevented from fulfilling their mission due to heavily armed citizens, gangs and groups that target peacekeeping forces and the civilians and resources to which they are assigned to. At least fifteen AU peacekeepers have been killed in Darfur since the force was deployed in 2004.[18] In many cases, the insecurity caused by small arms proliferation reinforces a cycle of violence that requires even more peacekeeping aid and diverts resources from much-needed development assistance. According to Alfred Fawundu of the United Nations Development Programme (UNDP), the UN spends more than $200 billion annually on peacekeeping, roughly four times what it spends on development assistance.[19]

Slowed economic development

Economic development is often slowed and impeded by the proliferation and threat of conventional arms. According to the Control Arms Campaign, a civil war in a low-income country can cost the international economy an estimated $50 billion annually.[20] One report on the nearly twenty-year conflict in Uganda found that the conflict cost the country at least 3 per cent of its annual Gross Domestic Product (GDP), or $100 million a year.[21]

Impoverished communities may suffer additional hardships from weapons proliferation and misuse. Widespread insecurity and a proliferation of weapons prevent citizens from seeking safe access to food, water and other key resources. US Army General David Petraeus told National Public Radio in July 2007 that continued armed violence in Iraq has created fear throughout the country, which has forced markets and banks to close, as well as prevented the implementation of many basic services, including sanitation, which has created numerous problems for the Iraqi public and economy.[22]

Impeded business investment and opportunities

In the worst cases, businesses are unable to open and operate effectively, as armed violence and persistent insecurity increase the costs of conducting business, while reducing profits. In Nicaragua, for example, the Association of Coffee Growers of Matagalpa has reported that the country's lucrative coffee crop has been harmed by armed violence that is concentrated in the coffee-growing regions. Growers were forced to increase their production costs by over 10 per cent due to the implementation of increased security measures that became necessary when the weapons – particularly AK-47s – provided to the coffee farmers by the Nicaraguan army were stolen and lost and ended up in the hands of criminal gangs. Moreover, the coffee growers reported that, had armed violence not plagued the region, production could have increased by up to 30 per cent.[23] Other reports estimated the loss of coffee production in 1999 was worth 300,000 quintals, or roughly $25 million.[24]

Foreign investment and business may also be harmed by weapons proliferation and violence. The fishing industry in Bangladesh – which is a major source of Bangladeshi commerce, employment and food – has been negatively harmed by arms proliferation and resulting violence. Fishermen have been killed, their ships hijacked and their fish stolen. Moreover, both domestic and foreign ships are hesitant to use Bangladeshi ports to conduct business, because of the increased violence and insecurity. Indeed, some foreign companies have raised the costs for using the ports, which raises the price of imports and exports.[25] In some cases, the perpetual economic disparity and deficient future opportunities fuel a cycle of poverty and disenchantment with peaceful processes. These conditions may encourage disgruntled ex-combatants to return to fighting, as well as fuel crime – and plentiful supplies of weapons make that choice easy to execute.

Loss of tourism

Tourism, a significant source of revenue for many countries, may also be affected by weapons proliferation and conflict. The shooting deaths of nearly sixty tourists in Luxor, Egypt, in 1997 harmed the entire country's tourism industry. In the first year after the massacre, tourism revenues fell drastically, with a loss of approximately 50 per cent of Egypt's annual $3.7 billion tourism industry. One year after the attack, estimates placed the number of tourists in Luxor at 3,000 per day, or 75 per cent of the pre-massacre total.[26] Similarly, Kenya experienced a fall in tourism in the late 1990s. Numbers of foreign tourists, who are a major source of income to the country, fell as violent clashes plagued the areas around Mombasa and Nairobi. When the US government issued travel warnings and British Airways halted flights to the country, Kenya saw the amount of foreign tourism – and thus tourism revenue – halved from its late 1980s high of 900,000 tourists per year.[27] A similar trend also occurred in the Balkans after the violence of the 1990s.

Increasing violence and crime

Conflict and crime at the barrel of a gun interfere with the efforts of individuals to pursue their livelihoods. In many post-conflict areas, economic recovery is thwarted as the basic infrastructure – such as supply and transportation routes – may be threatened or destroyed. In many cases markets remain closed, supplies are difficult to obtain, and arable land is unusable. Comprehensive studies of the human security impacts of small arms proliferation in countries around the world have found that small arms and the insecurity they engender have had deleterious effects on agricultural and pastoral activities, as well as development and commercial investment.[28] Studies

have estimated that insecurity in Chad due to continued conflicts between 1960 and 1995 has prevented the country from
drilling up to 10 million tons of oil a year.[29] Similar trends
can be seen in Angola and the DRC as mining opportunities
were too dangerous or expensive due to armed violence and a
requirement for increased security.

Development of cultures of violence

Weapons proliferation is also responsible for consequential
effects on society. The two largest of these – cultures of violence
and the use of child soldiers – lengthen conflicts, undermine
community and family leaders and contribute to additional
pressures on peacekeeping and peace-building. Cultures of
violence – when weapons come to represent both power and
means of conflict resolution – cause more and more people to
take up arms, leading to greater violence and insecurity. In turn,
people arm themselves further to protect themselves against the
ever-increasing violence. As a result, crime and impunity are
rampant, and efforts to solve conflicts and rebuild are prevented
or slowed. Development also suffers as insecurity prevents economic investment.

The use of child soldiers

In addition, a tragic consequence of lengthened conflict and widespread small arms proliferation is the use of child soldiers. Young
children can easily be taught to use these weapons. When conflicts
rage for years, new ranks of traditional soldiers – adult males –
simply do not exist, and armed forces and non-state armed groups
use children to fill their dwindling numbers. Rebel groups, guerrilla armies, militias and armed gangs utilize child soldiers in their
violent conflicts against each other, against the state or to gain
control of resources and power. According to the International
Coalition to Stop the Use of Child Soldiers, at least twenty current conflicts use child soldiers, both as direct combatants and in

support roles, such as cooks, messengers, porters and sex slaves. At least nine governments actively use children in conflicts around the world. Countries such as Burma, Uganda and Colombia have some of the largest numbers of child soldiers fighting in their ongoing conflicts. Many of these armed groups would be unable to wage war without the added troop strength provided by child soldiers. For example, experts believe the Lord's Resistance Army in Uganda has child soldiers making up a considerable percentage of its fighting force.[30]

The arms trade and terrorism

The global arms trade is inextricably linked to international terrorism. Although the world's attention is focused on the danger of terrorists armed with nuclear, chemical, biological or radiological devices, the reality is that terrorists already have possession of and easy access to some of the most deadly tools of their trade: conventional weapons, and small arms in particular. Several factors make these weapons highly desirable to terrorists – their lethality, portability and easy concealment make them extremely effective weapons, and small arms are readily available most everywhere in the world. The appearance of assault rifles alone can induce panic and terror, allowing individuals or groups to take control of situations and hold groups of people hostage.[31] According to analysis by the Federation of American Scientists, small arms and light weapons alone were used to perpetrate the roughly 175 terrorist incidents identified in the 2004 US State Department's annual Patterns of Global Terrorism report.[32] From small-scale attacks to large-scale operations, terrorists rely on conventional arms to conduct their business.

The terrorist link

With few exceptions, information about the linkages between conventional arms and terrorism is difficult to come by. The

United Nations Programme of Action on Small Arms vaguely refers to terrorism in multiple places, but these references include statements such as 'concerned also about the close link between terrorism, organized crime, trafficking in drugs and precious minerals and the illicit trade in small arms and light weapons', without elaborating on those links and connections.[33] This imprecision arises from the fact that it is difficult, if not nearly impossible, to research fully the supply networks of terrorist groups, because of the clandestine nature of the organizations. Moreover, because researchers and policymakers have focused on terrorists' potential for future violence, scant research has specifically examined the tools of their trade.

But even though any discussion of terrorism undoubtedly invokes images of momentous, well-coordinated attacks, such as those of 11 September 2001, or organized bands of militants operating in Chechnya, Iraq or Afghanistan, in reality conventional weapons – and small arms specifically – make even small groups of individuals extremely effective at terrorizing civilian populations. Indeed, several high-profile terrorist incidents in the last few years have been executed solely with conventional weapons. Among the most notable of these attacks are the October 2002 seizure of the Russian Palace of Culture Theatre by Chechen militants brandishing guns and armed with explosives; the November 2002 shoulder-fired surface-to-air missile attack on an Israeli airliner in Mombasa, Kenya, by al Qaeda-linked terrorists; and the September 2004 Beslan School siege by Chechen rebels, who held more than 1,000 adults and children hostage before detonating explosives and killing more than 300 of the captives.[34] Lower-profile terrorist incidents have also been perpetrated with conventional weapons. In March 2007, a disgruntled day-care centre owner in the Philippines held more than 30 people hostage on a bus, armed with grenades and guns. The hostage taker was not affiliated with any terrorist organization, and protested against corruption and the needs of poor children.[35]

MANPADS

Man-portable air defence systems, or MANPADS, have received increased attention in the past several years due to their attractiveness to terrorists. These weapons can be fired by only one or two people but can bring down military and commercial aircraft in dramatic fashion. Although recent MANPADS strikes – such as the 2002 Mombasa attack – have prompted international action on establishing tighter controls over these weapons, terrorists have adeptly used MANPADS since the 1970s. In thirty-plus years, MANPADS have hit over forty civilian aircraft, causing twenty-five crashes. In fact, over 600 deaths can be blamed on these deadly weapons, according to the US State Department.[36] For example, the September 1978 downing of Air Rhodesia flight 825, the April 1994 crash of the jet carrying the Presidents of Rwanda and Burundi, and the UN transport planes shot down in December 1998 and January 1999 by UNITA rebels in Angola were all a result of MANPADS attacks.[37]

Terrorist procurement of weapons

Terrorists are often portrayed armed with AK-47s, pistols and grenades, supplied by the illicit arms trade. As described in chapter 4, the illicit arms trade is thriving. Terrorists take advantage of the many channels available to divert weapons from the legal to the illegal market – including theft and craft production – to acquire weapons. For example, weapons are believed to flow from Burma to Indian rebels across the two countries' porous borders, supporters of Sri Lanka's Tamil Tigers have sought to divert US conventional weapons illegally, and Iran is believed to provide weapons to al Qaeda-affiliated militants in Iraq. Terrorists are also creative when it comes to producing weapons. In Pakistan, craft production has been part of the local business economy in the Northwest Frontier Province for decades. In fact, what started as a reliable source of weapons for the region's many tribes is now a sophisticated operation that provides arms for militants and separatists throughout South Asia.[38] In the Philippines, craft production fills the arsenals of criminal gangs and Islamic separatist groups. Although large terrorist groups such as Abu Sayyaf prefer more sophisticated and better-quality weapons, smaller terrorist groups and organized criminals rely on the cheap locally produced *sumpak* to carry out their illicit activities.[39]

Flouting US law

Terrorists have also become experts at acquiring weapons through legal means, by utilizing loopholes in existing laws and regulations. Even countries with sophisticated export controls and national legislation are not immune from terrorist exploitation. Although the United States has a vast array of federal and state laws governing arms purchasing and ownership, as well as elaborate and comprehensive arms export regulations, significant loopholes have allowed terrorist networks to acquire US weapons with relative ease. In fact, according to interviews and material found at terrorist training camps, the United States has been identified by terrorist networks, including al Qaeda, as a promising source for weapons. The Violence Policy Center in Washington, DC, obtained a pamphlet entitled 'How I Can Train Myself for Jihad', which was allegedly discovered at terrorist safe houses in Kabul, Afghanistan. The pamphlet highlights the benefits of firearms training and acquisition in the United States, and encourages visits to US shooting ranges and participation in the many firearms courses offered to the public. The pamphlet goes on to recommend legally obtaining an assault rifle and training in its proper uses, stressing that because these things can be done legally, employing illicit avenues is unnecessary.[40]

According to data and information provided by the Violence Policy Center and the US government, it appears terrorists are indeed purchasing firearms and other conventional weapons in the United States. A Violence Policy Center report reveals significant purchases of .50-calibre sniper rifles by terrorist organizations working in the United States – two by the Irish Republican Army in 1995, and twenty-five by al Qaeda in 1988 or 1989.[41]

After the attacks of 11 September 2001, the Brady Center to Prevent Gun Violence detailed the weaknesses of existing US gun laws and policies and described how terrorists take advantage of these loopholes to acquire weapons.[42] The Brady Center report exposed several cases where terrorists were able to exploit US law – through gun shows, straw purchasing, the purchase of assault rifles and high-capacity ammunition magazines, ordering gun kits through the mail and by employing corrupt gun dealers. The report features numerous examples in which would-be terrorists were caught by the Federal Bureau of Investigation (FBI) and other federal authorities acquiring weapons. Although these cases were prevented, they probably represent only a small percentage of the attempts by foreign terrorists to acquire US weapons for malevolent purposes.

Three particular cases in the Brady Center report underscore the reality of foreign terrorists seeking US weapons. Keith Glaude of Trinidad was arrested in June 2001 in Florida after trying to purchase sixty AK-47s and ten machine guns to send to Jamaat Al Muslimeen, an extreme Islamic group in Trinidad. The group, responsible for the 1990 coup attempt in Trinidad and Tobago, used weapons purchased in Florida in their failed plot. In a second case, Ali Boumelhem was convicted of attempting to supply the terrorist group Hezbollah in 2000 after he and his brother Mohamed purchased weapons at gun shows in Michigan to avoid background checks. Although his brother was legally allowed to purchase weapons, Boumelhem was a convicted felon and took advantage of the lack of federal and state laws requiring private sellers to conduct background checks. He was caught only because of the information provided by a police informant. And in a third instance, IRA soldier Conor Claxton, convicted of supplying guns to the IRA in 2000, purchased $18,000 worth of weapons, including rifles, handguns and high-powered ammunition, from a legal gun dealer, whom Claxton then bribed to persuade him not to file paperwork on the sales. British police intercepted the weapons, which had been mailed in packages and disguised in toys, computers and clothes, and traced them back to the corrupt dealer.[43]

Nongovernmental organizations are not the only sources of information on terrorist acquisition of weapons. The US government has also begun investigating the role of US law and terrorist weapons acquisition. A 2003 CRS report found 'foreign terrorists could exploit, and appear to have exploited in limited cases, the general availability of firearms in the United States to carry out terrorist attacks in the United States or abroad'.[44] According to the CRS, terrorist networks used both legal and illegal channels to acquire weapons, including gun shows. The CRS report also cautions that 'a terrorist could plausibly stockpile weapons, since multiple firearm purchases would only be reported by licensed dealers if such purchases exceeded more than one handgun from a single dealer within 5 consecutive days'.[45] Under US law, background checks for gun purchases do not include cross-checks of terrorist watchlists. The GAO reported in 2005 that 'membership in a terrorist organization does not prohibit a person from owning a gun under current law'.[46] According to the GAO report, between 3 February and 20 June 2004 forty-four firearm-related background checks that were conducted by the FBI and relevant state agencies had matches with terrorist watchlist records. However, only six of these background checks resulted in a denied purchase, because the checks failed to uncover any conditions that prohibited gun purchases (for three more, either a decision is pending or records were not available).[47] The frightening truth is that patience and creativity can allow terrorists to assemble massive arsenals through legal means in the United States.

Other sources of terrorist weapons

Poorly monitored covert arms transfers are also a source of terrorist weaponry. US covert weapons provided to the Afghan *mujahideen* during the Cold War have been linked to al Qaeda and Osama bin Laden. In addition, Islamic fundamentalists from North Africa and Saudi Arabia hired by the CIA during the 1980s to fight in Afghanistan were all trained and armed with US expertise and weapons.[48] Terrorist groups also rely on theft from weapons stockpiles and illegal sales from soldiers to fill their arsenals. In 2003, Saudi Arabia investigated the illegal sale of automatic rifles and other weapons by Saudi National Guard soldiers to al Qaeda operatives.[49]

The United States may be an unwilling supplier of weapons to terrorists, but other governments have been complicit in the arming of terrorist networks around the world. Countries such as Syria and Iran have been repeatedly implicated in arms transfers to terrorist groups. After the summer 2006 war between Hezbollah and Israel, intelligence revealed that Hezbollah used weapons, including rockets, that were made in Syria. The discovery marked a shift in the relationship between Syria and Hezbollah. Previously, Syria had been known to permit Iranian weapons to flow into Lebanon. Israeli investigators also identified Russian-made weapons – that were originally transferred from Russia to Syria – and were also able to pinpoint specific cross-border routes the arms were likely to have taken.[50] Hezbollah made no secret of its plans or interest in rearming following the war and, in December 2006, reports surfaced that Hezbollah was looking to rearm and replace its lost and used equipment. According to US officials, Hezbollah had an arms shopping list including anti-ship cruise missiles, anti-tank missiles and MANPADS. The US source claimed that Iran was Hezbollah's main arms supplier and had access to the list.[51]

The impact of terrorist weapons

Terrorism, guns and other commodities, such as diamonds, are linked in the murky and shadowy world of arms and conflict. The area between Paraguay, Argentina and Brazil is believed to be a source of financing and recruiting for Hezbollah and Hamas, as well as other Middle Eastern terrorist networks. The area is home to cigarette, gun and drug trafficking and is known for money laundering and producing falsified documents.[52] Former Liberian President Charles Taylor is alleged to have sold diamonds from Sierra Leone to a number of terrorist and criminal organizations, including Hezbollah and al Qaeda, as part of a large money laundering, diamonds and gun running scheme.[53] As mentioned in chapter 4, this nexus between weapons and the illicit trade in a variety of commodities fuels illegal activity around the world.

Although conventional weapons are used directly to support terrorist activities, they also indirectly support terrorism. Because the violence perpetuated by weapons proliferation impedes the activities of peacekeepers, stifles economic growth and foreign investment and development and prevents the delivery of assistance by humanitarian and relief organizations, societies are unable to recover from conflict and poverty. As a result, an insecure environment, coupled with a stagnating economy, allows hostility, isolation and dissatisfaction to grow and breed among a desperate population. Terrorists and criminal organizations use these conditions to their advantage. These conditions permit unscrupulous actors to enlist and indoctrinate new recruits, and foster a culture of impunity and violence.

Somalia fits this tragic pattern. In a report by the United Nations Monitoring Group in November 2006 – a month before the Islamic Courts Union was ousted by invading troops from Ethiopia – ten foreign governments were implicated in supplying arms to warring parties in Somalia, despite a UN arms embargo forbidding such transfers.[54] Somalia has long been suspected of harbouring terrorist groups, and groups and individuals operating in the failed state are believed to have ties to al Qaeda. The country has been accused by the United Nations and the United States of playing a key role in both the 1998 East African embassy bombings and 2002 attacks in Mombasa, Kenya,[55] prompting the United States to conduct air raids against Somali targets in January 2007.[56]

The international arms trade contributes to a variety of complex and multifaceted consequences. No country, region or community is immune from these deleterious effects, which bind many sectors of society. Addressing the consequences of the international arms trade requires a multitude of approaches, involving many different segments of society. As will be demonstrated in chapter 6, specifically addressing the costs of the international arms trade requires creativity and patience.

6

Controlling the international arms trade

In February 2008, twenty-eight states[1] took part in the first session of the UN Group of Governmental Experts on an Arms Trade Treaty. The group was tasked with determining the possible feasibility, scope and parameters of a legally binding international agreement that establishes common international standards for international arms transfers. The initiative marked recognition by the international community that the legal trade in arms has had negative consequences for global peace and security, human rights and development, and marked an evolution of existing control mechanisms covering the conventional weapons trade.

Yet, developing an Arms Trade Treaty will not be an easy task. Although many governments have demonstrated increased interest in global arms trade controls, some states – particularly those that have a significant stake in the arms trade, from either a security or economic perspective – challenge such undertakings and constrain efforts to limit weapons transfers. When discussing controls, states are constantly mindful of the intersection between foreign policy, security and humanitarian concerns on the one hand, and financial issues such as 'trade, jobs and profit' on the other.[2] Indeed, throughout history, balancing responsible arms trade practices with security and human rights has always been challenging and has had implications for the ways in which the global weapons trade system is controlled and managed.

In general, the international trade in conventional arms has proven to be difficult to control. Unlike weapons of mass destruction (nuclear, chemical and biological weapons), conventional arms are considered legitimate weapons with purposes ranging from national defence and security force use to policing purposes, sport and hunting activities and personal security use. Conventional arms, therefore, are viewed as legitimate commodities that can be fairly sold, provided and traded, making arms control efforts all the more complicated and fraught with obstacles and challenges. Nonetheless, numerous efforts have been made at the international, regional and national levels to control the trade in arms, with varying degrees of success. This chapter provides an in-depth look at theses efforts. It first provides a historical overview of past efforts to control the weapons trade before focusing on more recent arms control activities at the international, regional and national levels. Within the context of these various levels of activities, the chapter discusses the relevant arms control actors and their roles in limiting the arms trade. Finally, the chapter examines the various challenges and obstacles facing arms control today and concludes with a discussion of the prospects for weapons control measures in the future.

Conventional arms control of the past

Attempts to control the international arms trade date back as far as the Middle Ages, when informal understandings among nations regarding the sale of arms were used to limit weapons transfers to potential enemies. European Christian nations, for example, collectively agreed not to transfer arms to the Turks.[3] Formal controls on the arms trade were first considered in the context of regulating the slave trade. The General Act for the Repression of the African Slave Trade of 1890 was a formal agreement among thirteen European states, the United States, and three non-European nations to regulate the arms traffic to North Africa.[4] In 1925, the Geneva Disarmament Conference focused on limiting the trade of poisonous, asphyxiating and other noxious gases that may be used in warfare, as well as bacteriological weapons. The Conference, however, was never fully enforced given that the primary signatories (the United States, United Kingdom, France and the Soviet Union) added a condition that if any of their enemies, or their enemies' allies, failed to implement the agreement and respect the limitations, they too would not comply. From 1925 to 1938, the League of Nations published a statistical yearbook disclosing arms exports and imports around the world. Yet, beyond this transparency measure, the discussion of arms trade regulation floundered and little progress was made.[5]

At the beginning of the Cold War, a renewed interest in conventional arms control emerged. However, the interest focused less on conventional weapons and more on nuclear capabilities and sensitive, dual-use technologies and equipment relevant for military weapons programmes. One of the first international organizations to focus strictly on trade control issues emerged in 1949 when North Atlantic Treaty Organization members (minus Iceland and Japan) created the Coordinating Committee for Multilateral Export Controls (COCOM) to control the sale of strategic goods to Communist bloc countries.[6] After the Cold War ended, COCOM was replaced by the Wassenaar Arrangement on Export Controls for Conventional Arms and Dual-Use Goods and Technologies (discussed more fully below) – the only multilateral organization that today focuses on conventional weapons and critical dual-use items.[7]

By the 1970s a number of attempts to control the conventional arms trade materialized. Some were focused on regional controls, others on controlling certain types of weaponry. The first regional attempt to control large arms purchases was created by eight Andean states with the Ayacucho Declaration of 1974. This agreement, however, failed to prevent the acquisition of large weapons systems by several member states.[8]

The Conventional Arms Transfer Talks
The Conventional Arms Transfer (CAT) Talks of 1977 and 1978 were organized during the Carter Administration because of 'a

general political perception . . . that the international market in arms was outstripping the ability of policymakers to control it'.[9] These talks between the United States and Soviet Union failed not only because of Cold War politics, but because of competing international and domestic objectives and a failure to start with a small, clear goal that could be expanded later. Moreover, during the CAT Talks, European states such as France, the United Kingdom and Germany refused to work with the United States on arms controls unless an agreement was first reached with the Soviet Union. However, the Soviet Union refused to consider the control of conventional arms transfers as a legitimate arms control concern. Thus, the talks in December of 1977 ended with little agreement. Any optimism that had been built up during minor agreements through 1978 were dashed when the United States and Soviet Union collided over whether to discuss regions allied with the United States (Iran, China, South Korea) during talks in Mexico City.[10]

The CCW
The UN Convention on Prohibitions or Restrictions on the Use of Certain Conventional Weapons which may be Deemed to be Excessively Injurious or to Have Indiscriminate Effects (also known as the Inhumane Weapons Convention or CCW) was originally adopted on 10 October 1980 with three annexed Protocols. Fifty states signed the Convention and it entered into force on 2 December 1983. The Convention contains general provisions, with the goal of banning or restricting the use of those weapons that cause unnecessary or unjustifiable suffering to combatants or affect civilians indiscriminately.[11] Protocol I on Non-Detectable Fragments prohibits the use of any weapon that is intended to injure by fragments that are undetectable by X-ray, and has 100 states parties.[12] Protocol II on Prohibitions or Restrictions on the Use of Mines, Booby Traps and Other Devices prohibits the use of such weapons against civilians, through indiscriminate

means, or in most towns, and has 89 states parties.[13] Protocol III on Prohibitions or Restrictions on the Use of Incendiary Weapons prohibits their use against civilians, a military target located among civilians, or plant cover and has 95 states parties.[14]

Additional work on the CCW took place in the 1990s with the adoption of Protocol IV on Blinding Laser Weapons on 13 October 1995 at the First Review Conference. While the original Convention only applied to international armed conflict situations, the states parties amended the Convention at the Second Review Conference held on 11–21 December 2001 to apply to situations of non-international armed conflict. Protocol V on Explosive Remnants of War was adopted on 28 November 2003 and entered into force on 12 November 2006, requiring states that use explosives that leave remnants to assist in the marking, clearance, removal or destruction of such weapons after the conflict. Moreover, states are required to record, retain and transmit information on the use and abandonment of explosive ordinances. Protocol V also calls on members to take steps to protect civilians and humanitarian missions in the conflict area.[15] Today, 102 states are parties to the Protocol and another 6 are signatories.[16]

The CCW is not without its difficulties. The implementation of and compliance with the agreement have suffered some inconsistencies as reports have emerged about the development and use of items found on the CCW control lists, especially regarding laser weapons.[17] Moreover, parties to the CCW have not been able to achieve consensus on issues such as the creation of a mechanism to ensure compliance with the Treaty and the addition of provisions to ban small-calibre bullets because of the significant damage they may cause to the human body.[18] Other problematic issues include whether the CCW states should add restrictions on cluster munitions – weapons that distribute small 'sub munitions' over a large area – or limitations on the deployment of anti-vehicle mines. The United States supports adding measures on both issues (although they had opposed limits on cluster munitions

until June 2007). China and Russia, however, object to both measures. Because of the frustrations, a number of Treaty members
began a negotiating process outside the CCW in February 2007 to
ban cluster munitions.[19]

The CFE Treaty

One of the most significant conventional arms control treaties of
the twentieth century emerged near the end of the Cold War. The
Treaty on Conventional Forces in Europe (the CFE Treaty) was
signed on 19 November 1990 by twenty-two NATO and Warsaw
Pact countries. The agreement was meant to bring parity, enhance
transparency and increase stability regarding conventional forces
in Europe. Covering the area from the Atlantic Ocean to the Ural
Mountains, the CFE Treaty outlined limits for five categories of
conventional weapons systems: armoured combat vehicles, battle
tanks, combat aircraft, attack helicopters and large artillery. The
limits were set at a total of 30,000 armoured vehicles, 20,000
tanks, 20,000 pieces of artillery, 6,800 aircraft, and 2,000 helicopters. Limits were set for each individual country within the
Treaty area, and no one state could possess more than one-third
of the total limit in each category. All weaponry in excess of these
limits was to be destroyed within forty months of the Treaty entering into force, and a rigorous verification and inspection regime
was established to oversee the process.[20] Not all of the weapons
that exceed Treaty limits, however, have been removed and
destroyed. Disagreements between states parties have emerged,
and former Soviet weapons in Moldova and Georgia, for example, remain today. Moreover, due to Russian concerns about the
deployment of a US missile defence system and the placement
of US military bases in Central and Eastern Europe, the Russian
Duma voted unanimously in November 2007 to suspend the
country's implementation of the CFE Treaty, leaving the future of
this groundbreaking conventional arms treaty in question.[21]

Contemporary arms trade controls

Conventional arms control today is unlike arms control of the past. The comprehensive legalistic arms control treaties that focus on large conventional weaponry are being replaced by voluntary, political agreements and the development of global norms, principles and standards of behaviour that mould and constrain, but do not necessarily require significant limitations on, state arms trade practices. Moreover, today's conventional arms control initiatives are more likely to involve a wider range of actors, including numerous international governmental and nongovernmental organizations, rather than simply national governments. States, of course, remain a necessary component of any arms control effort as they continue to be the primary actors in the international political system, but states can no longer ignore the pressure and requirements of international organizations and nongovernmental actors that push, prod, encourage and facilitate state behaviour. The role of these international governmental and nongovernmental groups in relation to the specific national practices that governments have put in place is remarkable. Although many conventional arms control activities have occurred throughout the post-Cold War period, current control efforts demonstrate that much remains to be done to limit effectively the destabilizing and dangerous spread of conventional weapons.

Current international arms control efforts

The United Nations is the primary international governmental organization that has been active in implementing controls on the international arms trade. The UN has a long history of facilitating arms control matters, and in the 1990s this role increased. The trade of large conventional weapons was the subject of early 1990s discussion and activities at the UN. In 1991, in the wake of the Gulf War, for example, the permanent members of the United

Nations Security Council (United States, Britain, France, China and Russia) established guidelines for conventional arms transfers, including advance notification of arms sales, considerations of human rights consequences, and concerns for destabilizing arms build-ups. These guidelines, however, were never fully implemented because China opposed US arms sales to Taiwan and refused to abide by the guidelines until such sales ceased.[22] Future discussions about the role and purpose of arms transfer guidelines continued with the UN Disarmament Commission reiterating the importance of restraint in its 1996 report.[23] Perhaps the most significant conventional arms control development of the 1990s was the creation of the UN Register of Conventional Arms in December of 1991. Since then, numerous working groups, reports, meetings and agreements have been arranged, focusing on the international trade in small arms and light weapons. The United Nations is not, however, the only forum for conventional arms controls. The Wassenaar Arrangement on Export Controls for Conventional Arms and Dual-Use Goods and Technologies also plays a significant role.

The UN Register of Conventional Arms

Following the recommendations of an expert group appointed by the UN Secretary-General, the United Nations General Assembly established the UN Register of Conventional Arms under Resolution 46/36 L 'Transparency in Armaments' in December 1991. The Resolution requested Member States to provide annual data on conventional arms exports and imports in seven categories[24] and to provide background information on military holdings, procurement through national production, and any other relevant information and policies.[25] To date, the UN Arms Register remains the only cooperative global security instrument that focuses on the proliferation of conventional weapons.

The UN Register of Conventional Arms was the result of a long history of attempted arms registers. After World War I, the League of Nations agreed to create an office to compile and publish arms export licences. In 1924, the League published the Armaments Yearbook with information on states' armed forces and occasional information on arms procurement activities. After World War II, proposals for arms registers were submitted to the UN by Malta in 1965 and Denmark in 1967. In 1976, Japan asked the UN Secretary-General to begin a study of arms transfer activities. However, these suggestions did not gain much support until 1991 with the collapse of the Warsaw Treaty Organization (which had been hostile to the idea of an arms register) and the Gulf War (because Iraq had benefited significantly from an uncontrolled international arms trade system). The Gulf War, in fact, ushered in a new era in arms control. After it was clear that Iraq had been able to build up its weapons capabilities secretly with the aid of US and European arms exports, governments became more receptive to increased transparency in the arms trade.[26] States began to focus more closely on the trans-national nature of the arms trade, moving away from the bilateral superpower efforts that prevailed during the Cold War. Moreover, states began to monitor more carefully the spread of small arms and light weapons as it became more evident that various civil conflicts were heating up or spreading in the post-Cold War period. Accordingly, governments and international actors realized that weapons suppliers needed to accept responsibility for their contributions to the international arms trade.

The foundational idea and 'underlying assumption' of the UN Register of Conventional Arms is that transparency in the trade of conventional arms 'will encourage prudent restraint by arms exporting and importing nations'.[27] UN Member States are asked to submit voluntarily information on their annual imports and exports of conventional weapons, as well as military procurement through national production. Since the Register's inception, 170 member states have at some point reported information on the trade in major conventional arms, including tanks, artillery systems, missiles, aircraft and warships.[28] Reviews of, and updates to, the Register are made regularly. In 2003, the expert review report recommended that MANPADS be included in the Register within the missile category.[29] The Report of the Group of Government Experts on the continuing operation and further development of the UN Register, dated 15 August 2006, made the following recommendations: (1) international transfers of conventional arms involving only UN member states should be reported to the Register; (2) member states should report transfers of small arms and light weapons on a standardized form as additional background information; and (3) the reporting weight threshold for submarines should be lowered. The Group also observed that the Register captures 'the great bulk of the global arms trade in the seven categories of conventional arms' as well as many transfers with non-participating states.[30]

The UN focus on small arms and light weapons

Although it has been suggested that states submit small arms transfer data to the UN Conventional Arms Register, this is a new provision that is only suggested in the background information and, to date, little information on small arms and light weapons exports has been provided. However, the United Nations has addressed the small arms trade in other ways. The UN first tackled the illicit trade of small arms and light weapons in the 1995 General Assembly Resolution A/RES/50/70/B, which requested a report from the Secretary-General detailing the illicit trade in small arms and making recommendations for controlling the trade. In response, the Secretary-General appointed a Panel of Government Experts to study the small arms issue. The Panel submitted a detailed report that the Secretary-General presented to the General Assembly in 1997, which detailed the various consequences of the illicit small arms trade, as well as the modes of small arms transfers and the causes of illicit trafficking. The report also outlined the specific steps UN member states should take to curb the illicit trafficking of small arms.[31] A follow-up Group of Governmental Experts on Small Arms and Light Weapons was established in 1999 to evaluate progress made on small arms and recommend future UN involvement in the issue. The Group's 1999 report set the stage for a UN Conference on small arms.[32] The Secretary-General also created an internal UN mechanism, the Coordinating Action on Small Arms (CASA), which is intended to help implement small arms activities and agreements within the UN system.[33]

On 8 June 2001, UN member states adopted the *Protocol against the Illicit Manufacturing of and Trafficking in Firearms, Their Parts and Components and Ammunition* (known as 'the Firearms Protocol'). The Firearms Protocol supplements the United Nations Convention against Trans-national Organized Crime and entered into force on 3 July 2005. The Firearms Protocol is the first international legally binding small arms control agreement. Ratifying states commit to adopting certain crime control measures and implementing domestic legislation to: (1) make the illegal manufacturing or trafficking of firearms a criminal offence; (2) establish a governmental arms licensing system; and (3) create a system for marking and tracing firearms.[34] The Firearms Protocol negotiations were often arduous and resulted in an agreement that allows individual countries to use their own, individual coding systems, which, some argue, could hamper and obstruct inspection activities because weapons may not necessarily be identified individually but in batches. Solutions to this problem, however, are currently under discussion.[35]

The United Nations held the Conference on the Illicit Trade in Small Arms and Light Weapons in All Its Aspects on 9–20 July 2001, which resulted in the UN *Programme of Action to Prevent, Combat and Eradicate the Illicit Trade in Small Arms and Light Weapons in All Its Aspects*. The Programme of Action (PoA) established a voluntary process for member states to take action on small arms at the national, regional and global levels. In the PoA, member states expressed their concern about the illicit trade of weapons; pledged to enact at the national level small arms control measures such as export licensing procedures, brokering controls and stockpile security practices; promised to create regional networks to share information and promote arms trafficking controls; and at the international level pledged to work with the UN to enforce embargoes, circulate data and encourage international laws governing the arms trade. Member states also vowed to assist interested states in implementing the PoA, exchange information on the arms trade, and take efforts to improve their own legal arms transfer systems.[36] However, because the PoA is a voluntary, politically binding agreement, with no enforcement mechanism, implementation has been spotty.

The PoA discussions and agreement, however, were not without debate and controversy. At the 2001 UN Small Arms Conference, the United States was openly hostile to the PoA negotiations and made clear its opposition to a PoA that contained any restrictions on ownership of weapons by civilians, restrictions on the legal trade and manufacture of small arms and light weapons, restrictions on the sale of small arms and light weapons to entities other than governments, and a commitment to begin discussions on legally binding agreements. The United States was silently supported by China and Cuba, among others. After closed-door sessions and all-night negotiations, the PoA did not contain any language to which the United States would be opposed, leaving small arms control as a narrowly defined, voluntary effort. Although the UN Conference on the Illicit Trade in Small Arms did not live up to the hopes of many governments and nongovernmental organizations, it did begin an international dialogue on small arms controls.

As a follow-up to the 2001 PoA Conference, the United Nations hosted the First Biennial Meeting of States (BMS) to Consider the Implementation of the PoA from 7–11 July 2003, the Second BMS from 11–15 July 2005, the 2006 Review Conference (see below) and the third BMS from 14–18 July 2008.[37] The report from the first BMS noted international progress regarding the disclosure of information about arms transfers, implementation of new national legislation to combat the illicit arms trade, and strengthening of institutions tackling small arms problems. The report also noted, however, that there remained a need for greater transparency and assistance in stockpile management. The BMS report revealed that, since 2001, twenty-one member states had adopted or revised arms control legislation and twelve had added end-user certificate requirements. Most states, however, still had not enacted brokering controls.[38] The 2005 BMS also reiterated and reaffirmed member state commitment to the PoA and noted that, although progress had been made, much more action was needed to implement the 2001 agreement more effectively. Moreover, states began a discussion at the 2005 BMS about expanding and strengthening the PoA to include additional controls on small arms transfers not currently covered by it.[39]

One tangible result of the 2001 PoA was the adoption in December 2005 of the *International Instrument to Enable States to Identify and Trace, in a Timely and Reliable Manner, Illicit Small Arms and Light Weapons*.[40] In addition to identifying and tracing weapons, the instrument is also meant to enhance international cooperation in the marking and tracing of weapons. While the method of marking arms is up to the individual states, member states agreed to ensure that weapons receive a unique mark at the time of manufacture, allow for marking of the year and country of import, and mark or destroy unmarked weapons found in their territory. Also, while the mode of record keeping is at state discretion, states agreed to keep accurate and comprehensive records of marked small arms and light weapons in their territory, including manufacturing records, for thirty years, and import and export records for twenty years. States may also choose their own tracing systems. Moreover, a state may request a trace on illicit weapons found in their territory, and should be prompt in responding to tracing requests from other states. States agreed to enact such legislation and regional cooperation as necessary to put in place such an instrument, but, again, such action is voluntary.[41]

The PoA also created a Group of Government Experts to address the prevention and eradication of illicit brokering of small arms and light weapons in December 2005. The Group submitted a report to the United Nations in July 2007, outlining a number of specific recommendations. Specifically, the Group urged nations to enhance national implementation of brokering legislation, strengthen international cooperation and the sharing of information about brokering activities, increase international assistance and the building of capacity at local levels to respond to illicit arms brokering, promote more effective reporting on brokers and brokering activities and enhance national implementation of UN Security Council arms embargoes and relevant sanctions.[42]

In an effort to assess global small arms control activities related to the 2001 PoA, member states held the UN Conference to Review Progress Made in the Implementation of the Programme of Action (RevCon) from 26 June to 7 July 2006. Unfortunately, the conference ended without the parties agreeing to an outcome document, although member states did reiterate their commitment to implementing the 2001 PoA.[43] Before the 2006 UN RevCon, the International Action Network on Small Arms (IANSA) published their review of the PoA thus far and offered recommendations for the conference. The report noted that the current PoA does not provide controls on transfers to non-state actors nor on civilian possession. The PoA also does not offer any restrictions on the transfer of certain small arms and light weapons such as MANPADS, or address issues to reduce the demand for small arms. Moreover, most states have not implemented even the minimal systems of control required by the PoA. Some additional problems include the vagueness of national guidelines for authorizing arms transfers, non-existent or non-binding international controls over arms brokering, the underdeveloped nature of international stockpile security and surplus arms destruction

programmes and the failure to establish fully international information-sharing frameworks. The report recommends a more
effective and comprehensive PoA.[44] However, as in 2001, the
United States, backed by a few key countries such as India,
Pakistan, China, Indonesia and Iran, was able to block any
agreement on a final result, and the PoA was not expanded or
improved.

The UN focus on landmines

One conventional category of weapons not covered by the UN
Register or the PoA is landmines. The United Nations Mine
Action Service (UNMAS) was created in 1997 by the General
Assembly to work with thirteen other UN branches as the focal
point for mine action and to help create a coordinated and effective
approach to eliminating the international threat from landmines.
UNMAS is the chair of the UN Inter-Agency Coordination Group
on Mine Action, which meets to discuss policies and strategies
of mine action. UNMAS also establishes and manages country-
based mine action projects, including mine clearance, mine-risk
education, data collection, victim assistance, technical assistance
for stockpile destruction, and destruction of explosive weapons.
UNMAS manages mine action programmes in Afghanistan,
Burundi, the Democratic Republic of the Congo, the Ethiopia/
Eritrea Temporary Security Zone (TSZ), southern Lebanon and
Sudan. UNMAS also coordinates UN support for landmine treaties and administers the Voluntary Trust Fund for Assistance in
Mine Action, a fund created by the Secretary-General in 1994 to
fund UNMAS-managed programmes and assess state activities in
dealing with landmine problems.[45] The UN Inter-Agency Mine
Action Strategy for 2006–10 specifies continued UN work with
countries and organizations to address the threat of landmines,
build national capacities to tackle the threat and provide assistance
to mine survivors. The strategy notes that the use, production,
transfer and sale of anti-personnel landmines (APLs) decreased

dramatically between 1999 and 2005.[46] The most significant landmine effort, however, was led not by the UN, but by a group of NGOs and a few like-minded states. Their work resulted in the 1997 *Convention on the Prohibition of the Use, Stockpiling, Production and Transfer of Anti-Personnel Mines and on their Destruction*. This agreement, known as the Ottawa Treaty, is discussed in more detail below.

The UN and an international Arms Trade Treaty

On 6 December 2006, 153 state members of the UN General Assembly approved a non-binding resolution calling on the UN Secretary-General to ascertain the views of the General Assembly on the feasibility of a treaty 'establishing common international standards for the import, export and transfer of conventional arms'.[47] The Secretary-General was asked to submit a report to the September 2007 session of the General Assembly and establish a group of government experts to assess the feasibility of such a treaty beginning in 2008. This resolution is considered the first step toward the creation of an international Arms Trade Treaty (ATT). The United States was the only country to vote against the resolution, and 24 other states abstained. Nonetheless, Former High Commissioner for Human Rights Mary Robinson said that if the UN receives many positive responses from other General Assembly members, the UN might have an Arms Trade Treaty in place by 2010.[48]

As requested, Secretary-General Ban Ki-moon asked General Assembly member states to submit their views on the possible contents of the treaty by 30 April 2007. Ban Ki-moon confirmed at a press conference in June 2007 that the proposed treaty would cement common international standards to control conventional arms imports, exports and transfers. More than 100 governments have responded thus far with varying degrees of support and opposition. The European Union collectively supported the consideration of an Arms Trade Treaty, as have state members of the Economic Community of West African States (ECOWAS).[49] Many states, however, do not support the Arms Trade Treaty process. China, for example, favours measures that focus on the illicit arms trade, but argues that the legal weapons trade is of key importance to most governments and that a legal instrument addressing this issue is likely to be both complex and sensitive. Russia expressed similar doubts. While acknowledging the humanitarian and other concerns that result from illegal weapons transfers and trafficking, the Russian Federation suggests that universal regulations focused on the legal arms trade will be very difficult to achieve.[50]

The Wassenaar Arrangement

The United Nations does not have a monopoly on multilateral controls over the international arms trade. *The Wassenaar Arrangement on Export Controls for Conventional Arms and Dual-Use Goods and Technologies* (WA) was created in the early 1990s as a successor to COCOM, and is the first and only multilateral organization that focuses on both conventional weapons and sensitive dual-use goods and technologies.[51] The organization seeks to prevent the accumulation of arms by promoting greater transparency and responsibility in the trade of conventional arms and dual-use goods and technologies. While participating states have final say over their arms transfers, they have pledged to create national legislation to prohibit arms transfers that would create international instability or insecurity. Specifically, Wassenaar member states agree to share information on arms transfers for two reasons: (1) opening a state's arms exports to international scrutiny may make it act with more restraint, and (2) it allows exporters to see if an area is accumulating a threatening number of weapons.[52]

The WA has moved beyond transparency mechanisms in the past several years. At the WA Plenary Session of 11–12 December 2002, the group established the Best Practices Guidelines for Exports of Small Arms and Light Weapons. In the Guidelines, member states pledged to deny small arms export licences if it was deemed that the arms might encourage terrorism, hinder the security of another state, be diverted to terrorists, go against any other international arms control agreements, aggravate existing conflicts, endanger the peace or regional security, be re-exported or sold without licences, be used for repression or human rights abuses, facilitate organized crime or be used for any other purpose besides the 'legitimate defence and security needs of the recipient country'.[53] States also agreed to notify the original exporting state if arms are to be re-exported and give special consideration to the export of small arms to non-state entities. Finally, states agreed to consider the stockpile management and security procedures of a state before exporting weapons to that recipient. States pledged to reflect these guidelines in national legislation and policy documents, to assist other states in implementing effective weapons trade control measures, and to control strictly and to punish the brokering of small arms through national laws and procedures.[54]

In December 2003, the Wassenaar Plenary adopted the 'Elements of Export Controls of Man-Portable Air Defence Systems'. The agreement requires individual licences for exports of MANPADS and prohibits the use of nongovernment brokers in their transfer. Exporting governments will evaluate exports in light of other WA agreements and report transfers of MANPADS. The authorizations process should consider if exports will be diverted, re-exported, or kept in insecure locations. The importing government must submit certain paperwork to assure the exporter of the security and proper use of the MANPADS. States will help insecure states get rid of stockpiles of MANPADS, and share information about states that have failed to meet the requirements for importing MANPADS and non-state actors who are trying to do so. As with other WA agreements, the exporting state will have the final say over what is transferred, but only if the decision is reached by competent authorities.[55]

Finally, the WA has focused on the problem of arms brokering with the development of 'Elements for Effective Legislation on Arms Brokering', also adopted at the December 2003 Plenary. In the agreement, states pledged to implement laws and regulations to control strictly the activities of conventional arms brokers. According to the Elements, states should require licensing of certain transactions carried out by brokers and keep records of them, penalize illicit brokers and exchange information on arms brokering activities.[56]

Regional arms trade controls

Numerous regional organizations have also addressed the issue of conventional arms control in recent years. These organizations have particularly focused on the destabilizing spread and illicit trafficking of small arms and light weapons. Several regions of the world that have been affected by armed conflict in the post-Cold War era – from the Americas to Europe to West Africa – have developed regional agreements and local mechanisms for addressing the arms trade. Moreover, these regional agreements have often served as models for state arms control behaviour worldwide, as well as for arms trade discussions in global forums, such as the United Nations.

The Organization of American States (OAS)

The OAS set a global example in 1997 when it adopted the first legally binding regional agreement on illicit firearms trafficking.[57] *The Inter-American Convention Against the Illicit Manufacturing of and Trafficking in Firearms, Ammunition, Explosives, and Other Related Materials* (CIFTA) was signed in Washington, DC on 13 November 1997, and entered into force on 1 July 1998. Twenty-six states in Central and South America have ratified the treaty. Eight more, including Canada and the United States, have signed but not ratified it.[58] CIFTA requires that member states: adopt legislation making illicit arms trafficking a crime under state jurisdiction; require the marking of firearms with manufacturer and importer information; confiscate illicitly made or transferred firearms; ensure the security of transferred weapons; issue licences for import, export and transit of arms; strengthen security at export points; keep tracing records of illicit trades; guarantee the confidentiality of shared information, and share information, on arms production and transfers with other member states; and provide assistance and cooperation in implementing the Convention.[59]

The OAS continues to focus on the issues of conventional weapons control in its region. *The OAS Model Regulations for the Control of the International Movement of Firearms, Their Parts and Components and Ammunition*, dated 15 September 1997, outlines the recommended procedure for the export of firearms and ammunition by member states, including suggested templates for export, import and transit certificates for firearms.[60] *The Inter-American Convention on Transparency in Conventional Weapons Acquisitions* was adopted in Guatemala City on 7 June 1999 and entered into force on 21 November 2002. The goal of the Convention is to facilitate the sharing of information on weapons acquisitions and thus promote regional transparency and trust. Eleven states have ratified the treaty, and another nine, including Mexico and the United States, have signed but not yet ratified.[61] The Convention requires each state to provide an annual report of relevant imports and exports of conventional weapons to the OAS Depository (which is the same as the UN Register) and notify the Depository of acquisitions of conventional weapons within ninety days.[62]

In the *OAS Declaration on Small Arms and Light Weapons*, which was adopted on 5 June 2000, the OAS General Assembly resolved to:

> request that the Permanent Council, through its Committee on Hemispheric Security (the Committee), study the feasibility of developing a declaration on all aspects of the excessive and

destabilizing accumulation and transfer of small arms and light weapons, in the context of the work being carried out by the United Nations in relation to the United Nations Conference on the Illicit Trade in Small Arms and Light Weapons in All Its Aspects.[63]

Finally, the *OAS Model Regulations for the Control of Brokers of Firearms, Their Parts and Components and Ammunition* encouraged member states to adopt the Model Regulations as part of their national legislation to control arms brokers. The Regulations include guidelines and forms for the registration and licensing of arms brokers, as well as on which activities should be prohibited, and suggested penalties for illicit brokering.[64] Moreover, funding and financial assistance for all of these activities is available to help OAS member states implement small arms controls.[65]

Despite the activities at the OAS focused on weapons issues, the agreements are not binding on state members, remain relatively narrow in scope, and are not evenly implemented due to financial and political constraints in some countries. The agreements, therefore, remain limited in their effect, but are illustrative of collective desires to address illicit weapons trafficking.[66]

The European Union

The EU was very active on the issue of arms trade controls throughout the 1990s. The *European Code of Conduct on Arms Exports* (see chapter 3) is one of the most often cited arms control documents outlining standards of appropriate arms trade behaviour. The *EU Code of Conduct* was adopted on 8 June 1998 and includes the first denial notification and consultation mechanism ever applied to conventional arms exports. All member states must apply the Code when considering export applications for any items listed in the EU Common Military List.[67] Specifically, the Code of Conduct requires member states to reject arms export licence requests if they do not meet with the obligations of UN,

OSCE and EU arms embargoes and the Wassenaar Arrangement. Export licences may not be issued if there is a risk that the weapons may be used for internal repression or they will provoke or prolong conflict, or if the arms will be used aggressively against another country, and only with discretion to areas where human rights abuses have taken place. States must also take into account the national security of member states, the international behaviour of the buyer country, the risk of undesirable re-export and the compatibility of the arms with technology in the buyer nation when considering the issuance of export licences. Arms export information is shared with other member states in a diplomatic manner.[68]

Recognizing that small arms and light weapons pose significant challenges to stability and development in southeastern Europe and elsewhere, the EU adopted a Joint Action on Small Arms on 17 December 1998 to fight the accumulation and spread of small arms. The Joint Action was updated on 12 July 2002 to include small arms ammunition. The Joint Action is legally binding for member states, who must implement the provisions in their national laws and procedures. The Joint Action, however, applies only to military-style small arms, and not firearms intended for civilian or sporting use. Member states also promise to share any relevant arms control information with their fellow members and to improve their own arms control measures. Accordingly, the EU publishes annual reports on the implementation of the Joint Action.[69]

The Common Position on the Control of Arms Brokering was adopted by the EU on 23 June 2003 to help ensure compliance with UN, EU and OSCE arms embargoes. The Common Position requires member states to control arms brokering by enacting specified legislation, to assess certain brokering licence applications against the Code of Conduct, to establish a system to exchange information on arms brokering, and to establish sanctions to ensure that controls are enforced.[70]

Organization for Security and Co-operation in Europe (OSCE)

Work on limiting the international arms trade began at the OSCE in the early 1990s when it adopted the *Principles Governing Conventional Arms Transfers*. In the document, participating states affirmed the need to ensure that arms are not transferred illegally, to build transparency in the conventional arms trade and to enhance effective national controls over the conventional arms trade. States agreed to consider a country's respect for human rights, internal and regional environment, record of compliance with international agreements, the nature of the arms to be shipped and the defence requirements of the country before exporting conventional arms. States also pledged to avoid transfers that could be used in violation of human rights or to threaten other states, that violate other international control agreements, that would prolong an existing conflict or endanger the peace or that might be diverted or re-exported or be used to support terrorism, human rights abuses or any other non-defence-related purpose. In addition, states will implement these policies in their national legislation, provide assistance to other states to establish arms control measures, and share information about practices to control the transfer of conventional arms.[71]

On 24 November 2000, OSCE member states adopted the *OSCE Document on Small Arms and Light Weapons*. With this agreement, member states pledged to combat the illicit trade in small arms by adequately marking and tracking weapons and ensuring national control over weapons manufacturers. States also agreed to specific criteria that must be met before exporting arms to another state, and to situations where licences to transport arms would not be granted. The states also agreed to follow certain import, export and transit criteria and pledged to enforce international arms transfer codes with police action, and to exchange information on arms transfers. Finally, states vowed to enhance security of arms stockpiles and encourage the destruction of surplus weaponry.[72] Because meeting these requirements is often

difficult for developing member states, the OSCE provides assistance to those requesting help implementing the provisions of the
document.[73] For example, the Kazakhstan government requested
OSCE assistance in implementing the agreement in December
2004 and, after coordinating a workshop, OSCE experts went to
Kazakhstan to assess weapons stockpiles in advance of helping the
government with their destruction.[74]

   To further their focus on small arms control, in 2003 the OSCE
published the *Handbook of Best Practices on Small Arms and Light
Weapons*. Specifically, the *Handbook* provides a Best Practices
Guide on: (1) national controls over the manufacture of small arms
and light weapons; (2) marking, recordkeeping and traceability
of small arms; (3) national procedures for stockpile management
and security; (4) national control of brokering activities; (5) export
control of small arms; (6) definitions and indicators of surplus
weaponry; (7) national procedures for the destruction of small
arms; and (8) guidance for disarmament, demobilization and
reintegration processes.[75] Moreover, the OSCE extended its work
on weapons stockpiles in November 2003 when it adopted the
Document on Stockpiles of Conventional Weapons. This agreement
established identification and management processes for 'surplus
stockpiles of conventional ammunition, explosive material or detonating devices that pose a security risk'.[76]

Economic Community of West African States (ECOWAS)

West African states have been significantly affected by the spread,
accumulation and misuse of small arms and light weapons. In
response, the member states of ECOWAS issued the *Declaration of
a Moratorium on Importation, Exportation, and Manufacture of Light
Weapons* in West Africa in December 1998. In this agreement,
member states acknowledged the destabilizing effects of light
weapons in the region and declared a moratorium on weapons production, transfer and trade for a renewable three-year period.[77] The

ECOWAS Moratorium grew out of a 1994 UN advisory mission on the control and collection of small arms in the Sahara–Sahel region, which found that curbing the spread of small arms in the region was a necessary step for greater regional security and development. The UN Programme for Coordination and Assistance on Security and Development (PCASED) was developed to help West African countries enact small arms control measures, and to help build National Commissions to implement better the ECOWAS Moratorium.[78]

Despite the excitement about the development of the ECOWAS Moratorium, difficulties with its implementation have been quite evident. For example, although the Moratorium was declared in 1998, the necessary instruments for its enactment were not ready until several years later.[79] The Moratorium was renewed for an additional three years in October 2001, but, because the Moratorium was not legally binding and written in weak and ambiguous language, it proved hard to enforce sanctions against violators.[80] Ultimately, slow and irregular implementation characterized the initial ECOWAS Moratorium.[81]

In 2004, the UN-run PCASED was replaced by the Economic Community of West African States Small Arms Project (ECOSAP) to provide the technical assistance needed in implementing small arms controls. Meanwhile a Small Arms Unit was created within ECOWAS. These measures stemmed from the widespread impression that PCASED had failed. The shift also allowed African states to have greater regional ownership of the initiative.[82] On 19 February 2005, ECOWAS established its first ever arms embargo against a member state when it sanctioned Togo after Faure Gnassingbé illegally took over as President. The embargo was removed on 26 February when he stepped down.[83]

Because of continued breaches of the Moratorium, the ECOWAS heads of state decided, at the Dakar Summit on 30 January 2003, to move toward a legally binding Convention.[84] NGOs, namely the West African Action Network on Small Arms with the support of Oxfam, provided their own draft of a Convention when states were slow to develop their own.[85] Finally, on 14 June 2006, the ECOWAS Moratorium became a legally binding Convention: the *ECOWAS Convention on Small Arms and Light Weapons, Their Ammunition, and Other Related Materials*. The objectives of the ECOWAS Convention are to control and prevent the accumulation of small arms, to consolidate the gains of the Moratorium, to promote trust and the exchange of information among member states and to build the capacities of ECOWAS and its member states to control the spread of small arms.[86] It remains to be seen, however, whether implementation of the Moratorium will improve now that member states are legally obligated to comply.

Other regional arms control efforts

Various other regional efforts to combat the spread of small arms and light weapons have emerged in recent years. NATO learned firsthand the destabilizing effects of small arms in a region during its intervention in the Balkans in the mid-1990s. Still, NATO was relatively late to consider the control of small arms when it announced the NATO/EAPC (Euro-Atlantic Partnership Council) Working Group in July 1999. NATO had previously argued that controlling stockpiles, export security and transparency in the arms trade are the responsibility of member states. After a September 1999 workshop, however, the Working Group decided on three areas of concern: (1) training in stockpile management and security, disposal and destruction of weapons and reintegration of former combatants; (2) assistance programmes to individual nations on border controls, export control regulations and customs enforcement; and (3) the exchange of information on export control and marking systems.[87] Moreover, the NATO Partnership for Peace Trust Fund Policy was created in September 2000 to help NATO members safely destroy stockpiled anti-personnel landmines. The Trust Fund has since been expanded to assist states in the destruction of small arms and light weapons.[88]

The Stability Pact for South Eastern Europe, which was created on 10 June 1999 by forty states, works toward creating a regional approach to control the trade of small arms and light weapons by working with arms control organizations in the region. The Stability Pact joined with the United Nations Development Programme (UNDP) to create the South Eastern and Eastern Europe Clearinghouse for the Control of Small Arms and Light Weapons (SEESAC), to control the spread of small arms in the region.[89] SEESAC works to educate governments and civil society on small arms issues, help create national strategies to control small arms, and incorporate small arms issues into the UNDP agenda.[90]

The *Southern African Development Community (SADC) Firearms Protocol*, which was signed in 2001 and entered into force in November 2004, and the *Nairobi Declaration for Prevention, Control and Reduction of Small Arms and Light Weapons*, which was signed in April 2004, represent the commitment of twenty-five African states to developing effective and coordinated legislation to control the civilian possession of firearms.[91] Central American organizations have also been involved in weapons control with the development of the *Central American Integration System Code of Conduct on the Transfer of Arms, Ammunition, Explosives, and Other Related Material* in 2005.

National arms control measures

National arms control efforts are ultimately the first line of defence in preventing the unchecked spread of conventional arms. Without strong national controls, arms transfers can easily move from the legal to the illicit market. Despite the need for common practices to harmonize national laws and regulations, national controls have been implemented haphazardly. Some states have robust arms control systems and fully comply with internationally accepted standards, while others lack even basic control measures.

While three-quarters of UN member states have legislation to control the import and export of weapons, only half control the transit of weapons through their country. Moreover, only two-thirds of states criminalize the illicit trafficking of weapons, and only forty countries have some form of legislation to control arms brokering.[92]

Elements of an arms trade control system

Based on the numerous international and regional agreements discussed above, we can outline the various arms control activities, laws and procedures states can develop to check the transfer of weapons around the world. Ultimately, the agreements developed at both the international and regional levels provide guidance to and guidelines for national-level arms trade behaviour. These are, however, significant tasks, and many countries require assistance and support to develop and implement the elements in table 6.1.

Arms trade legislation

While most governments have enacted some kind of law, policy or regulation that outlines the legal responsibilities of officials and representatives within their territory engaged in the arms trade, many states do not cover all important aspects of arms control. Moreover, many governments have relatively weak arms control laws or have established regulations with numerous gaps and loopholes, allowing arms brokers, dealers or corrupt officials to circumvent the law and perpetuate the illicit trade in arms. For example, every central European state provides some legal basis for the regulation of arms exports, but some states do not adequately regulate the import, re-export, transit or transshipment of weapons.[93] The same is true for countries in the Black Sea region. All have a legal basis for arms transfer controls, but they do not necessarily sufficiently address all aspects of the arms trade.[94] Legislation in the states of West Africa to control the spread of

Table 6.1: Elements of a national arms trade control system

Elements	Description
Arms trade legislation	Legal instruments, in the form of laws or decrees, serve to provide government authorities the legal basis to register and license weapons producers, brokers, traders, transporters and owners – as well as to authorize individual weapons transactions.
Licensing procedures	Licensing procedures work to control the export, import, re-export, transit and transshipment of weapons into, out of and through national territory, including brokering activities.
Export criteria and control lists	Arms control lists detail those weapons and weapons systems that are subject to licensing procedures and must be authorized by government authorities. Lists of controlled goods also include lists of proscribed destinations, such as those subject to an arms embargo. Export criteria based on international norms and standards help to determine whether a weapons transfer should be authorized. End-user criteria such as respect for human rights, involvement in armed conflict, involvement in terrorist activities and level of democratic development are often considered when making licensing decisions.
Interagency coordination	Multiple parties within government work together to manage weapons licensing activities and jointly consider and approve arms transfers. Open communication and coordination among relevant agencies allows for an effective licensing process.
Customs authority and border controls	Border control agents and Customs officers work to provide security at points of entry and exit, as well as to inspect and verify weapons moving into, out of and through national territory. These officials need to be granted the authority to investigate arms activities and enforce breaches of the law.
Verification documentation	Arms transfers are verified with the use of standardized documentation. Import certificates, end-use and end-user statements and post-delivery checks can all be required and their authenticity verified in order to confirm and validate the legality of weapons transactions.
Penalties and enforcement	Appropriate civil and criminal penalties can prevent illicit weapons activities and punish illegal actions. Appropriate authorities must enforce the law, investigate violations, arrest and prosecute offenders, and ultimately punish those found guilty of illicit arms transfers.

Transparency and oversight	Information regarding arms production, possession, trade and control is shared and reported domestically and internationally. Transparency in the arms trade allows for greater oversight in order to prevent destabilizing and dangerous weapons transfers.
Marking and tracing	Weapons producers stamp their wares with identifying marks in order to allow for the tracing of weapons that have been diverted and misused.
Stockpile management	Weapons storage facilities are secured and effectively managed to prevent loss and theft.
Collection and destruction	Surplus weapons are collected from among the public (particularly after conflict has ended and reconstruction begins) as well as from official stockpiles, and destroyed in order to prevent additional build-ups, loss and theft.
Regional and international cooperation	Because the international arms trade is a trans-national issue, countries are engaged in regional and international cooperative activities regarding weapons transfers and controls. Collective, consistent, comprehensive and compatible arms trade controls require multilateral engagement, guidance and governance.

arms is virtually non-existent, outdated or weak. Moreover, the unwillingness of many states in the region to share information on their national legislation hampers the quest to create regional control mechanisms.[95] The states of Central America do have good laws to combat the illicit trade in arms, but they do not always take action on them, and there is poor intergovernmental and interagency communication, which makes it more difficult to implement the laws.[96] With the exception of the United States and Canada, most OAS states lack legislation to regulate arms brokers.[97] All of the countries in Eurasia have laws, including export controls, to regulate the trade of arms, but their enforcement can be non-existent.[98]

Licensing procedures

Procedures for licensing weapons imports, exports, re-exports, transits and transshipments are implemented so that weapons flowing into, out of or through national territory can be authorized and permitted on the basis of law. Moreover, weapons producers, exporters, importers, shippers and brokers are registered so that they are held accountable to the law for their activities. Like legislation, licensing procedures across governments vary. Some countries, such as the United States and the United Kingdom, have established elaborate licensing systems, while others, such as governments in Eastern Europe and the Balkans, have implemented minimal requirements and do not sufficiently capture all aspects of, and actors involved in, the arms trade.[99] All countries in the Black Sea region, for example, have developed weapons licensing procedures, but they mainly control arms exports and imports and ignore re-export, transits and transshipments.[100]

Export criteria and control lists

As with weapons licensing, some countries have established elaborate and solid export criteria and lists of controlled armaments, while others pay nominal lip-service to arms export criteria and fail to incorporate even international and regional arms embargoes into lists of controlled destinations. While the United States and EU member states outline a number of criteria that guide their arms transfer decisions, some states do not incorporate limiting language into their legislation, or enforce international agreements regarding arms control. All of the countries in Eurasia, for example, have reportedly developed arms export criteria, and they have agreed to the common OSCE export criteria, but a lack of resources and political will hampers their effective implementation.[101]

Interagency coordination

Of primary consideration in controlling the arms trade is the role of multiple parties in approving weapons transfers. As a check and balance in the arms trade process, multiple agencies knowledgeable in various aspects of the arms trade (e.g. security, foreign policy, commercial, legal aspects, etc.) are involved in licensing procedures. Ministries or Departments of Foreign Affairs, Defence, Internal Affairs, Economy, to name a few, can be consulted in order to prevent the domination of only one agenda and, therefore, an unchecked weapons transfer process. Interagency processes vary across countries, with some governments including numerous agencies in the process while others incorporate rather few. There remain, however, some countries that are yet to establish an interagency process – such as Albania where the Ministry of Defence has sole responsibility for arms transfer decisions – and other countries where interagency processes might exist on paper, but are not implemented in practice. Croatia, for example, reportedly includes the Ministry of Foreign Affairs, Ministry of Economy, and Ministry of Defence in its decision making, but officials report that the Ministry of Defence dominates the process and other agencies are not regularly involved in weapons trade decisions.[102]

Customs authority and border controls

One of the most important aspects of physical control of the arms trade is border control and customs activities. Customs agents are authorized to actively review, verify and investigate arms-related transactions. Border police are knowledgeable of, and authorized to inspect, documents and goods to prevent illegal weapons movements. Like all other elements, customs authorities and border controls vary across countries. Because few people live along the previously war-torn Croatian–Bosnian border, for example, there is little border control and ample opportunity for arms smugglers to transport weapons. Similar porous borders exist throughout the Black Sea region, the Western Balkans, Africa, the Middle East, Central America and many other regions of the world.[103] Starting in late 2007, large numbers of weapons were reported flowing across the US–Mexican border, contributing to other illegal activity such as drug trafficking and a series of high-profile drug cartel murders.[104] The United States has responded, however, with a new Border Enhancement Security Task Force in an effort to prevent criminal organizations from acquiring weapons and other dangerous materials such as explosives.[105] Ultimately, without strong border controls, it is impossible to control the arms trade. Moreover, customs authorities and border officials require adequate resources in an effort to prevent bribery and corruption.

Verification documentation

The use of standardized and harmonized documents, such as import and export certificates, and post-delivery checks help to control the flow of weapons and ensure that arms are not destined for undesirable end-users or for inappropriate end-uses. One of the challenging aspects of verification documentation, however, is that no universal standard exists from one country to the next, resulting in a mix of certification and opening the door to forgery and inaccurate documents. Moreover, not all states even require the use of import and export certificates, and even fewer require and conduct post-delivery checks. Verifying the authenticity of a weapons transaction is a key aspect of arms control, but remains elusive in terms of consistent and compatible implementation. There are verification programmes, however, that may serve as a model for the creation of other systems around the world. For example, the US State Department's Blue Lantern end-use monitoring programme includes a comprehensive process of verifying documents and arms transfers. In FY 2006, the Directorate of Defense Trade Controls conducted 613 Blue Lantern checks, a record number, and made unfavourable determinations in 94 cases. This means that in some way the transfer did not comply with the licence granted – the end-user was perhaps different, the weapon could no longer be accounted for, etc. The largest percentage of unfavourable checks occurred in transfers to the Americas (40 per cent), even though that region only accounts for 19 per cent of all checks and 6 per cent of all licences.[106] The DDTC has also found that firearms and ammunition have a high incidence of unfavourable checks. Moreover, the French government requires all arms exporters to create an internal compliance programme that incorporates procedures for internal verification of arms transfers.[107] Verification programmes such as these are an important method of catching inappropriate and illegal weapons transfers.

Penalties and enforcement

Any law or legal process is only as strong as its enforcement. Law enforcement agencies, therefore, must be involved in arresting, prosecuting and sanctioning those who violate legal arms trade practices to ensure those who break arms trade laws are held accountable and punished appropriately, with the use of civil and/ or criminal penalties. For example, in 2005 the United States arrested, prosecuted and imprisoned several individuals caught smuggling weapons into and out of the country. Specifically, weapons were being trafficked from the United States to Colombian terrorists, to individuals in Japan, and from Vietnam to a former law enforcement officer in the United States.[108] Moreover, countries like Sweden have indicted citizens who have been caught transporting weapons illegally.[109] Such prosecutions occur regularly in some countries, but in other areas enforcement procedures are lax and penalties are rarely levied against offenders. There is a significant disparity in enforcement capacities across countries, requiring assistance and support to enhance enforcement practices in areas such as the Balkans, Central America, Africa and elsewhere. Moreover, all states need to do more to incorporate legal controls on arms brokering activities so that illicit arms dealers can no longer operate with impunity and instead must face the enforcement of arms trade laws.

Transparency and oversight

Improved transparency in arms trade activities will serve to check, balance and control destabilizing arms sales and weapons build-ups, prevent violent conflict and minimize misuse.[110] Public oversight of the weapons trade provides a natural restraint on arms transfers and infuses responsibility into the arms trade system. Many of the largest weapons producers and exporters, in fact, share the most information about their arms sales. The US arms export system is more transparent than in the rest of the world, with publicly available reports and explanations of processes, licences and end-user checks involved with US exports. The State Department, Defense Department and Library of Congress all assemble annual reports with US arms transfer data. Most of these reports, as well as arms sales notifications that are over the reporting threshold, are publicly available. However, there is no standard for what kind of arms trade information is shared with other countries. Nonetheless, some countries say they would increase transparency in the arms trade if other governments, such as the United States, set an example and took the lead.[111] The reality is, however, that many states remain quite elusive when it comes to arms trade information and that much work remains regarding more transparent arms trade practices.[112]

Marking and tracing of weapons

Marking of weapons is done in order to keep records on arms flows. Marking allows for tracing when and if weapons end up in violent conflict and there is suspicion that arms were acquired illegally. The concern of some states is that weapons that are illegally acquired or somehow diverted or re-exported will be traced back to the original producer who may or may not have any involvement in the diversion of the weapons. Nonetheless, marking and tracing has been a significant component of arms trade controls. The OAS CIFTA-CICAD Group of Experts, for example, approved a *Draft Proposed Model Legislation on the Marking and Tracing of Firearms and Ammunition* at their first meeting on 6–7 February 2006. This draft presents regulations on marking, record keeping and the tracing of arms.[113] The Firearms Protocol includes provisions regarding marking and tracing as well, although the negotiations were hampered when China objected to a universal standard for marking, instead preferring to maintain two marking methods during the manufacturing process.[114] The UN Programme of Action also outlines desires for marking and tracing, but leaves to state governments the responsibility for determining how best to implement these requirements.

Stockpile management

At a national level, preventing illicit trafficking requires tightening security of stockpiles to prevent theft.[115] Official military and police stockpiles, as well as surplus weaponry, must be kept in secure facilities, and appropriate accounting procedures should be used to prevent theft and loss. In 1993, for example, Poland created the Military Property Agency to control, manage and account for the surplus arms that were stockpiled after a drastic reduction in the size of the military. Trained guards protect the stockpiles, and the arms are accounted for by a computerized system. Yet, many central European, East European, Balkan and other countries do not adequately control their stockpiles of excess weapons, and some think that excess weapons should be sold and exported.[116] Leakages from weapons stockpiles in Eurasia have been a systematic problem and many of the weapons end up in conflict zones or in the hands of human rights abusers.[117]

Weapons collection and destruction

An important aspect of weapons control is the removal of excess weapons from society, as well as from the government and police authorities, and destroying – rather than stockpiling – them so that they are permanently removed from circulation. Weapons collection efforts have been undertaken in many post-conflict countries with varying degrees of success. Weapons buy-back programmes, for example, have been less effective in keeping weapons off the street and back in the hands of combatants than have weapons-for-development programmes.[118] SEESAC has reported success in destroying surplus arms in Central and Eastern Europe, in part because these states, as former conflict zones, have a greater impetus to destroy their arms.[119] In Hungary, there is pressure to sell surplus weapons because of the high costs of stockpiling or destroying them.[120] Countries in the Black Sea region have problems with the disposal of surplus weaponry,[121] while West African states that are emerging from conflict, including Liberia, Sierra Leone, Niger and Mali, as well as Senegal, have actively destroyed collected and surplus arms. However, other West African nations have only done so in annual symbolic demonstrations.[122]

Despite the various outcomes, the United States has spent $27 million (as of June 2006) to help other countries destroy their stockpiles of weapons.[123] Specifically, the United States maintains the largest assistance programme to help countries destroy sur-plus and obsolete weapons and safeguard those that remain in government arsenals. The destruction programme is overseen by the State Department's Office of Weapons Removal and Abatement. Six years after the programme's launch, the United States had destroyed more than 1 million weapons and more than 90 million rounds of ammunition in twenty-five countries. In addition, the United States has helped destroy more than 24,000 MANPADS in twenty-one countries.[124] The Physical Security and Stockpile Management (PSSM) programme is run by the Defense Threat Reduction Agency (DTRA) at the Department of Defense. The PSSM programme has helped secure stockpiles in more than thirty-seven countries, and conducted thirty-eight assessments and thirty seminars.[125] The two programmes work closely together and conduct evaluations and assessments in order to provide com-prehensive control strategies.

Regional and international cooperation

Because the international arms trade is inherently trans-national in nature, cross-border cooperation and coordination are neces-sary to ensure the effectiveness of national activities. Each national arms control system is only as strong as its neighbours', because of border controls, information sharing and transparency, among other control initiatives. States can engage and coordinate their arms control practices with others in their region and further abroad, and also be willing and able to implement regional and international commitments at home to enhance global control of the international arms trade. One way in which the United States works to enhance regional and international cooperation is via the State Department's Export Control and Related Border Security Assistance (EXBS) programme. EXBS works to assist countries in developing adequate and effective export control systems. US experts provide training and model regulations to foreign govern-ments eager to curb weapons proliferation.[126]

Nongovernmental organizations (NGOs)

Although states remain the primary actors involved in arms control activities, numerous NGOs, working individually and collectively, have managed to inform the public, and to pressure governments to develop more responsible weapons practices. NGOs play a role in encouraging states to adopt more rigorous arms transfer controls, raising awareness about irresponsible arms trade activities, and facilitating the development of international standards and agreements that limit state arms trade behaviour. Some NGO networks have been more successful than others, but ultimately these organizations are significant actors in current arms control efforts.

The International Campaign to Ban Landmines (ICBL)

The ICBL was created in October 1992 by six NGOs dedicated to finding a comprehensive solution to stop the indiscriminate horrors of anti-personnel landmines. Within a few short years, the network grew to more than 1,400 NGOs in 90 countries. After five years of developing its network and strengthening its campaign through awareness activities, the symbolic use of landmine survivor stories, and the leveraging of celebrity and high-level actors, the Diplomatic Conference on an International Total Ban on Anti-Personnel Land Mines was held in Oslo on 18 September 1997. The Conference resulted in the *Convention on the Prohibition of the Use, Stockpiling, Production and Transfer of Anti-Personnel Mines and on their Destruction*, which was opened for signatures in Ottawa on 3 December 1997.[127] The Convention, more commonly referred to as the 'Mine Ban Treaty' or the 'Ottawa Treaty', was signed by 122 governments in Ottawa and is the 'most comprehensive instrument' for eliminating the use of landmines internationally. The Treaty became binding in March 1999 under international law, as the fortieth state, Burkina

Faso, ratified it six months earlier in September 1998.[128] As of 21 February 2007, 155 countries had signed and 153 had ratified the 1997 Mine Ban Treaty.[129] There are 40 countries, including the United States, Russia and China, which have not ratified the agreement.[130] In 2004, the ICBL held the first Review Conference of the Mine Ban Treaty in Nairobi, after which the ICBL continued its anti-landmine activities, but in a more decentralized fashion, through national campaigns and organizations.[131] Because of the ICBL's success in facilitating a landmine ban, the organization won the Nobel Peace Prize in 1997. The ICBL annually produces the Treaty's evaluation and implementation report, known as the *Landmine Monitor*, which is a country-by-country analysis of Treaty implementation, including mine use, production, trade, stockpiling, humanitarian demining and mine survivor assistance. Despite the success, the Mine Ban Treaty and the ICBL have been criticized for weak language regarding survivor assistance, for not preventing continued landmine activity in states that have signed (but not ratified) the agreement, and for not doing more to encourage ratification in several important states, such as the United States, Russia and China.[132]

The International Action Network on Small Arms (IANSA)

IANSA is a network of 700 civil society organizations from 100 countries working together to stop the spread and misuse of small arms and light weapons through stronger regulations on gun ownership and arms export controls.[133] IANSA was founded in 1998 when 45 individuals representing 33 NGOs from 18 countries met in Canada from 17 to 19 August to explore how civil society organizations could better respond to the devastating effects of small arms by tightening arms controls. The members at the meeting decided that forming a network of NGOs to work on various arms issues was the best approach. The scope and nature of IANSA was decided at a second international meeting of 100

NGOs in Brussels on 14 October 1998. The outcomes of these two meetings are contained in the IANSA Founding Document. In the document, members outline some approaches IANSA might take to controlling the supply of arms by regulating legal transfers of small arms between states, preventing and combating the illicit trade of small arms, collecting and removing surplus arms, increasing transparency and accountability and supporting research and information-sharing on the arms trade. The document also lists ways in which IANSA might reduce the demand for small arms, as well as possible activities and requirements for membership.[134]

IANSA has been an active participant in the UN PoA process, and has been directly involved in pushing for an international Arms Trade Treaty. Governments around the world and the public in general are much more informed about the small arms and light weapons issue because of IANSA's work. However, IANSA has suffered from a scattered agenda and remains an organization with multiple objectives and many voices.[135]

Cluster Munitions Coalition

On 13 November 2003, 80 NGOs joined together in the Cluster Munitions Coalition (CMC) to launch a global campaign to ban cluster bombs. The CMC wants to ban the production and trade of cluster bombs until the humanitarian problems associated with unexploded bomblets are solved. In addition to stopping the unrestricted use of cluster munitions, the CMC wants countries that use cluster bombs to be responsible for clearing unexploded remnants and aiding victims.[136] Currently, the CMC is composed of around 200 member organizations. In order to achieve its goal of protecting civilians from cluster munitions, the Coalition has adopted the following three strategic objectives: (1) to help establish a successful international ban on cluster munitions; (2) to promote national measures to reduce the threat to civilians from cluster bombs; and (3) to raise public awareness of the harm caused to civilians by cluster munitions and the efforts to prevent such harm.[137] In response, the UN Secretary-General Ban Ki-moon urged states in November 2007 to consider soon a legally binding instrument that would ban the manufacture, stockpiling, transfer and use of these weapons.[138] In December 2007, 138 states then met in Vienna to discuss a comprehensive treaty banning cluster munitions, and in December 2008, 97 states signed the Convention on Cluster Munitions in Oslo, Norway.[139]

The Stockholm International Peace Research Institute (SIPRI)

SIPRI is a long-standing and key promoter of transparency in the arms trade. Its Arms Transfer Project maintains a computerized database of all major international conventional arms transfers since 1950.[140] The SIPRI Arms Control and Disarmament Documentary Survey keeps records of states that have signed and ratified arms control agreements. Information from both branches is published in the annual SIPRI Yearbook.[141] Today, SIPRI continues to provide the most comprehensive and reliable public information about the conventional arms trade.

The Norwegian Initiative on Small Arms Transfers (NISAT)

NISAT was founded on 17 December 1997 by four Norwegian organizations: the Norwegian Red Cross, Norwegian Church Aid, and two research and foreign policy institutions. Funded by the Norwegian government. NISAT was founded with the goal of combining resources to prevent the proliferation of small arms and light weapons, particularly to areas where they may cause violent conflict and diminish the security of humans. The International Peace Research Institute, Oslo (PRIO) works through NISAT to maintain an online database of international arms transfers, the world's only online database of small arms transfers.[142]

The Control Arms Campaign

The Control Arms Campaign was established in October 2003 by two NGOs (Amnesty International and Oxfam) and one NGO network (IANSA) to enhance awareness of the international arms trade and gather public support for global arms control efforts. The Campaign has gathered the support of over 1 million people to push for a global Arms Trade Treaty.[143]

Other arms control organizations

Various other NGOs have focused on conventional arms control, highlighted flaws in state arms trade practices, and worked to inform the general public about weapons issues. Human Rights Watch, for example, studies and publicizes arms trade activities around the world.[144] The Small Arms Survey provides the public with information on the international trade in small arms and light weapons.[145] Networks of NGOs have sprung up around the world, often with the help and guidance of IANSA. In May 2002, ten West African NGOs joined together to create the West African Action Network on Small Arms (WAANSA) to coordinate civil society actions to fight weapons proliferation. Now a group of over fifty organizations, WAANSA serves to exchange information and strategies to help control the spread of weapons in West Africa and played an instrumental role in the development of the legally binding ECOWAS Convention.[146] NGOs in Central America have played a vital role in getting information on small arms trafficking and arms control laws to the public. The Central America Forum on Small Arms Proliferation, in particular, has helped create an abundance of research, leading the public in Central America to be some of the best informed in the world.[147] Viva Rio in Brazil has been one of the most dynamic and active. Moreover, Central America has the most NGO participation in IANSA.[148] In 1999, International Alert, Saferworld and the University of Bradford joined together to create Biting the Bullet, a project to promote international understanding of the 2001 UN Conference on Small Arms.[148]

Challenges and obstacles to conventional arms control

Despite the many international, national and NGO activities that have been undertaken regarding conventional arms control in recent years, numerous challenges and obstacles remain in enhancing arms control measures. The first challenge is the legitimacy of the weapons. Conventional weapons, unlike weapons of mass destruction, serve many purposes. They provide for the national defence and support policing activities – and small arms are regularly and legitimately used for sport and hunting activities. It is undesirable and unlikely that conventional weapons will be banned. The challenge, then, is to limit and constrain the trade in conventional weaponry to prevent destabilizing build-ups and misuse. Checks on weapons transfers and a focus on demand are ultimately the primary avenues for conventional arms control.

Because conventional arms serve legitimate purposes, a second challenge arises and that is the role of arms producers and exporters. Many countries produce weapons, but the role of the major weapons producers and exporters cannot be overstated. The United States, Russia, China, Britain and France hold the lion's share of the global arms market – with the United States leading the way. Hesitance on their part to enhance conventional arms trade controls has a significant impact on the will and capability of the entire international community to engage in stricter arms trade practices. A negotiator who helped craft the Wassenaar Arrangement, for example, argued that changes in the organization that would 'provide meaningful restraint in conventional arms transfers and still be acceptable both to the United States and Europe' were quite unlikely. Furthermore, 'the negotiations during the early 1990s that led to the creation of the Wassenaar Arrangement made clear that mutual restraint in transfers of advanced technology and arms is impossible when foreign policies diverge. And with the end of the Cold War, any Atlantic consensus was fast eroding over sales to commercially important nations in Asia and the Middle East.'[150]

A third challenge to the development of stronger arms trade controls goes beyond great power and major supplier concerns. Existing ideas and norms of state sovereignty, national self-defence, self-determination and territorial integrity have an impact on political will more generally in the international community. Many recent international agreements on weapons control have, in fact, reiterated the norms of sovereignty, national self-defence, self-determination and territorial integrity, which are grounded in the UN Charter itself.[151] Moreover, Article 223 of the Treaty of Rome, which established the basis for the European Community and today's European Union, specifies that national governments have exclusive control over national arms industries, arms sales and arms control decisions, providing additional hindrance to state interests in multilateral arms trade controls in Europe.[152] Ultimately, while there is an international consensus that the sale of nuclear weapons should be restricted, 'there is no such consensus that there should be general controls on the sales of conventional weapons, since a state's right to self-defence, embodied in the UN Charter, gives it the right to buy arms from abroad'.[153]

A fourth challenge, particularly for the control of small arms and light weapons, is the existence of competing coalitions that promote diverging ideas and norms regarding arms trade controls. The work of NGO groups goes beyond that of those promoting arms control efforts, but includes a small, but vocal, cadre of groups and individuals who seek to prevent stricter controls on weapons acquisition and possession. The American National Rifle Association (NRA), for example, has become a global actor on the issue of international arms control. The NRA helped to create a global counterpart, the World Forum on the Future of Sport Shooting Activities (WFSA), headquartered in Brussels, Belgium. The WFSA is comprised of approximately two dozen pro-gun groups and arms manufacturers, and serves as the lead pro-gun, anti-gun-control coalition at the United Nations and other international arenas.[154] Their primary purpose is to counter any measure that may negatively affect a citizen's right to own and use a firearm. The work of IANSA and other organizations that promote stricter and more responsible arms trade practices, therefore, is countered by the work of the NRA and WFSA who largely oppose stricter controls, especially as they relate to civilian possession and acquisition.

Ultimately, the fifth and perhaps the primary challenge facing arms control today is the sheer complexity of the issue. The conventional arms trade is comprised of weapons both big and small and is concerned with issues such as supply and demand. Many factors affect demand and there are many sources of supply to provide the arms that states, non-state actors and individuals seek. It has become increasingly difficult to control the flow of weapons in a growing global economy, and even more difficult reaching all relevant arms trade actors and limiting or constraining their behaviour. Today, cross-border mergers and acquisitions spread weapons technology and governments become less able to control arms-producing corporations. Weapons are increasingly assembled in more than one country, making it hard to control the end product. Moreover, developing countries have improved their own weapons industries, lessening their reliance on traditional trading partners if avenues to arms are closed. In addition, a growing illicit trade significantly hampers the development and implementation of arms control measures. Furthermore, the economic benefits of arms sales are increasingly considered more important than the possible political consequences. All of these factors signify more trouble enacting comprehensive and compatible national controls.[155]

Because of these challenges, most conventional arms control agreements at international and regional levels remain politically binding at best, and only voluntarily implemented. Thus, states' adherence to them cannot be ensured.[156]

Despite the many challenges, there are also many prospects for the future of international arms trade controls. The past several years have indicated that there has been increased attention and activity surrounding control of the international arms trade. Indeed, the issue has risen in global salience to the extent that the subject will not just easily fade away. NGOs and interested arms control advocates will persist and states must face their pressure. Ideally, a more cooperative environment will emerge and states, NGOs and relevant arms trade actors will work together to find common ground and agree to limitations on the arms trade that will meet everyone's needs in forums that are not necessarily based on consensus rule. The international community may also continue to use economic tools, such as development assistance and trade, investment and technology transfers, as enticements when negotiating arms controls in the developing world, and individual governments can also use persuasion, through political dialogue, to help enact arms controls in a bilateral agreement.[157] Moreover, other international, regional and national measures regarding the protection of human rights, reform of security sectors, enhancement of the rule of law and good governance will also have an impact on the international arms trade as safer and more secure environments emerge.[158] Ultimately, governments need to continue interacting, and NGOs must keep advising and pressuring, for progress to be made regarding control of the international arms trade.

7
Conclusion

The international arms trade is big business, valued at tens of billions of dollars each year. Although worth only half a percentage of all global trade,[1] the international arms trade contributes to tremendous economic costs. The average civil war in a poor country costs the international economy an estimated $50 billion annually.[2] Economics aside, the international arms trade leads to serious human consequences as well. Moreover, in the wake of 11 September 2001, terrorist access to weapons has also been front and centre in the debate. As numerous conflicts have erupted or escalated in the post-Cold War period, increasing attention has been given to controlling the tools of this violence: controlling the international weapons trade.

Ultimately, the international trade in conventional arms is a global enterprise that reflects the interests and actions of various state, sub-state and individual actors. Although conventional weapons transfers are not as visible or concerning to a general audience as is the spread of weapons of mass destruction, conventional weapons are and will continue to be responsible for significant mass destruction. Understanding the dynamics and effects of the international arms trade is, therefore, exceedingly important, as governments and policy makers strive to create a more peaceful world. The purpose of this book has been to heighten such awareness and enhance knowledge regarding the global trade of the weapons that kill, injure and destroy on a daily basis. Based on the analysis and information provided in the preceding chapters, we draw five main conclusions.

First, the supply and demand of conventional arms, both legal and illegal, have fluctuated throughout history. Certain global events have often marked changes in the international arms trade, particularly throughout the twentieth century. From World War I to the 'global war on terror', we have seen the growth of the state as the primary authority over the arms trade. However, in recent years, we have also witnessed the rise of non-state actors and international terrorist organizations as participants in the global arms trade, which creates significant challenges for arms trade controls. For states, we see that foreign policy objectives, goals and concerns predominantly drive the supply and transfer of arms, but we also see economic considerations playing an increasingly important role in determining weapons production and sales. Moreover, the global supply of and trade in arms are only part of the picture, given weapons are in demand by many and for various reasons. Whether for personal security, national defence, conflict avoidance, violence suppression or aggressive tendencies, conventional weapons, and increasingly small arms and light weapons, are sought, acquired and used by actors of all kinds. Both weapons supply and demand, therefore, must be examined and understood to comprehend fully the entirety of the international arms trade.

Second, conventional arms are a much more difficult class of weapons to control, given their legitimate uses. While taboos regarding the acquisition, transfer and use of weapons of mass destruction have emerged to constrain the trade of fissile, chemical and biological weaponry, as well as their component parts, no such taboo exists regarding conventional weapons.[3] In fact, Article 51 of the UN Charter guarantees states the right to produce, import, export, deploy and use conventional weaponry as needed for self-defence. Weapons are legitimately acquired and used for and by national militaries, police forces and civilians throughout the world. And states regularly assert this right and reiterate the importance and legitimacy of conventional weapons and the legal arms trade.[4] Moreover, national and international actors, such as the National Rifle Association and World Forum on the Future of Sport Shooting Activities, seek to protect the rights of individuals to buy and use firearms.[5] The legitimacy of conventional arms, therefore, poses significant challenges for controlling the international arms trade.

Third, the international trade in conventional arms generates a significant amount of revenue, and arms sales have proven to be quite profitable. In 2007, the value of legal arms sales around the world amounted to approximately $60 billion. Black and grey market sales most likely account for another $5 billion. Although it is difficult to know with exact certainty what the total value of the international arms trade is, it is clear that weapons transfers not only serve political and security interests but also contribute to financial gain and economic wherewithal. This is true for large-scale, legal government-to-government transfers, as well as for smaller-scale, illicit transactions among non-state actors and individual gun runners. In fact, weapons traffickers highlight the profitability of illegal arms transfers, indicating that weapons are often viewed like any other commodity from which a profit can be made.[6] With few restraints on the international arms trade, and with continued and occasionally heightened demand for conventional weapons, the profitability of arms transfers, both legal and illegal, will likely continue.

Fourth, the lack of restraints on the international conventional arms trade has significant consequences for human security. Day after day, year after year, millions of people are injured and killed by conventional weapons. Peacekeeping missions are hampered by widespread availability and circulation of arms, as are the work of relief organizations and the delivery of humanitarian assistance. Post-conflict reconstruction is impeded without the implementation of effective disarmament, demobilization and reintegration efforts. Economic development is often prevented or damaged due to ongoing violent conflict in the wake of war and continued weapons transfers. Overall, general peace and security are negatively affected as the international arms trade grows and remains unchecked.

Finally, national, regional and global controls on the conventional arms trade are underdeveloped and face tremendous challenges. A primary challenge is the lack of support from the major weapons producers, suppliers and exporters for existing and proposed controls on the international trade in arms. Countries such as the United States, Russia and China, in particular, are reluctant to support and implement greater restraints on the legal arms trade. And although they offer much rhetoric regarding controls on illicit arms transfers, major weapons exporters such as the United States often fail to make changes in their own domestic laws and policies to ensure that weapons do not end up in the hands of undesirable actors. The need for greater control of the international arms trade, however, is bigger than these primary producers and suppliers. Ultimately, restraints on the conventional arms trade require multiple and varied solutions with the involvement of multiple and varied actors operating in multiple and varied forums. States, sub-state actors and individuals are involved in the arms trade process, which occurs concurrently at various local, national, regional and global levels. A simultaneous response is, therefore, required at all levels. National laws, regional agreements and global standards that constrain state, sub-state and individual behaviour and hold them accountable are all necessary components of international arms trade controls – and both legal and illegal transactions are essential issues with which these various actors and forums must grapple.

At the end of the day, we have learned much about the international arms trade, but much more remains to be done. We are more aware of how, why and to what extent the conventional weapons trade matters for national, international and human security, but more awareness must be raised and more attention must be paid to the issue. Although concerns with weapons of mass destruction dominate our interests, conventional weapons of individual destruction should not be overlooked and neglected. Ignoring the international trade in conventional arms will have only negative consequences, either directly or indirectly, for us all.

The EU Code of Conduct on Arms Transfers

On 25 May 1998, the European Union adopted a Code of Conduct on Arms Transfers, a politically binding agreement that established criteria for states to take into consideration when determining whether to grant an arms export. The Code also has twelve operative provisions, which outline state implementation of the Code, including granting licences for arms exports to countries previously denied by other EU states. It also allows for public reporting of arms transfers to improve the transparency about the international arms trade. The Code's criteria are as follows:

CRITERION ONE

Respect for the international commitments of EU member states, in particular the sanctions decreed by the UN Security Council and those decreed by the Community, agreements on non-proliferation and other subjects, as well as other international obligations

An export licence should be refused if approval would be inconsistent with, inter alia:

a) the international obligations of member states and their commitments to enforce UN, OSCE [Organisation for Security and Cooperation in Europe] and EU arms embargoes;
b) the international obligations of member states under the Nuclear Non-Proliferation Treaty, the Biological and Toxin Weapons Convention and the Chemical Weapons Convention;
c) their commitments in the frameworks of the Australia Group, the Missile Technology Control Regime, the Nuclear Suppliers Group and the Wassenaar Arrangement;

d) their commitment not to export any form of anti-personnel landmine.

CRITERION TWO

The respect of human rights in the country of final destination

Having assessed the recipient country's attitude towards relevant principles established by international human rights instruments, Member States will:

a) not issue an export licence if there is a clear risk that the proposed export might be used for internal repression;
b) exercise special caution and vigilance in issuing licences, on a case-by-case basis and taking account of the nature of the equipment, to countries where serious violations of human rights have been established by the competent bodies of the UN, the Council of Europe or by the EU.

For these purposes, equipment which might be used for internal repression will include, inter alia, equipment where there is evidence of the use of this or similar equipment for internal repression by the proposed end-user, or where there is reason to believe that the equipment will be diverted from its stated end-use or end-user and used for internal repression. In line with operative paragraph 1 of this Code, the nature of the equipment will be considered carefully, particularly if it is intended for internal security purposes. Internal repression includes, inter alia, torture and other cruel, inhuman and degrading treatment or punishment, summary or arbitrary executions, disappearances, arbitrary detentions and other major violations of human rights and fundamental freedoms as set out in relevant international human rights instruments, including the Universal Declaration on Human Rights and the International Covenant on Civil and Political Rights.

CRITERION THREE

The internal situation in the country of final destination, as a function of the existence of tensions or armed conflicts

Member States will not allow exports which would provoke or prolong armed conflicts or aggravate existing tensions or conflicts in the country of final destination.

CRITERION FOUR

Preservation of regional peace, security and stability

Member States will not issue an export licence if there is a clear risk that the intended recipient would use the proposed export aggressively against another country or to assert by force a territorial claim.

When considering these risks, EU Member States will take into account inter alia:

a) the existence or likelihood of armed conflict between the recipient and another country;
b) a claim against the territory of a neighbouring country which the recipient has in the past tried or threatened to pursue by means of force;
c) whether the equipment would be likely to be used other than for the legitimate national security and defence of the recipient;
d) the need not to affect adversely regional stability in any significant way.

CRITERION FIVE

The national security of the member states and of territories whose external relations are the responsibility of a Member State, as well as that of friendly and allied countries

Member States will take into account:

a) the potential effect of the proposed export on their defence and security interests and those of friends, allies and other member states, while recognising that this factor cannot affect consideration of the criteria on respect of human rights and on regional peace, security and stability;
b) the risk of use of the goods concerned against their forces or those of friends, allies or other member states;
c) the risk of reverse engineering or unintended technology transfer.

CRITERION SIX

The behaviour of the buyer country with regard to the international community, as regards in particular to its attitude to terrorism, the nature of its alliances and respect for international law

Member States will take into account inter alia the record of the buyer country with regard to:

a) its support or encouragement of terrorism and international organised crime;
b) its compliance with its international commitments, in particular on the non-use of force, including under international humanitarian law applicable to international and non-international conflicts;
c) its commitment to non-proliferation and other areas of arms control and disarmament, in particular the signature, ratification and implementation of relevant arms control and disarmament conventions referred to in sub-paragraph b) of Criterion One.

CRITERION SEVEN

The existence of a risk that the equipment will be diverted within the buyer country or re-exported under undesirable conditions

In assessing the impact of the proposed export on the importing country and the risk that exported goods might be diverted to an undesirable end-user, the following will be considered:

a) the legitimate defence and domestic security interests of the recipient country, including any involvement in UN or other peace-keeping activity;
b) the technical capability of the recipient country to use the equipment;
c) the capability of the recipient country to exert effective export controls;
d) the risk of the arms being re-exported or diverted to terrorist organisations (anti-terrorist equipment would need particularly careful consideration in this context).

CRITERION EIGHT

The compatibility of the arms exports with the technical and economic capacity of the recipient country, taking into account the desirability that states should achieve their legitimate needs of security and defence with the least diversion for armaments of human and economic resources

Member States will take into account, in the light of information from relevant sources such as UNDP, World Bank, IMF and OECD reports, whether the proposed export would seriously hamper the sustainable development of the recipient country. They will consider in this context the recipient country's relative levels of military and social expenditure, taking into account also any EU or bilateral aid.

Source: European Union, EU Code of Conduct on Arms Transfers, at http://ec.europa.eu/external_relations/cfsp/sanctions/codeofconduct.pdf, last accessed 5 April 2009.

Notes

CHAPTER 1 INTRODUCTION TO THE
INTERNATIONAL ARMS TRADE

1 See, for example, Cassady Craft, *Weapons for Peace, Weapons for
War: The Effect of Arms Transfers on War Outbreak, Involvement, and
Outcomes* (New York: Routledge, 1999).
2 Richard F. Grimmett, *Conventional Arms Transfers to Developing
Nations 2000–2007* (Washington, DC: Congressional Research
Service, Library of Congress), 23 October 2008, p. CRS-4.
3 See global trade data at http://stat.wto.org/StatisticalProgram/
WSDBViewData.aspx?Language=E, last accessed 31 March 2009.

CHAPTER 2 THE INTERNATIONAL ARMS TRADE IN
HISTORICAL PERSPECTIVE

1 William D. Hartung, *And Weapons for All* (New York: HarperCollins,
1994), pp. 21–6.
2 Keith Krause, *Arms and the State: Patterns of Military Production
and Trade* (Cambridge: Cambridge University Press, 1992), p. 34;
Thucydides, *The History of the Peloponnesian War*, trans. Steven
Lattimore (Indianapolis: Hackett Publishing Co., 1998).
3 Frederic S. Pearson, *The Global Spread of Arms: Political Economy of
International Security* (Oxford: Westview Press, 1994), pp. 10–11.
4 Krause, *Arms and the State*, pp. 37–9.
5 Ibid., pp. 40–2.
6 Ibid., pp. 44–6.
7 Ibid., pp. 46–7.
8 Ibid., pp. 44–5, 47–8.
9 Pearson, *The Global Spread of Arms*, pp. 10–11.

10 Krause, *Arms and the State*, pp. 48–51.
11 Ibid., p. 54.
12 Pearson, *The Global Spread of Arms*, p. 11.
13 Krause, *Arms and the State*, p. 53; Donald J. Stoker and Jonathan A. Grant, eds., *Girding for Battle: The Arms Trade in a Global Perspective, 1815–1940* (London: Praeger, 2003); John Stanley and Maurice Pearton, *The International Trade in Arms* (New York: Praeger, 1972).
14 Krause, *Arms and the State*, pp. 58, 60–1.
15 Fenner Brockway, *The Bloody Traffic* (London: Victor Gollancz, 1933); see also Bernt Engelmann, *The Weapons Merchants* (New York: Crown, Inc., 1964); Basil Collier, *Arms and the Men: The Arms Trade and Governments* (London: Hamish Hamilton, 1980); William Manchester, *The Arms of Krupp* (Boston: Little, Brown and Company, 1968); Anthony Sampson, *The Arms Bazaar* (New York: The Viking Press, 1977).
16 Stanley and Pearton, *The International Trade in Arms*.
17 Collier, *Arms and the Men*, p. 132.
18 Ibid., pp. 132, 183.
19 Pearson, *The Global Spread of Arms*, pp. 62–3.
20 Stanley and Pearton, *The International Trade in Arms*, pp. 5, 7.
21 Ibid., p. 8.
22 Collier, *Arms and the Men*, p. 166.
23 Ibid., pp. 178–9.
24 Stanley and Pearton, *The International Trade in Arms*, p. 8.
25 Ibid., pp. 104, 105, 110–18.
26 Ibid., pp. 110–18.
27 Ibid., pp. 8, 24–61.
28 Andrew J. Pierre, *The Global Politics of Arms Sales* (Princeton: Princeton University Press, 1982); Stanley and Pearton, *The International Trade in Arms*.
29 The SIPRI Arms Transfers Database at http://armstrade.sipri.org, last accessed 31 March 2009. Due to a lack of transparency and international standards, arms sales data are often difficult to acquire and compare. Thus, the authors have been particularly conscientious in using data that are widely accepted, respected and used. In addition, the authors have not compared data from multiple sources. Instead, the authors have relied on data compiled by either the Stockholm International Peace Research Institute (SIPRI) or the Congressional Research Service's (CRS's) annual Report for

Congress, *Conventional Arms Transfers to Developing Nations*. Yet, these two sources are also limited. SIPRI compiles its data from open sources and covers only actual deliveries of conventional arms, while the CRS reports rely on US government data, which are impossible to verify or disaggregate.

30 Pearson, *The Global Spread of Arms*, p. 30.
31 Krause, *Arms and the State*, pp. 97–8.
32 Stoker and Grant, eds., *Girding for Battle*; Stephanie G. Neuman and Robert E. Harkavy, eds., *Arms Transfers in the Modern World* (New York: Praeger, 1979).
33 Krause, *Arms and the State*, p. 2.
34 Stanley and Pearton, *The International Trade in Arms*, p. 101.
35 Stoker and Grant, eds., *Girding for Battle*.
36 Stanley and Pearton, *The International Trade in Arms*, p. 66.
37 Ibid., p. 83; Neuman and Harkavy, eds., *Arms Transfers in the Modern World*.
38 Pierre, *The Global Politics of Arms Sales*, pp. 19, 22–3; see also Neuman and Harkavy, eds., *Arms Transfers in the Modern World*.
39 Pierre, *The Global Politics of Arms Sales*, p. 23.
40 For more on arms acquisitions, see Andrew L. Ross, 'On Arms Acquisitions and Transfers', in Edward A. Kolodziej and Patrick M. Morgan, eds., *Security and Arms Control*. Vol. I (New York: Greenwood Press, 1989).
41 Edward A. Kolodziej, 'Arms Transfers and International Politics: The Interdependence of Independence', in Neuman and Harkavy, eds., *Arms Transfers in the Modern World*, p. 9.
42 Krause, *Arms and the State*, pp. 31–2.
43 Stanley and Pearton, *The International Trade in Arms*, p. 101.
44 Pierre, *The Global Politics of Arms Sales*, pp. 25–7.
45 Ibid.; Kolodziej, 'Arms Transfers and International Politics', p. 9.
46 The SIPRI Arms Transfers Database at http://armstrade.sipri.org, last accessed 31 March 2009.
47 Michael Brzoska and Thomas Ohlson, eds., *Arms Production in the Third World* (London: Taylor & Francis, 1986); Pearson, *The Global Spread of Arms*; Geoffrey Kemp, 'Introduction: The Global Arms Trade: Past and Present', in Gary E. McCuen, ed., *The Global Arms Trade* (Hudson: Gary E. McCuen, Inc., 1992), pp. 9–19.
48 The SIPRI Arms Transfers Database at http://armstrade.sipri.org/, last accessed 31 March 2009.
49 Pierre, *The Global Politics of Arms Sales*, p. 12.

50 Martin Edmonds, ed., *International Arms Procurement: New Directions* (New York: Pergamon Press, 1981).

51 Kemp, 'Introduction'.

52 Pierre, *The Global Politics of Arms Sales*, pp. 5, 13.

53 Kemp, 'Introduction', p. 16.

54 The SIPRI Arms Transfers Database. See also Sampson, *The Arms Bazaar*.

55 Kemp, 'Introduction', p. 11.

56 Pierre, *The Global Politics of Arms Sales*, pp. 8–9, 12.

57 SIPRI, *Yearbook 1994, Armaments, Disarmament and International Security* (New York: Oxford University Press, 1994), p. 511.

58 SIPRI, *Yearbook 1999, Armaments, Disarmament and International Security* (New York: Oxford University Press, 1999), p. 451.

59 SIPRI, *Yearbook 2006, Armaments, Disarmament and International Security* (New York: Oxford University Press, 2006), p. 482.

60 Grimmett, *Conventional Arms Transfers to Developing Nations 2000–2007*, p. CRS-24.

61 Ibid., p. CRS-4.

62 Pearson, *The Global Spread of Arms*, p. 14.

63 Richard F. Grimmett, *CRS Report for Congress: Trends in Conventional Arms Transfers to the Third World by Major Supplier, 1982–1989* (Washington, DC: Congressional Research Service, Library of Congress, 19 June 1990), p. CRS-2.

64 SIPRI, *Yearbook 2003, Armaments, Disarmament and International Security* (New York: Oxford University Press, 2003), p. 374.

65 SIPRI, *Yearbook 1995, Armaments, Disarmament and International Security* (New York: Oxford University Press, 1995), p. 459.

66 SIPRI, *Yearbook 2003*, p. 375.

67 Pearson, *The Global Spread of Arms*, p. 14.

68 Neuman and Harkavy, eds., *Arms Transfers in the Modern World*, p. 25.

69 Alexei Izyumov, 'The Soviet Union: Arms Control and Conversion – Plan and Reality', in Herbert Wulf, ed., *Arms Industry Limited* (Stockholm and Oxford: SIPRI and Oxford University Press, 1993), pp. 90–5, 109–10.

70 Ian Anthony, ed., *Russia and the Arms Trade* (Oxford: Oxford University Press, 1998), p. 4.

71 Pearson, *The Global Spread of Arms*, p. 16.

72 All data in this paragraph are from Richard F. Grimmett, *CRS Report for Congress, U.S. Arms Sales: Agreements with and Deliveries to Major*

Clients, 1999–2006 (Washington, DC: Congressional Research
Service, Library of Congress, 20 December 2007).

73 All data in this paragraph are from Richard F. Grimmett, *CRS Report
for Congress, U.S. Arms Sales: Agreements with and Deliveries to Major
Clients* (Washington, DC: Congressional Research Service, Library of
Congress, 15 December 2006).

74 United States Department of State, Bureau of Political–Military
Affairs, *Foreign Military Training: Joint Report to Congress, Fiscal Years
2006 and 2007* (Washington, DC: United States Department of States
August 2007), and Sharon Weinberger, 'Seller's Market', *Aviation
Week*, 19 November 2006.

75 Grimmett, *Conventional Arms Transfers to Developing Nations
2000–2007*, p. CRS-7.

76 McCuen, *The Global Arms Trade*, p. 24.

77 Pearson, *The Global Spread of Arms*, p. 14.

78 Neuman and Harkavy, (eds.), *Arms Transfers in the Modern World*, p. 26.

79 Richard F. Grimmett, *CRS Report for Congress: Conventional Arms
Transfers to Developing Nations, 1998–2005* (Washington, DC:
Congressional Research Service, Library of Congress, 23 October
2006), p. CRS-12.

80 Grimmett, *CRS Report for Congress: Trends in Conventional Arms
Transfers to the Third World by Major Supplier, 1982–1989*, p. CRS-3.

81 Matthew Schroeder and Rachel Stohl, 'U.S. Export Controls,' in
SIPRI, *Yearbook 2005, Armaments, Disarmament and International
Security* (New York: Oxford University Press, 2005), Appendix 17A,
pp. 720–40.

82 The White House, Office of the Press Secretary, 'Fact Sheet: Criteria
for Decisionmaking on U.S. Arms Exports', 17 February 1995.

83 Viktor Litovkin, 'Russian Arms Exports Break Records', *RIA Novosti*
(8 March 2007), at www.spacewar.com/reports/Russian_Arms_
Exports_Break_Records_999.html; and Viktor Litovkin, 'An Arms
Export Bonanza for Russia', *UPI Moscow* (20 March 2007), at
www.spacewar.com/reports/Am_Arms_Export_Bonanza_For_
Russia_999.html. For more on the value of Russian arms exports,
see the SIPRI database at http://armstrade.sipri.org/arms_trade/
trade-register.php. Websites last accessed 31 March 2009.

84 Congressional Research Service, *Conventional Arms Transfers to
Developing Nations, 1998–2005* (Washington, DC: Congressional
Research Service, 2006), at www.opencrs.com/document/RL33696,
last accessed 31 March 2009.

85 Grimmett, *Conventional Arms Transfers to Developing Nations 2000–2007*, p. CRS-6.

86 Richard F. Grimmett, *CRS Report for Congress: Conventional Arms Transfers to the Third World, 1983–1990* (Washington, DC: Congressional Research Service, Library of Congress, 2 August 1991), p. CRS-10.

87 Ibid., pp. CRS-10 and CRS-11.

88 D. Hartung, *And Weapons for All*, p. 223.

89 Ibid., p. 168.

90 McCuen, *The Global Arms Trade*, p. 62.

91 Hartung, *And Weapons for All*, p. 273.

92 SIPRI, *Yearbook 2000, Armaments, Disarmament and International Security* (New York: Oxford University Press, 2000), p. 374.

93 Richard F. Grimmett, *CRS Report for Congress: Conventional Arms Transfers to Developing Nations, 1992–1999* (Washington, DC: Congressional Research Service, Library of Congress, 18 August 2000), p. CRS-72.

94 Richard F. Grimmett, *Conventional Arms Transfers to Developing Nations, 2000–2007* (Washington, DC: Congressional Research Service, Library of Congress, 23 October 2006), p. CRS-64 and CRS-69.

95 Algeria, Armenia, Azerbaijan, Bahrain, Chad, Djibouti, Ethiopia, Georgia, India, Indonesia, Kazakhstan, Kenya, Kyrgyzstan, Mali, Mauritania, Nepal, Niger, Oman, Pakistan, Philippines, Tajikistan, Thailand, Turkmenistan, Yemen, Uzbekistan.

96 For more information, and data on the twenty-five case studies, see 'U.S. Arms Exports and Military Assistance in the "Global War on Terror"', at www.cdi.org, last accessed 31 March 2009.

97 Grimmett, *Conventional Arms Transfers to Developing Nations 2000–2007*, pp. CRS-63 and CRS-9.

98 Richard F. Grimmett, *CRS Report for Congress: Trends in Conventional Arms Transfers to the Third World by Major Supplier, 1999–2006*, (Washington, DC: Congressional Research Service, Library of Congress, 26 September 2007), pp. CRS-4 and CRS-13; Richard F. Grimmett, *CRS Report for Congress: Trends in Conventional Arms Transfers to the Third World by Major Supplier, 1998–2005* (Washington, DC: Congressional Research Service, Library of Congress, 23 October 2006), p. CRS-139; and Grimmett, *Conventional Arms Transfers to Developing Nations 2000–2007*, p. CRS-63.

99 Grimmett, *CRS Report for Congress: Conventional Arms Transfers to Developing Nations, 1998–2005*, p. CRS-16.

100 Ibid., pp. CRS-56 and CRS-57.

101 Grimmett, *CRS Report for Congress: Trends in Conventional Arms Transfers to the Third World by Major Supplier, 1999–2006*, p. CRS-36.

102 Grimmett, *Conventional Arms Transfers to Developing Nations 2000–2007*, p. CRS-17.

103 Ibid., p. CRS-43.

104 Grimmett, *CRS Report for Congress: Trends in Conventional Arms Transfers to the Third World by Major Supplier, 1999–2006*, p. CRS-16.

105 Grimmett, *CRS Report for Congress, U.S. Arms Sales: Agreements with and Deliveries to Major Clients, 1999–2006*, p. CRS-3.

106 SIPRI, *Yearbook 2006*, p. 401.

107 United States Government Accountability Office, 'Defense Industry: Trends in DOD Spending, Industrial Productivity, and Competition', January 1997, p. 4, at www.gao.gov/archive/1997/pe97003.pdf, last accessed 31 March 2009.

108 SIPRI, *Yearbook 2006, Armaments, Disarmament and International Security* (New York: Oxford University Press, 2006), p. 397–8.

109 'Joint Strike Fighter', *Federation of American Scientists*, 30 May 2008, at www.fas.org/man/dod-101/sys/ac/jsf.htm, last accessed 3 April 2009.

110 The nine countries are Australia, Canada, Denmark, Italy, the Netherlands, Norway, Turkey, the United Kingdom and the United States; see John R. Kent and John Smith, 'Denmark Joins F-35 Program's Next Phase, Completes JSF Partner Participation', Lockheed Martin, 27 February 2005, at www.lockheedmartin.com/news/press_releases/2007/DENMARKJOINSF35PROGRAMSNEXTPHASECOM.html, last accessed 3 April 2009.

111 Jay Stowsky, 'The History and Politics of the Pentagon's Dual-Use Strategy', in Ann R. Markusen and Sean Costigan, eds., *Arming the Future: A Defense Industry for the 21st Century* (New York: Council on Foreign Relations Press, 1999), p. 107.

112 SIPRI, *Yearbook 2006*, pp. 398–9.

113 Ibid.

114 See global trade data at http://stat.wto.org/StatisticalProgram/WSDBViewData.aspx?Language=E, last accessed 3 April 2009.

115 SIPRI, *Yearbook 2008*, p. 295.

CHAPTER 3 THE LEGAL SUPPLY AND TRANSFER OF
ARMS

1 'The First Two Serially Produced Su-30MKM Fighters for the Royal
Malaysian Air Force Have Been Demonstrated, Irkut Corp', 24 May
2007, at www.irkut.com/en/news/press_release_archives/index.
php?id48=252, last accessed 3 April 2009.
2 Grimmett, *Conventional Arms Transfers to Developing Nations
2000–2007*, p. CRS-4.
3 'Boeing Arms Chief Warns Against "Peace Dividend"', Reuters, 24
May 2007.
4 'Ferengi Rules of Acquisition', *Wikia Entertainment* at http://
memory-alpha.org/en/wiki/Rules_of_Acquisition, last accessed 3
April 2009.
5 French Ministry of Defence, 'Press Kit: Report to the French
Parliament Regarding Defence Equipments Exports in 2006,' 4
December 2007, p. 12.
6 See Kevin Speers and RADM Stephen H. Baker (ret.), 'Economic
Arguments for Arms Export Reform', in Tamar Gabelnick and
Rachel Stohl, eds., *Challenging Conventional Wisdom: Debunking the
Myths and Exposing the Risks of Arms Export Reform* (Washington,
DC: Center for Defense Information and Federation of American
Scientists, June 2003), pp. 53–64.
7 Alexi Nikolsky, 'The Defense Industry Switches to Euros', *Vedemosti*,
4 June 2007, p. 13.
8 Alexi Nikolsky, 'The Defense Industry Switches to Euros', *Vedemosti*,
4 June 2007, p. 13.
9 Mark P. Sullivan, 'Chile: Political and Economic Conditions and
U.S. Relations', CRS Report for Congress, updated 5 August 2003,
at http://fpc.state.gov/documents/organization/23586.pdf, last
accessed 3 April 2009.
10 International Monetary Fund, *Chile: Report on Observance of
Standards and Codes – Fiscal Transparency* (Washington, DC:
International Monetary Fund, August 2003) at www.imf.org/
external/pubs/ft/scr/2003/cr03237.pdf, last accessed 3 April 2009.
11 Andrew Chuter and Martin Agüera, 'Copper Helps Chile Make
Deals for Ships, Planes', *Defense News*, 24 June 2005.
12 Richard F. Grimmett, *Conventional Arms Transfers to Developing
Nations 1993–2000* (Washington, DC: Congressional Research

Service, Library of Congress, 16 August 2001), pp. CRS-4 and CRS-5.

13 Paul Rivlin, 'The Russian Economy and Arms Exports to the Middle East', *Jaffee Center for Strategic Studies, Memorandum 79*, November 2005, at http://sel.isn.ch/serviceengine/FileContent?serviceID=47& fileid=2A7C5105-3FF9-3561-8852-AC025C91F339&lng=en, p. 35, last accessed 3 April 2009.

14 Gethin Chamberlain, 'Iran Fears Spark Sunni Arms Spree: $50 Billion Shopping List from Saudi Arabia Alone', *The Gazette (Montreal)*, 11 February 2007.

15 US Department of Commerce, *Offset in Defense Trade*, 10th Study (Washington, DC, 2005), at www.bis.doc.gov/DefenseIndustrialBasePrograms/OSIES/Offsets/OffsetXFinalReport.pdf, last accessed 3 April 2009.

16 Leslie Wayne, 'A Well-Kept Military Secret', *New York Times*, 16 February 2003.

17 Brooks Tigner, 'EDA Strives to Rein in Offsets', *Defense News*, 28 August 2006.

18 Gripen International, 'Latest Hungarian Gripen Offset Claim Approved', *defense-aerospace.com* (5 August 2005).

19 Lee Stokes, 'Kuwait–Soviet Arms Deal Signals Shift from U.S.', UPI, 10 July 1988.

20 Michael Brzoska, 'The Economics of Arms Imports After the End of the Cold War', *Defence and Peace Economics*, 15(2) (April 2004).

21 'United States: New Allegations of Nicaraguan Arms Buildup', Inter Press Service, 19 April 1985; James M. Dorsey, 'Sandinista Buildup at Border Stirs U.S. Concern', *Washington Times*, 6 December 1989.

22 Marius Zaharia, 'Romania To Buy 48 New Fighter Jets: Official', *Defense News*, 22 February 2007; Agence France Presse, 'Czech Republic Signs 835 Million Euro Contract for Armored Transporters', *Defense News*, 9 June 2006; Hil Anderson, 'F16s Arrive in Poland; Renamed "Hawks"', UPI, 13 November 2006.

23 One author's meeting with senior State Department official, 16 May 2007.

24 Rivlin, 'The Russian Economy and Arms Exports to the Middle East', p. 34.

25 One author's meeting with senior State Department official, 16 May 2007.

26 Jim Wolf, 'U.S. Looks to Arm Iran's Neighbors: General', Reuters, 18 May 2006.

27 Jim Wolf, 'Iran, North Korea Spur PAC-3 Missile Demand: Lockheed', Reuters, 24 August 2006.

28 US Department of Defense, *Joint Publication 1–02, Department of Defense Dictionary of Military and Associated Terms* (Washington, DC, 12 April 2001 as amended through 22 March 2007), at www.dtic. mil/doctrine/jel/new_pubs/jp1_02.pdf, last accessed 3 April 2009.

29 Col. Daniel M. Smith (USA, ret.), 'U.S. Arms Exports and Interoperability: Fighting with Each Other', in Tamar Gabelnick and Rachel Stohl, eds., *Challenging Conventional Wisdom: Debunking the Myths and Exposing the Risks of Arms Export Reform* (Washington, DC: Center for Defense Information and Federation of American Scientists, June 2003), p. 67. For more on interoperability, see the entire chapter.

30 For more information on military diplomacy, see Cassady Craft, 'Military Diplomacy: The Myth of Arms for Influence', in Tamar Gabelnick and Rachel Stohl, eds., *Challenging Conventional Wisdom: Debunking the Myths and Exposing the Risks of Arms Export Reform* (Washington, DC: Center for Defense Information and Federation of American Scientists, June 2003), pp. 86–103.

31 David S. Cloud, 'Inquiry Opened Into Israeli Use of U.S. Bombs', *New York Times*, 25 August 2006; and David S. Cloud and Greg Myre, 'Israel May Have Violated Arms Pact, U.S. Says', *New York Times*, 28 January 2007.

32 One author's interview with senior State Department official, 16 May 2007.

33 Center for Public Integrity, 'U.S. Foreign Lobbying, Terrorism Influencing Post 9/11 U.S. Military Aid and Human Rights', Washington, DC, 18 May 2007.

34 Agence France Presse, 'Hungarian Tanks Leave for Iraq', *Defense News*, 17 October 2005.

35 Richard Speier, Robert Gallucci, Robbie Sabel and Victor Mizin, 'Iran–Russia Missile Cooperation', in Joseph Cinnicione, ed., *Repairing the Regime: Preventing the Spread of Weapons of Mass Destruction*, New York: Routledge, May 2000 at www. carnegieendowment.org/files/Repairing_12.pdf, last accessed 3 April 2009.

36 Rivlin, 'The Russian Economy and Arms Exports to the Middle East', p. 35.

37 For more in-depth information on the US arms export system, see Schroeder and Stohl, 'U.S. Export Controls', pp. 720–40.

38 The White House, Office of the Press Secretary, 'Fact Sheet: Criteria for Decision-making on US Arms Exports' (Washington, DC, 17 February 1995), at www.fas.org/asmp/resources/govern/whcrit. html, last accessed 3 April 2009. PDD 34 remains US conventional arms policy, as the Bush Administration never released its own.

39 See White House, Office of the Press Secretary, 'White House Memo For The Secretary of State on Waiver of Nuclear-Related Sanctions on India and Pakistan' (Washington, DC, 23 September 2001), at www.fas.org/terrorism/at/docs/2001/Ind-PakWaiver. htm, last accessed 3 April 2009; and US Department of State, Office of the Spokesman, 'Fact Sheet: Sanctions on Pakistan and India' (Washington, DC, 28 September 2001), at www.fas.org/terrorism/ at/docs/2001/Ind-PakSanctions.htm, last accessed 3 April 2009.

40 The 1961 Foreign Assistance Act (PL87–195) is available on the Internet site of the Federation of American Scientists at FAA – www.fas.org/asmp/resources/govern/109th/FAA0106.pdf, last accessed 3 April 2009. The 1976 Arms Export Control Act (PL90-629) is available on the Internet site of the Federation of American Scientists at AECA – www.fas.org/asmp/resources/govern/109th/ AECA0106.pdf, last accessed 3 April 2009.

41 For more information, see L. Lumpe and J. Donarski, *The Arms Trade Revealed: A Guide for Investigators and Activists* (Washington, DC: Federation of American Scientists Arms Sales Monitoring Project, 1998).

42 Until 1994, dual-use items were regulated by the Export Administration Act (EAA), administered by the Bureau of Industry and Security at the Department of Commerce. When the EAA expired in 1994, dual-use items became regulated by the International Emergency Economic Powers Act, which gives the President 'temporary authority to continue controls and most enforcement activities'. David Fite, 'A View from Congress', in Tamar Gabelnick and Rachel Stohl, eds., *Challenging Conventional Wisdom: Debunking the Myths and Exposing the Risks of Arms Export Reform* (Washington, DC: Center for Defence Information and Federation of American Scientists, 2003).

43 United States Department of State, *End-Use Monitoring of Defense Articles and Defense Services Commercial Exports FY 2007* (Washington, DC: Directorate of Defense Trade Controls).

44 Ibid.
45 United States Bureau of Industry and Security, *Annual Report Fiscal Year 2007* (Washington, DC: United States Department of Commerce, 2006), pp. 16 and 23, at www.bis.doc.gov/news/2008/ annreport07/bis_annual_report07.pdf, last accessed 3 April 2009.
46 United States Immigration and Customs Enforcement, 'FY07 Accomplishments', at www.ice.gov/doclib/pi/news/factsheets/ fy07accmplshmntsweb.pdf, last accessed 3 April 2009.
47 United States Department of Homeland Security, Immigration and Customs Enforcement, Counter-Proliferation Investigations Factsheet, 28 October 2008, at www.ice.gov/pi/news/factsheets/ counter_proliferations.htm, last accessed 9 April 2009; and US Immigration and Customs Enforcement, 'FY07 Accomplishments'.
48 Ibid.
49 Anthony, ed., *Russia and the Arms Trade*, p. 10.
50 'Putin to Reform Russian Arms Exporter', Reuters, 20 June 2005, at http://asia.news.yahoo.com/070620/3/33n08.html, last accessed 5 April 2009.
51 See the Russian report in the SIPRI database at http://first.sipri.org/ db/dbf/export_reg_display, last accessed 5 April 2009.
52 Ibid.
53 Lionel Beehner, 'Russia–Iran Arms Trade', *Council on Foreign Relations Backgrounder* (1 November 2006), at www.cfr.org/ publication/11869/, last accessed 5 April 2009.
54 'Chinese Fighter Jets to Reach Pakistan', *Kommersant: Russia's Daily Online*, 26 April 2007, at www.kommersant.com/p762182/r_500/ deal_fighter_jets_Pakistan, last accessed 5 April 2009.
55 'Russia to Supply over $2.2bln Weapons to Libya', *Iran Defence Forum*, 4 May 2007, at www.irandefence.net/showthread. php?t=14570, last accessed 5 April 2009.
56 'Russia's Sukhoi Fighter is State-of-the-Art Warplane – Chavez', 18 April 2007, at http://209.157.64.200/focus/f-news/1819804/posts; and Jason Bush, 'Russia's Back in the Arms Game', *Business Week*, 10 April 2007, at www.businessweek.com/globalbiz/content/apr2007/ gb20070409_470397.htm. Websites last accessed 5 April 2009.
57 Ariel Cohen, 'The Russian Effect', *FrontPageMagazine.com*, 20 March 2007, at http://bsimmons.wordpress.com/2007/03/20/the-russian-effect, last accessed 5 April 2009.
58 Bush, 'Russia's Back in the Arms Game'.
59 Guy Faulconbridge, 'No One Can Limit Russian Arms Exports:

Putin', Reuters, 31 October 2007, at www.reuters.com/articlePrint?
articleID=USL3183608320071031, last accessed 5 April 2009.

60 Ibid.

61 Center for International Trade and Security, *Nonproliferation Export Controls: A Global Evaluation* (Athens, GA: Center for International Trade and Security).

62 Department for Business Enterprise and Regulatory Reform, 'UK Legislation on Strategic Export Controls', July 2007, at www. berr.gov.uk/whatwedo/europeandtrade/strategic-export-control/ legislation/index.html, last accessed 5 April 2009.

63 Mark Curtis, Helen Close, Vanessa Dury and Ray Iskister, *The Good, the Bad, and the Ugly: A Decade of Labour's Arms Exports* (London: Saferworld, 2007), pp. 9–10.

64 Department for Business Enterprise and Regulatory Reform, 'SPIRE – Background information', 2008, at www.berr.gov.uk/whatwedo/ europeandtrade/strategic-export-control/licensing-policy/spire/ index.html, last accessed 5 April 2009.

65 Department for Business Enterprise and Regulatory Reform, 'Export Control Organization: Controlling UK Export of Strategic Goods, Technology and Software', 2008, at www.berr.gov.uk/whatwedo/ europeandtrade/strategic-export-control/index.html, last accessed 5 April 2009.

66 Author correspondence with Saferworld staff, 30 January 2008.

67 Ibid.

68 *Explanatory Notes to Export Control Act 2002* (London: Queen's Printer of Acts of Parliament), 2002, at www.opsi.gov.uk/acts/ acts2002/en/ukpgaen_20020028_en_1, last accessed 5 April 2009.

69 Neil Mackay, 'Revealed: The Extent of Britain's Arms Trade', *The Sunday Herald*, 8 July 2006, p. 8.

70 Grimmett, *Conventional Arms Transfers to Developing Nations 1999–2006*, p. CRS-4.

71 Mackay, 'Revealed: The Extent of Britain's Arms Trade', p. 8.

72 Ibid.

73 'About DESO: Our History, Mission, and Vision', retrieved January 2008 from www.deso.mod.uk/about.htm.

74 Symon Hill, 'How to Get Ahead in Arms Dealing', *Morning Star*, 6 October 2006.

75 Adam Plowright, 'OECD has "serious concerns" about Halt to BAE–Saudi Probe', Agence France Presse, 18 January 2007.

76 SIPRI, *Yearbook 2006*, p. 421.
77 Rob Evans, 'Export Department Closure Leaves Defence Firms Out in the Cold', Thursday 26 July 2007, at www.guardian.co.uk/business/2007/jul/26/1, last accessed 5 April 2009.
78 Wassenaar Arrangement, 'French Policy On Export Controls for Conventional Arms and Dual-Use Goods and Technologies', www.wassenaar.org/natdocs/fr1_fr.pdf, last accessed 5 April 2009.
79 Commission to Assess the Ballistic Missile Threat to the United States, Appendix III: Unclassified Working Papers, System Planning Corporation: 'Non-Proliferation Issues', France, Executive Summary, at www.fas.org/irp/threat/missile/rumsfeld/pt3_france.htm, last accessed 5 April 2009.
80 Ministère de la Défense, 'Press Kit: Report to the French Parliament Regarding Defence Equipments Exports in 2006', p. 6.
81 Commission to Assess the Ballistic Missile Threat to the United States, 'Non-Proliferation Issues.'
82 Ibid.
83 Wassenaar Arrangement, 'French Policy On Export Controls for Conventional Arms and Dual-Use Goods and Technologies.'
84 Pierre Tran, 'France Works to Review Flagging Arms Exports,' *Defense News*, 17 December 2007.
85 French Ministry of Defence, 'Export of Defense and Security Equipment: A Strategy for Growth', 13 December 2007, unofficial translation by www.defense-aerospace.com.
86 Ibid.
87 Tran, 'France Works to Review Flagging Arms Exports.'
88 Ibid.
89 Ibid.
90 For a detailed discussion of the conventional arms licensing process, see Evan S. Medeiros, *Chasing the Dragon: Assessing China's System of Export Controls for WMD-Related Goods and Technologies* (Santa Monica: RAND Corporation, 2005), pp. 59–64.
91 Ibid., p. 60.
92 Ibid., p. 35.
93 Ibid., pp. 59–64.
94 'China Refutes Amnesty International's Slams on Arms Trade', *People's Daily Online*, 12 June 2006, http://english.peopledaily.com.cn/200606/12/eng20060612_273325.html; and 'China Always Prudent in Arms Trade: FM Spokeswoman', *People's Daily*

Online, 13 June 2006, at http://english.people.com.cn/200606/13/eng20060613_273707.html. Websites last accessed 5 April 2009.

95 'China Always Prudent in Arms Trade: FM Spokeswoman,' *People's Daily Online*, 13 June 2006.

96 Canadian Security Intelligence Service, *Weapons Proliferation and the Military Industrial Complex of the PRC*, Ottawa, Ont., 27 August 2003, at www.csis-scrs.gc.ca/pbectns/cmmntr/cm84-eng.asp#top, last accessed 5 April 2009.

97 'China Voices Firm Opposition to Illegal Trade in Small Arms', *People's Daily Online*, 10 July 2001, at http://english.peopledaily.com.cn/200107/10/eng20010710_74551.html, last accessed 5 April 2009.

98 Ibid.

99 According to SIPRI, China regularly exports arms worth hundreds of millions of US dollars each year, but rarely transfers billions of dollars' worth of arms in any given year, with the exception of 1987 and 1988 when Chinese weapons exports were valued at $3 billion and $2 billion, respectively. See the SIPRI Arms Transfers Database at http://armstrade.sipri.org/arms_trade/values.php, last accessed 5 April 2009.

100 China submitted arms export information to the UN Registry of Conventional Arms from 1992 to 1996, but then suspended its participation in the Registry after other countries reported arms transfers to Taiwan, a province of China. The Chinese government submitted its first report to the Registry in ten years in 2006. See The People's Republic of China, Ministry of Foreign Affairs, *UN Register of Conventional Arms*, 21 May 2005, at www.fmprc.gov.cn/eng/wjb/zzjg/jks/kjlc/cgjkwt/cgjm/t321038.htm, last accessed 5 April 2009.

101 See, for example, Clifford Coonan, 'China is Arming World's Regimes to Fuel Economic Boom, says Amnesty', *The Independent*, 12 June 2006, at www.independent.co.uk/news/world/asia/china-is-arming-worlds-worst-regimes-to-fuel-economic-boom-says-amnesty-482018.html; Amnesty International, 'China: Secretive Arms Exports Stoking Conflict and Repression', 11 June 2006, at www.amnesty.org/en/library/asset/ASA17/033/2006/en/dom-ASA170332006en.html. Websites last accessed 5 April 2009.

102 See, in particular, Amnesty International, *Sudan: Arms Continuing to Fuel Serious Human Rights Violations in Darfur* (London: Amnesty International, 8 May 2007), at www.amnesty.org/en/library/

info/AFR54/019/2007; and Esther Pan, *China, Africa and Oil* (Washington, DC: Council on Foreign Relations, 2007), at www.cfr. org/publication/9557, last accessed 6 April 2009.

103 See Nicholas D. Kristof, 'China's Genocide Olympics', *The International Herald Tribune*, 24 January 2008, at www. nytimes.com/2008/01/24/opinion/24kristof.html?_ r=1&scp=1&sq=china's%20genocide%20olympia&st=cse; and www.dreamfordarfur.org. Websites last accessed 6 April 2009.

104 Medeiros, *Chasing the Dragon*, p. 59; and Daniel Byman and Roger Cliff, *China's Arms Sales: Motivations and Implications* (New York: RAND Corporation, 2000).

105 Pan, *China, Africa and Oil*; for specifics on Chinese transfers to these countries, see the UN Registry of Conventional Arms at http://disarmament.un.org/UN_REGISTER.nsf, last accessed 6 April 2009.

106 Bates Gill and Evan S. Medeiros, 'Foreign and Domestic Influences on China's Arms Control and Nonproliferation Policies,' *The China Quarterly*, 161 (March 2000), pp. 66–94, at http://cns.miis.edu/ research/china/pdfs/evancq.pdf, last accessed 6 April 2009.

107 Author interviews with Chinese authorities and experts, Beijing, China, August–December 2007.

108 Grimmett, *Conventional Arms Transfers to Developing Nations 2000–2007*, p. CRS-6.

109 All data in this paragraph are from Grimmett, *CRS Report for Congress, U.S. Arms Sales: Agreements with and Deliveries to Major Clients, 1999–2006*.

110 'Damaged U.S. Spy Plane Arrives in Georgia', CNN (5 July 2001), at http://archives.cnn.com/2001/US/07/05/spy.plane.return/index. html, last accessed 6 April 2009.

111 Jonathan Reingold, 'U.S. Arms Sales to Israel End Up in China, Iraq', *CommonDreams.org* (9 May 2002), at www.commondreams. org/views02/0509–07.htm, last accessed 6 April 2009.

112 SIPRI Arms Transfers Database.

113 John Rossant with Dexter Roberts, 'An Arms Cornucopia for China?' *Business Week* (21 February 2005), at www.businessweek. com/magazine/content/05_08/b3921073_mz054.htm; and Marcel DeHaas, 'Russia–China Security Cooperation', *Power and Interest News Report* (27 November 2006), at www.pinr.com/report/ php?ac=view_printable&report_id=588&language_id=1. Websites last accessed 6 April 2009.

114 SIPRI Arms Transfers Database, and Dettaas, 'Russia–China Security Cooperation'.

115 Rachel Stohl, 'Wrangling Over Arms Sales to China', *Foreign Policy in Focus* (December 2006), at www.fpif.org/pdf/papers/0612arms.pdf, last accessed 6 April 2009.

116 Ibid.

117 'UK Breaks EU Rule, Trains Chinese Officer', *UPI.com* (7 September 2008), at www.upi.com/Top_News/2008/09/07/UK_breaks_EU_rule_trains_Chinese_officer/UPI-82381220793189/, last accessed 6 April 2009.

118 Adam Segal, 'New China Worries', *The International Economy* (Fall 2007), at www.cfr.org/content/publications/attachments/TIE_F07_Segal.pdf, last accessed 6 April 2009.

119 David Lague, 'Russia and China Rethink Arms Deals', *International Herald Tribune* (2 March 2008), at www.chinaelections.net/newsinfo.asp?newsid=16018, last accessed 6 April 2009.

120 Segal, 'New China Worries.'

121 See, for example, Amnesty International, 'People's Republic of China: Sustaining Conflict and Human Rights Abuses; The Flow of Arms Accelerates' (London: Amnesty International, 2007), at www.amnestyusa.org/document.php?id=ENGASA170302006&lang=e; and Office of the US Secretary of Defense, *Annual Report to Congress: Military Power of the People's Republic of China* (May 2007), available at www.defenselink.mil/pubs/pdfs/070523-China-Military-Power-final.pdf. Websites last accessed 6 April 2009.

122 Hartung, *And Weapons for All*, p. 5.

123 Richard Norton-Taylor, 'Countries Listed by Foreign Office as Poor on Human Rights Invited to Arms Trade Fair', *The Guardian*, 13 September 2005.

124 Chamberlain, 'Iran Fears Spark Sunni Arms Spree: $50 Billion Shopping List from Saudi Arabia Alone.'

125 Richard Norton-Taylor, 'Countries Listed by Foreign Office as Poor on Human Rights Invited to Arms Trade Fair.'

126 Amnesty International, 'Arms Without Borders: Why a Globalised Trade Needs Global Controls', 2 October 2006, at web.amnesty.org/library/Index/ENGPOL340062006?open&of=ENG-EGY, last accessed 6 April 2009.

127 For more specific information on Letters of Offer, Acceptance, etc., see chapter 3.

128 Krause, *Arms and the State*.

129 See table 3.1.

130 The SIPRI list does not include Chinese companies – which are possibly among the top 100 – due to lack of data.

131 Kevin Speers and Stephen H. Baker, 'Economic Arguments for Arms Export Reform', in Tamar Gabelnick and Rachel Stohl, eds., *Challenging Conventional Wisdom: Debunking the Myths and Exposing the Risks of Arms Export Reform* (Washington: Center of Defense Information and Federation of American Scientists, June 2003), p. 60.

132 David Gold, 'The Changing Economics of the Arms Trade', in Sean S. Costigan and Ann R. Markusen, eds., *Arming the Future: A Defense Industry for the 21st Century* (New York: Council on Foreign Relations Press, 1999), p. 252.

133 SIPRI, *Yearbook 2006*, p. 392.

134 'Boeing Arms Chief Warns Against "Peace Dividend"', Reuters, 24 May 2007.

135 SIPRI, *Yearbook 2006*, pp. 391–3, and SIPRI, *Yearbook 2007, Armaments, Disarmament and International Security* (New York: Oxford University Press, 2007), pp. 345–73.

136 One author's meeting with senior State Department official, 16 May 2007.

137 Ibid.

138 Human Rights Watch, 'Arsenals on the Cheap: NATO Expansion and the Arms Cascade', April 1999, at www.hrw.org/legacy/reports/1999/nato/, last accessed 6 April 2009.

139 Leslie Wayne, 'Free To A Good Country', *New York Times*, 31 October 2006, p. C1.

140 Ibid.

141 United Nations General Assembly, *Report of the Panel of Governmental Experts on Small Arms*, A/52/298 (27 August 1997) at www.un.org/Depts/ddar/Firstcom/SGreport52/a52298.html, last accessed 6 April 2009.

142 Small Arms Survey, *Small Arms Survey 2007: Guns in the City* (Cambridge: Cambridge University Press, 2007), p. 39.

143 Small Arms Survey, *Small Arms Survey 2002: Counting the Human Cost* (Oxford: Oxford University Press, 2002), p. 104.

144 Small Arms Survey, *Small Arms Survey 2007*, p. 39.

145 R. T. Naylor, 'The Structure and Operation of the Modern Arms Black Market', in Jeffrey Boutwell, Michael T. Klare and Laura W.

Reed, eds., *Lethal Commerce: The Global Trade in Small Arms and Light Weapons* (Cambridge, MA: American Academy of Arts and Sciences, 1995), p. 48.

146 The Norwegian Initiative on Small Arms Transfers (NISAT) database of authorized transfers of small arms and light weapons, at www.nisat.org, last accessed 6 April 2009.

147 Taras Kuzio, 'Ukraine: Look into Arms Exports', *The Christian Science Monitor*, 12 February 2002.

148 Nunn-Lugar Report, *Lugar, Obama Urge Destruction of Conventional Weapons Stockpiles*, August 2005, pp. 4–5, at http://lugar.senate.gov/nunnlugar/pdf/trip_report_2005.pdf.

149 Small Arms Survey, *Small Arms Survey 2003: Development Denied* (Oxford: Oxford University Press, 2003), p. 13.

150 *Small Arms Survey 2002: Counting the Human Cost*, p. 109.

151 'The Small Arms Manufacturing Industry's Revenue for the Year 2006 Was Approximately $2,150,000,000', *Business Wire*, 11 April 2007.

152 Small Arms Survey, *Small Arms Survey 2006* (Oxford: Oxford University Press, 2006).

153 Small Arms Survey, *Small Arms Survey 2004: Rights at Risk* (Oxford: Oxford University Press, 2004), p. 10.

154 Pablo Dreyfus, Benjamin Lessing and Júlio César Purcena, 'The Brazilian Small Arms Industry: Legal Production and Trade', in Rubem César Fernándes, ed., *Brazil: The Arms and the Victims* (Rio de Janeiro: 7 Letras Iser, 2005), p. 73, at www.smallarmssurvey.org/files/portal/issueareas/transfers/transfers_pdf/2005_Dreyfus_et_al.pdf, last accessed 6 April 2009.

155 Small Arms Survey, *Small Arms Survey 2006*, p. 7.

156 NISAT database of authorized transfers.

157 Ibid.

158 Small Arms Survey, *Small Arms Survey 2005: Weapons at War* (Oxford: Oxford University Press, 2005), p. 14.

159 Holger Anders and Reinhilde Weidacher, 'The Production of Ammunition for Small Arms and Light Weapons', in Stéphanie Pézard and Holger Anders, eds., *Targeting Ammunition: A Primer* (Geneva: Small Arms Survey, 2006), p. 57.

160 Mike Bourne and Ilhan Berkol, 'Deadly Diversions: Illicit Transfers of Ammunition for Small Arms and Light Weapons', in Stéphanie Pézard and Holgar Anders, eds., *Targeting Ammunition: A Primer*, (Geneva: Small Arms Survey, 2006), p. 121.

161 Anders and Weidacher, 'The Production of Ammunition for Small Arms and Light Weapons,' p. 62.

162 Anne-Kathrin Glatz, 'Buying the Bullet: Authorized Small Arms Ammunition Transfers', in Pézard and Anders, eds., *Targeting Ammunition*, p. 71.

163 Philip Alpers, *Gun-running in Papua New Guinea: From Arrows to Assault Weapons in the Southern Highlands*, Special Report No. 5 (Geneva: Small Arms Survey, 2005).

164 Defense Security Cooperation Agency, News Release, Transmittal No. 06–69, 'Iraq – Helicopters, Vehicles, Weapons and Support', 19 September 2006; Defense Security Cooperation Agency, News Release, Transmittal No. 06-68, 'Iraq – Logistics Support for Helicopters, Vehicles, and Weapons', 19 September 2006; Defense Security Cooperation Agency, News Release, Transmittal No. 07-09, 'Iraq – Trucks, Vehicles, Trailers, and Support', 7 December 2006; and Defense Security Cooperation Agency, News Release,Transmittal No. 07-20, 'Iraq – Various Small Arms Ammunition, Explosives, and Other Consumables', 4 May 2007.

165 Defense Secretary Cooperation Agency, 'Iraq – Helicopters, Vehicles, Weapons and Support'.

166 From Larry Kahaner, 'Lessons of the AK-47', defensetech.org, 25 October 2006, at www.defensetech.org/archives/002892.html, last accessed 6 April 2009.

167 Matthew Cox, 'Better than M4, but You Can't Have One', *Army Times*, 1 March 2007, at www.armytimes.com/news/2007/02/atCarbine070219/, last accessed 6 April 2009.

168 Special Inspector General for Iraq Reconstruction, *Iraqi Security Forces: Weapons Provided by the U.S. Department of Defense Using the Iraqi Relief and Reconstruction Fund* (Washington, DC: Office of the Special Inspector General for Iraq Reconstruction, 28 October, 2006), at www.sigir.mil/reports/pdf/audits/06-033.pdf, last accessed 6 April 2009.

169 United States Government Accountability Office, *Operation Iraqi Freedom* (Washington, DC, 22 March 2007), at www.gao.gov/new.items/d07639t.pdf, last accessed 6 April 2009.

170 Jason Campbell, Michael O'Hanlon and Amy Unikewicz, 'Op-Chart: The State of Iraq: An Update', *New York Times*, 10 June 2007.

CHAPTER 4 THE ILLICIT ARMS TRADE

1   For more on 'the Devil', see 'Victor Infante Charged with Weapons
    Exportation and Methamphetamine Distribution Arrested in
    the Philippines' (Washington, DC: U.S. Drug Enforcement
    Administration, 6 November 2003), at www.dea.gov/pubs/states/
    newsrel/2003/nyc110603.html, last accessed 6 April 2009.
2   'Security Council Extends Sanctions Against Liberia Until 7 May
    2004, Unanimously Adopted Resolution 1478 (2003)', United
    Nations Press Release, SC/7752, 5 June 2003, at www.un.org/News/
    Press/docs/2003/sc7752.doc.htm, last accessed 6 April 2009.
3   Dave Gilson, 'Ukraine: Cashing in on Illegal Arms', *Frontline World*,
    May 2002, at www.pbs.org/frontlineworld/stories/sierraleone/
    context.html, last accessed 6 April 2009.
4   The blockbuster Hollywood film *The Lord of War* was based on the
    life of Ukrainian-born gun runner, Victor Bout, who also advised
    during the making of the film.
5   'Insights and Mysteries: Global Small Arms Transfers', Small Arms
    Survey, *Small Arms Survey 2003*, p. 97.
6   Small Arms Survey, *Small Arms Survey 2001: Profiling the Problem*
    (Oxford: Oxford University Press, 2001), p. 167.
7   Ibid., p. 166. For more on defining the illicit arms trade, see Rachel
    Stohl, Matt Schroeder and Dan Smith, *The Small Arms Trade*
    (Oxford: Oneworld, 2006), p. 13.
8   Andrew J. Pierre, ed., *Cascade of Arms: Managing Conventional
    Weapons Proliferation* (Washington, DC: Brookings Institution Press,
    1997), pp. 47–8.
9   Lora Lumpe, *Running Guns: The Global Black Market in Small Arms*
    (London: Zed Books, 2000), p. 1.
10 See the Report of the 2006 Group of Governmental Experts on the
    UN Register of Conventional Arms at www.phxnews.com/fullstory.
    php?article=22505. For more on the UN Register, see http://
    disarmament.un.org/cab/register.html. Websites last accessed 6
    April 2009.
11 Despite the difficulty, researchers at the Small Arms Survey have
    attempted to enhance information on small arms transfers with the
    creation of the Small Arms Trade Transparency Barometer. The
    Barometer assesses the transparency of the major reported small-
    arms-exporting states on a twenty-point scale on the basis of the
    information states publish on their small arms exports in national

arms export reports and in customs data as reported to the UN
Comtrade. See Small Arms Survey, 'Reaching for the Big Picture: An
Update on Small Arms Transfers', in Small Arms Survey, Graduate
Institute of International Research (Geneva), *Small Arms Survey
2005: Weapons at War* (Oxford: Oxford University Press, 2005).

12 United Nations General Assembly, *General and Complete
Disarmament: Small Arms*, 27 August 1997, at www.un.org/Depts/
ddar/Firstcom/SGreport52/a52298.html, last accessed 6 April 2009.

13 Stohl, Schroeder and Smith, *The Small Arms Trade*, p. 12; and Small
Arms Survey, 'Crime, Conflict, Corruption: Global Illicit Small Arms
Transfers', *Small Arms Survey 2001*, p. 167.

14 Pierre, *Cascade of Arms*, pp. 44–6.

15 Mike Sunnucks, 'Red Flags Rise Over Military Surplus Sales', *Phoenix
Business Journal*, 27 April 2007, at www.bizjournals.com/phoenix/
stories/2007/04/30/story8.html, last accessed 6 April 2009.

16 Keith Epstein, 'F-14 Parts Anyone? How Iran Obtains Restricted
Military Technology from the Defense Department', *Business Week*,
11 June 2007, at www.businessweek.com/magazine/content/07_24/
b4038041.htm?chan=search, last accessed 6 April 2009.

17 Sharon Theimer, 'Pentagon Suspends Sale of F-14 Fighter Jet Parts
Sought by Iran', *ABC News*, 31 January 2007, The Associated Press,
at http://abcnews.go.com/Politics/wireStory?id=2835791, last
accessed 6 April 2009.

18 Sharon Theimer, 'Jets Shredded, Kept Away from "Bad Guys"', *ABC
News*, 2 July 2007, The Associated Press, at www.usatoday.com/
news/washington/2007-07-02-433055605_x.htm, last accessed 6
April 2009.

19 Stohl, Schroeder and Smith, *The Small Arms Trade*, p. 57.

20 David Atwood, Anne-Kathrin Glatz and Robert Muggah, *Demanding
Attention: Addressing the Dynamics of Small Arms Demand* (New
York: Quaker United Nations Organizations, 2006), p. xvi, at www.
smallarmssurvey.org/files/sas/publications/o_papers_pdf/2005-
op18-demand-eng.pdf, last accessed 6 April 2009.

21 Stohl, Schroeder and Smith, *The Small Arms Trade*, p. 58.

22 Atwood, Glatz and Muggah, *Demanding Attention*, p. 17.

23 Ibid., p. 24.

24 Although there is no universal definition of 'gun culture', it has
come to be understood largely as a 'set of values, norms – both social
and legal – and meanings that render the presence of firearms and
their possession by private individuals acceptable and legitimate'.

Small Arms Survey, '"Gun Culture" in Kosovo: Questioning the Origins of Conflict', in *Small Arms Survey 2005*, p. 205.

25 Atwood, Glatz and Muggah, *Demanding Attention*, pp. 29–31.

26 Ibid., p. 35.

27 Ibid., p. 45.

28 United Nations, General Assembly, *General and Complete Disarmament: Small Arms*, 27 August 1887, A/52/298, p. 16, at www.un.org/Depts/ddar/Firstcom/SGreport52/a52298.html, last accessed 6 April 2009.

29 Ibid., p. 17. For more on methods of arms transfers, see Michael T. Klare and Robert I. Rotberg, *The Scourge of Small Arms* (Cambridge, MA: World Peace Foundation, 1999); and Jeffrey Boutwell and Michael Klare, *Light Weapons and Civil Conflict: Controlling the Tools of Violence* (Lanham, MD: Rowman & Littlefield, 1999).

30 Stohl, Schroeder and Smith, *The Small Arms Trade*, p. 53.

31 Ibid., p. 13.

32 Small Arms Survey, 'Crime, Conflict, Corruption: Global Illicit Small Arms Transfers,' in *Small Arms Survey 2001*, p. 176.

33 Ibid., pp. 176–7.

34 Stohl, Schroeder and Smith, *The Small Arms Trade*, p. 13.

35 See Saferworld, *Turning the Page: Small Arms and Light Weapons in Albania* (London and Belgrade: Saferworld and the Southeastern and Eastern Europe Clearinghouse for the Control of Small Arms and Light Weapons [SEESAC], 2005), p. 16, at www.saferworld.org.uk/ images/pubdocs/Albania%20ENG%20report.pdf, last accessed 6 April 2009.

36 Stohl, Schroeder and Smith, *The Small Arms Trade*, p. 14.

37 Lumpe, *Running Guns*, p. 107. Also see The Brady Center to Prevent Gun Violence, *Shady Dealings: Illegal Gun Trafficking from Licensed Gun Dealers* (Washington, DC, January 2007), at www.bradycenter.org/ xshare/pdf/reports/shady-dealings.pdf, last accessed 6 April 2009.

38 Stohl, Schroeder and Smith, *The Small Arms Trade*, p. 15. Also see Lumpe, *Running Guns*, p. 107.

39 Stohl, Schroeder and Smith, *The Small Arms Trade*, pp. 43–5.

40 For an example of parliamentary and legislative efforts regarding the arms trade, see the Western Balkans Parliamentary Forum on Small Arms and Light Weapons at www.seeparliamentaryforum.org, last accessed 6 April 2009. This is the only international network of parliamentarians focused on arms control and the prevention of arms violence.

41 Stohl, Schroeder and Smith, *The Small Arms Trade*, p. 53. Also see
    The Brady Center to Prevent Gun Violence, *Smoking Guns: Exposing
    the Gun Industry's Complicity in the Illegal Gun Market* (Washington,
    DC: Brady Center to Prevent Gun Violence, 2003) at www.
    bradycenter.org/xshare/pdf/reports/smokingguns.pdf, last accessed
    6 April 2009.

42 *'Rosoboronexport to Sue Over Illegal Arms Production Abroad'*, 27 June
    2006, Global Security with RIA Novosti, at www.globalsecurity.org/
    wmd/library/news/russia/2006/russia-060627-rianovosti01.htm,
    last accessed 6 April 2009.

43 Stohl, Schroeder and Smith, *The Small Arms Trade*, p. 15. Also see
    Lumpe, *Running Guns*, p. 107.

44 Andrew Koch, 'The Nuclear Network – Khanfessions of a
    Proliferator', *Jane's Defense Weekly*, 26 February 2004, at www.janes.
    com/security/international_security/news/jdw/jdw040226_1_n.
    shtml, last accessed 6 April 2009.

45 Stohl, Schroeder and Smith, *The Small Arms Trade*, p. 56. For a
    discussion of a buy-back programme in the Republic of the Congo,
    see Small Arms Survey, *Small Arms Survey 2003*, p. 269.

46 Small Arms Survey, 'Crime, Conflict, Corruption', in *Small Arms
    Survey 2001*, pp. 165–8.

47 For more on arms embargoes, see Dominic Tierney, 'Irrelevant
    or Malevolent? UN Arms Embargoes in Civil Wars', *Review of
    International Studies*, 31 (2005), pp. 645–64; David Cortright and
    George A. Lopez, with Linda Gerber, 'Sanctions *Sans* Commitment:
    An Assessment of UN Arms Embargoes', Project Ploughshares
    Working Paper (Waterloo, Ont.: Project Ploughshares, May 2002),
    at www.ploughshares.ca/libraries/WorkingPapers/wp022.pdf; and
    Control Arms Briefing Note, 'UN Arms Embargoes: An Overview
    of the Last Ten Years' (London: Central Arms Campaign, March
    16, 2006), at www.oxfamamerica.org/newsandpublications/
    publications/briefing-papers/un_arms_embargoes. Websites last
    accessed 6 April 2009.

48 Lumpe, *Running Guns*, pp. 160–1.

49 Human Rights Watch, 'Arsenals on the Cheap', April 1999, available
    at www.hrw.org/legacyreports/1999/nato/index.htm, ch. 2, last
    accessed 6 April 2009.

50 Pierre, *Cascade of Arms*, p. 45.

51 The ex-FAR is the army of the Hutu-dominated Rwandan regime
    that led the genocidal killing of more than 500,000 Tutsis and

opponents of the Hutu regime. For more on the ex-FAR forces, see www.fas.org/irp/world/para/interahamwe.htm, last accessed 6 April 2009.

52 Brian Wood and Johan Peleman, 'Brokering Arms for Genocide', in *The Arms Fixers: Controlling the Brokers and Shipping Agents* (Oslo and Washington, DC: PRIO, NISAT and BASIC, 1999), at www.prio.no/ NISAT/Publications/the-Arms-Fixers-Controlling-the-Brokers-and-Shipping-Agents/, last accessed 6 April 2009.

53 Lumpe, *Running Guns*, p. 75.

54 Ibid., p. 66.

55 For more on the Iran–Contra affair, see *The Final Report of the Independent Counsel for Iran/Contra Matters*, 4 August 1993, at www.fas.org/irp/offdocs/walsh/, last accessed 6 April 2009; Jonathan Marshall, Jane Hunter and Peter D. Scott, *The Iran–Contra Connection* (Toronto: University of Toronto Press, 1987); and Lawrence Walsh, *Firewall: The Iran–Contra Conspiracy and Cover-Up* (New York: W.W. Norton, 1998).

56 Pierre, *Cascade of Arms*, pp. 55–6.

57 Lumpe, *Running Guns*, pp. 67–8.

58 Ibid., p. 277.

59 Ibid., p. 48.

60 Ibid.

61 Ibid., p. 54.

62 Ibid., p. 44.

63 Jordan Robertson, 'Dual-use Technologies Vex Export Regulators; Salesman Facing 100 years', Associated Press, 13 May 2007, at www.tmcnet.com/usubmit/2007/05/12/2609972.htm, last accessed 6 April 2009.

64 For definitions of 'gun broker' and 'brokering', see the United Nations, *Model Convention on the Registration of Arms Brokers and the Suppression of Unlicensed Arms Brokering* (2001), p. 3, available at www.iansa.org/issues/documents/model_convention.pdf, last accessed 6 April 2009.

65 See Lumpe, *Running Guns*; and Douglas Farah and Stephen Braun, *Merchant of Death: Money, Guns, Planes, and the Man Who Makes War Possible* (Hoboken, NJ: John Wiley & Sons, Inc., 2007).

66 Wood and Peleman, 'Arms Brokering Emerges from the Cold War' in *The Arms Fixers*.

67 Regarding Victor Bout, see Farah and Braun, *Merchant of Death*.

68 Lumpe, *Running Guns*, pp. 13–16.

69 Wood and Peleman, 'Brokering Arms for Genocide'.

70 Ibid.

71 Ibid.

72 Small Arms Survey, 'Fueling the Flames: Brokers and Transport Agents in the Illicit Arms Trade', in *Small Arms Survey 2001*; and Wood and Peleman, 'Introduction', in *The Arms Fixers*.

73 Douglas Farah, *Blood from Stones: The Secret Financial Network of Terror* (New York: Broadway Books, 2004), pp. 36–7. Also see Farah and Braun, *Merchant of Death*; and Stohl, Schroeder and Smith, *The Small Arms Trade*, pp. 16–17.

74 Farah and Braun, *Merchant of Death*, p. 40.

75 Rachel Stohl and Doug Tuttle, '"Merchant of Death" Arrested in Thailand', Center for Defense Information, 10 March 2008, at www. cdi.org/friendlyversion/printversion.cfm?documentID=4230, last accessed 6 April 2009.

76 '"Lord of War" Arms Dealer Victor Bout Arrested in Thailand', *Times Online*, 6 March 2008, at www.timesonline.co.uk/tol/news/ world/asia/article3498795.ece; 'Russian Charged with Trying to Sell Arms', *New York Times*, 7 March 2008, available at www.nytimes. com/2008/03/07/world/europe/07dealer.html. Websites last accessed 6 April 2009.

77 Farah, *Blood from Stones*, pp. 45–6.

78 Stohl, Schroeder and Smith, *The Small Arms Trade*, pp. 50–1.

79 United States Department of State, Bureau of Political–Military Affairs, 'Background Paper: The U.S. Approach to Combating the Spread of Small Arms', 2 June 2001, at www.disam.dsca.mil/ pubs/v.25_1&2/Stopping%20Spread%20Small%20Arms.pdf, last accessed 6 April 2009.

80 Fund for Peace, 'Model Convention on the Registration of Arms Brokers and the Suppression of Unlicensed Arms Brokering' (Washington DC: July 2001), at http://se1.isn.ch/serviceengine/ FileContent?serviceID=47&frleid=0332CD12-1164-8371-2303- A90549EFE888&lng=en, last accessed 6 April 2009.

81 See the United Nations, *Programme of Action to Prevent, Combat and Eradicate the Illicit Trade in Small Arms and Light Weapons in All Its Aspects*, at http://disarmament.un.org/cab/poa.html.

82 See the UN Group of Government Experts report (August 2007), at www.iansa.org/un/documents/UNGGEBrokering.pdf, last accessed 6 April 2009.

83 See IANSA's report, *Reviewing Action on Small Arms 2006: Assessing*

the First Five Years of the Programme of Action (London: IANSA and Biting the Bullet Project, 2006) available at www.iansa.org/un/review2006/redbook2006/index.htm, last accessed 6 April 2009.

84 For more on the connections between arms and other trafficking, see Dejan Anastasijevic, *Organized Crime in the Western Balkans: Trafficking in Drugs, Trafficking in Weapons, Trafficking in Human Beings*, HUMSEC Working Paper for the European Commission (Graz, Austria, 2006), at www.etcgraz.at/cms/fileadmin/user_upload/humsec/Workin_Paper_Series/Working_Paper_Anastasijevic.pdf; Glenn E. Curtis and Tara Karacan, *The Nexus Among Terrorists, Narcotics Traffickers, Weapons Proliferators, and Organized Crime Networks in Western Europe*, Study Prepared by the Federal Research Division, Library of Congress, December 2002, at www.loc.gov/rr/frd/pdf-files/WestEurope_NEXUS.pdf; Willem van Schendel and Itty Abraham, *Illicit Flows and Criminal Things* (Bloomington: Indiana University Press, 2005); and Robert J. Kelly, Jess Maghan and Joseph D. Serio, *Illicit Trafficking: A Reference Handbook* (Santa Barbara: ABC-CLIO, Inc., 2005). Websites last accessed 6 April 2009.

85 Moisés Naím, *Illicit: How Smugglers, Traffickers and Copycats are Hijacking the Global Economy* (New York: Random House, 2005), p. 229.

86 One author's interview with arms broker in Istanbul, Turkey, January 2003.

87 Naím, *Illicit*, p. 56.

88 See Farah, *Blood from Stones*; and Stohl, Schroeder and Smith, *The Small Arms Trade*.

89 A detailed discussion of arms control activities relevant for both the legal and illegal trades in weapons will be provided in chapter 6.

90 For US and other concerns regarding limits on the arms trade, see 'UN Conference on Illicit Trade in Small Arms', *The American Journal of International Law*, 95 (2001), p. 903.

CHAPTER 5 THE CONSEQUENCES OF THE INTERNATIONAL ARMS TRADE

1 Human Security Center, *Human Security Report 2005: War and Peace in the 21st Century* (New York: Oxford University Press, 2005), p. 8, at www.humansecurityreport.info/HSR2005_HTML/What_is_HS/index.htm, last accessed 6 April 2009.

2 UN Commission on Human Security, 'Report Outline' (New York, 2003), at www.humansecurity-chs.org/finalreport/Outlines/outline. html, last accessed 6 April 2009.

3 See, for example, Tim Prenzler, 'The Human Side of Security', *Security Journal*, 20(1) (2007), pp. 35–9; and Roland Paris, 'Human Security: Paradigm Shift or Hot Air?' *International Security*, 26(2) (2001), pp. 87–102.

4 Small Arms Survey, *Small Arms Survey 2004*, p. 174.

5 Ploughshares, 'Armed Conflict Report: Ethiopia–Eritrea' (February 2002), at www.ploughshares.ca/libraries/ACRText/ACR-EthEert. html, last accessed 6 April 2009.

6 United Nations Office on Drugs and Crime, 'Brazil 2006–2009, Strategic Programme Framework' (Vienna, August 2006), p. 4, at www.unodc.org/pdf/brazil/final2.pdf, last accessed 6 April 2009.

7 Olivia Ward, 'Congo's Women under Siege', *Toronto Star*, 8 June 2007.

8 UNHCR, *The State of the World's Refugees 2006* (Oxford: Oxford University Press, 2007), p. 10, at www.unhcr.org/publ/ PUBL/4444d3bf25.html, last accessed 6 April 2009.

9 Internal Displacement Monitoring Center, 'Internal Displacement: Global Overview of Trends and Developments in 2006', April 2007, pp. 6, 8, 23, at www.internal-displacement. org/8025708F004CFA06/(httpPublications)/6F9D5C47FA0DCCE 2C12572BF002B9212?OpenDocument, last accessed 6 April 2009.

10 Gregory Mthembu-Salter, 'The Wheel Turns Again: Militarization and Rwanda's Congolese Refugees', in Robert Muggah, ed., *No Refuge: The Crisis of Refugee Militarization in Africa* (London: Zed Books, 2006), pp. 196–7; and Robert Muggah and Edward Mogire, 'Introduction', in Muggah, ed., *No Refuge*, p. 6.

11 Arild Skedsmo, Kwong Danhier and Hoth Gor Luak, 'The Changing Meaning of Small Arms in Nuer Society', *African Security Review*, 12(4) (2003), pp. 57–67.

12 Musue N. Haddad, 'Arms Proliferation Increases Repression' (New York: UN, 20 July 2002), at www.theperspective.org/smallarms. html, last accessed 6 April 2009.

13 Robin Luckham, Ismain Ahmed, Robert Muggah and Sarah White, *Conflict and Poverty in Sub-Saharan Africa: An Assessment of the Issues and Evidence*, IDS Working Paper 128, March 2001 (Brighton, Sussex: Institute of Development Studies, 2001), p. 40.

14 United Nations Food and Agriculture Organization, 'Study on the Impact of Armed Conflicts on the Nutritional Situation of Children',

Rome, 1996, at www.fao.org/docrep/005/w2357e/W2357E02. htm#ch2.1, last accessed 6 April 2009.

15 Luckham et al., *Conflict and Poverty in Sub-Saharan Africa*, p. 41.

16 See for example ibid.; and Frances Stewart and Valpy FitzGerald, 'Introduction: Assessing the Economic Costs of War', in *War and Underdevelopment* Vol. I: *The Economic and Social Consequences of Conflict* (Oxford: Oxford University Press, 2000).

17 Cate Buchanan and Robert Muggah, 'No Relief: Surveying the Effects of Gun Violence on Humanitarian and Development Personnel', Geneva: Centre for Humanitarian Dialogue and SAS, June 2005, p. 26, at www.hdcentre.org/files/No%20relief%20intro. pdf, last accessed 6 April 2009.

18 BBC News, 'African Troops Killed in Darfur', 2 April 2007, at http:// news.bbc.co.uk/1/hi/world/africa/6517791.stm, last accessed 6 April 2009.

19 'Civil Society Consultation on the ECOWAS Moratorium: Beyond the UN 2001 Conference', Center for Democratic Development, June 2001, at www.cdd.org.uk/conferences/asdr.htm, last accessed 6 April 2009.

20 Control Arms Campaign, 'Towards an Arms Trade Treaty: Next Step for the UN Programme of Action' (June 2005), p. 3, at www. controlarms.org/en/documents%20and%20files/reports/english-reports/towards-an-arms-trade-treaty-next-steps-for-the-un, last accessed 6 April 2009.

21 Thomas Jackson, Nicholas Marsh, Taylor Owen and Anne Thurin, *Who Takes the Bullet?: The Impact of Small Arms Violence*. Understanding the Issues (Oslo: Norwegian Church Aid and the International Peace Research Institute, March 2005), p. 49.

22 'Petraeus: Increased U.S. Troops Yielding Results', *All Things Considered*, National Public Radio, 19 July 2007, at www.npr.org/ templates/story/story.php?storyId=12099511, last accessed 6 April 2009.

23 William Godnick, Robert Muggah and Camilla Waszink, 'Stray Bullets: The Impact of Small Arms Misuse in Central America', *Small Arms Survey Occasional Paper 5* (October 2002), at www. smallarmssurvey.org/files/sas/publications/o-papers-pdf/2002-op05-central_america.pdf, pp. 31–2, last accessed 6 April 2009.

24 Jackson et al., *Who Takes the Bullet*, p. 50.

25 Ibid.

26 BBC News, 'Middle East Tourists Return to Luxor', 17 November 1998, at http://news.bbc.co.uk/1/hi/world/middle_east/215997.stm, last accessed 6 April 2009.

27 Musambayi Katumanga with Lionel Cliffe, *Nairobi – a City Besieged: The Impact of Armed Violence on Poverty and Development* (Bradford: University of Bradford, Centre for International Cooperation and Security, March 2005), p. 6.

28 Eric Berman and Robert Muggah, *Humanitarianism under Threat: The Humanitarian Impacts of Small Arms and Light Weapons* (Geneva: Small Arms Survey, March 2001), p. 8.

29 Luckham et al., *Conflict and Poverty in Sub-Saharan Africa*, p. 37.

30 Laura Blue and Jonathan Woodward, 'Hope for Uganda's Child Soldiers?' *Time Magazine*, 14 August 2006, at www.time.com/time/world/article/0.8599.1226297.00.html, last accessed 7 April 2009.

31 Terry Gander, *Guerrilla Warfare Weapons: The Modern Underground Fighter's Armoury* (New York: Sterling Publishing Co., 1990), pp. 20–1.

32 Matt Schroeder, 'Issue Brief 3: The Illicit Arms Trade', Federation of American Scientists, at http://fas.org/asmp/campaigns/smallarms/IssueBrief3ArmsTrafficking.html, last accessed 6 April 2009.

33 United Nations, *Programme of Action to Prevent, Combat and Eradicate the Illicit Trade in Small Arms*, Section 1, paragraph 7.

34 Jill Dougherty 'Chechen "Claims Beslan Attack"', 17 September 2004, CNN.com, at http://edition.cnn.com/2004/WORLD/europe/09/17/russia.beslan/, last accessed 6 April 2009.

35 Paul Alexander, 'Philippines Bus Siege Ends in Surrender', Associated Press, 28 March 2007.

36 'Shoulder-Fired Anti-Aircraft Missiles Threaten Global Aviation', Bureau of International Information Programs, US Department of State, Washington, DC, 21 September 2005, at www.iwar.org.uk/news-archive/2005/09-21-2.htm, last accessed 6 April 2009.

37 Ibid.; see also Stohl, Schroeder and Smith, *The Small Arms Trade* (chapters 5–8).

38 Small Arms Survey, *Small Arms Survey, 2003*, pp. 32–3.

39 Ibid., pp. 34–5.

40 Tom Diaz, 'Credit Card Armies – Firearms and Training for Terror in the United States', Washington, DC: Violence Policy Center, November 2002, p. 5, at www.vpc.org/graphics/creditcardarmies.pdf, last accessed 6 April 2009.

41 Ibid., p. 6.

42 Brady Center to Prevent Gun Violence, *Guns and Terror* (Washington, DC: Brady Center to Prevent Gun Violence, 2001).

43 Ibid., pp. 6–7.

44 Congressional Research Service, *Foreign Terrorists and the Availability of Firearms and Black Powder in the United States*. Washington, DC: Congressional Research Service, 16 May 2003.

45 Ibid., p. CRS-5.

46 GAO, 'Gun Control and Terrorism: FBI Could Better Manage Firearm-related Background Checks Involving Terrorist Watch List Records', January 2005, p. 1, at www.gao.gov/new.items/d05127.pdf, last accessed 6 April 2009.

47 Ibid., p. 3.

48 Jim Hoagland, 'No More Frankensteins', *The Washington Post*, 13 July 1993, p. A15.

49 Peter Finn, 'Al Qaeda Arms Traced to Saudi National Guard; 3 Attackers Identified in Riyadh Bombings', *The Washington Post*, 19 May 2003, p. A1.

50 Peter Spiegel and Laura King, 'Israel Says Syria, Not Just Iran, Supplied Missiles to Hezbollah', *Los Angeles Times*, 31 August 2006.

51 Katherine Shrader, 'U.S.: Hezbollah Recovers, and Iran Helps', *The Washington Post*, 18 December 2006, at www.washingtonpost.com/wp-dyn/content/article/2006/12/18/AR2006121800552_pf.html, last accessed 6 April 2009.

52 Marcus Stern, 'Terrorism Takes Root in Jungle of S. America: Region Linked to Funds for Hezbollah, Hamas', *San Diego Union-Tribune*, 15 June 2003, p. 1.

53 Douglas Farah, 'Liberian Leader Again Finds Means to Hang On; Taylor Exploits Timber to Keep Power', *The Washington Post*, 4 June 2002, p. A1; and Douglas Farah, 'Standing By as a Brutal Warlord Plots his Return', *The Washington Post*, 2 October 2005, p. B3.

54 United Nations, *Final Report of the Monitoring Group on Somalia Pursuant to Security Council Resolution*, S/1676(2006)/913 (New York: United Nations, 22 November 2006).

55 Andrew Harding, 'UN Warns of Somali Terror Link', BBC, 4 November 2003, at http://news.bbc.co.uk/2/hi/africa/3241021.stm, last accessed 6 April 2009.

56 'U.S. "Targets Al Qaeda" in Somalia', BBC, 9 January 2007, at http://news.bbc.co.uk/2/hi/africa/6245943.stm, last accessed 6 April 2009.

CHAPTER 6 CONTROLLING THE INTERNATIONAL
ARMS TRADE

1 Algeria, Argentina, Australia, Brazil, China, Colombia, Costa Rica,
Cuba, Egypt, Finland, France, Germany, India, Indonesia, Italy,
Japan, Kenya, Mexico, Nigeria, Pakistan, Romania, Russia, South
Africa, Spain, Switzerland, Ukraine, the United Kingdom and the
United States.

2 Paul Levine and Ron Smith, *Arms Trade, Security, and Conflict* (New
York: Routledge, 1989), pp. 1.

3 Pierre, *Cascade of Arms*, pp. 373–4.

4 Ibid., p. 374. For more on early efforts to regulate the international
arms trade, see Robert E. Harkavy, *The Arms Trade and International
Systems* (Cambridge, MA: Ballinger Publishing Company, 1975).

5 Pierre, *Cascade of Arms*, p. 374.

6 Stanley and Pearton, *The International Trade in Arms*, p. 14. For
more on COCOM, see Michael Mastanduno, *Economic Containment:
CoCom and the Politics of East–West Trade* (Ithaca, NY: Cornell
University Press, 1992); and Richard T. Cupitt and Suzette R. Grillot,
'COCOM Is Dead, Long Live COCOM: Persistence and Change in
Multilateral Security Regimes', *British Journal of Political Science*, 27
(July 1997), pp. 361–89.

7 See Michael Lipson, 'The Reincarnation of CoCom: Explaining
Post-Cold War Export Controls', *The Nonproliferation Review* (Winter
1999), p. 1, at http://cns.miis.edu/pubs/npr/vol06/62/lipson62.pdf,
last accessed 6 April 2009.

8 Pierre, *Cascade of Arms*, p. 374.

9 Ibid., p. 140.

10 Thomas Ohlson, ed., *Arms Transfer Limitations and Third World
Security* (Oxford: Oxford University Press, 2000), pp. 116–19.

11 United Nations Office at Geneva (UNOG), Disarmament page,
'The Convention on Certain Conventional Weapons', at www.unog.
ch/80256EE600585943/(httpPages)/4F0DEF093B4860B4C125718
0004B1B30?OpenDocument, last accessed 6 April 2009.

12 UNOG, Protocol I of the 'UN Convention on Certain Conventional
Weapons', at www.unog.ch/80256EDD006B8954/(httpAssets)/D
F84B4D8659283DAC12571DE005B93C5/$file/Protocol+I.pdf, last
accessed 6 April 2009.

13 UNOG, Protocol II of the 'UN Convention on Certain Conventional
Weapons', at www.unog.ch/80256EDD006B8954/(httpAssets)/76

07D6493EAC5819C12571DE005BA57D/$file/PROTOCOL+II.pdf, last accessed 6 April 2009.

14 UNOG, Protocol III of the 'UN Convention on Certain Conventional Weapons', at www.unog.ch/80256EDD006B8954/(httpAssets)/B 409BC0DCFA0171CC12571DE005BC1DD/$file/PROTOCOL+III. pdf, last accessed 6 April 2009; also see United Nations Office at Geneva, 'The Convention on Certain Conventional Weapons', at www.unog.ch/80256EE600585943/(httpPages)/4F0DEF093B4860 B4C1257180004B1B30?OpenDocument, last accessed 6 April 2009.

15 UNOG, Protocol V of the 'UN Convention on Certain Conventional Weapons', at www.unog.ch/80256EDD006B8954/(httpAssets)/548 4D315570AC857C12571DE005D6498/$file/Protocol+on+Explosive+ Remnants+of+War.pdf, last accessed 6 April 2009.

16 UNOG Disarmament page, 'States Parties and Signatories. States Not Parties', at www.unog.ch/80256EE600585943/(httpPages)/3 CE7CFC0AA4A7548C12571C00039CB0C?OpenDocument, last accessed 6 April 2009.

17 See Jim Randle, 'Bosnia Laser Attack', *Federation of American Scientists*, 4 November 1998, at www.fas.org/nuke/control/ccw/news/981104-laser.htm; 'Lasers Burn U.S. Pilots' Eyes', ABC News.com, 4 November 1998, at www.fas.org/nuke/control/ccw/news/bosnia981104_laser. html; and 'HRW Questions U.S. Laser Programs as Blinding Laser Weapon Ban Becomes International Law', *Human Rights News*, 29 July 1998, at http://hrw.org/english/docs/1998/07/29/usint1194.htm. Websites last accessed 6 April 2009.

18 See 'Convention on Certain Conventional Weapons (CCW) at a Glance', *Arms Control Association*, October 2007, at www. armscontrol.org/factsheets/CCW.asp, last accessed 6 April 2009.

19 Ibid.

20 See the text of the CFE Treaty at www.osce.org/documents/ doclib/1990/11/13752_en.pdf, last accessed 6 April 2009.

21 See Peter Fedynsky, 'Russia's Parliament Suspends Arms Control Treaty Compliance', Global Security.org, 7 November 2007, at www. globalsecurity.org/wmd/library/news/russia/2007/russia-071107-voa01.htm, last accessed 6 April 2009.

22 James A. Lewis, 'Looking Back: Multilateral Arms Transfer Restraint: The Limits of Cooperation', *Arms Control Today*, November 2005, at www.armscontrol.org/act/2005_11/NOV-LOOKINGBACK.asp, last accessed 6 April 2009.

23 United Nations, *Report of the Disarmament Commission*, A/51/42
    (1996), at http://disarmament.un.org/Library.nsf/0bb8a163b66d62
    7f85256beb0073f596/adcb9adb12293ad585256ce500776b64/$FIL
    E/dc51.42.pdf, last accessed 6 April 2009.

24 The seven original categories of the UN Arms Register are: battle
    tanks, amoured combat vehicles, large-calibre artillery systems,
    combat aircraft, attack helicopters, warships, and missiles and
    missile launchers.

25 United Nations Department for Disarmament Affairs (DDA), *United
    Nations Register of Conventional Arms: Information Booklet 2007*
    (United Nations, *New York*: 2007), p. 28.

26 Pierre, *Cascade of Arms*, pp. 29–30, 161.

27 Ibid., p. 385.

28 UN Register of Conventional Arms webpage (2002) at http://
    disarmament2.un.org/cab/register.html, last accessed 6 April
    2009.

29 See the report at http://disarmament.un.org/cab/2003GRE.pdf, last
    accessed 6 April 2009.

30 See the report at http://daccessdds.un.org/doc/UNDOC/GEN/
    N06/468/71/PDF/N0646871.pdf?OpenElement, last accessed 6
    April 2009.

31 See the Report of the Panel of Government Experts at http://
    disarmament.un.org/cab/smallarms/docs/rep52298.pdf, last
    accessed 6 April 2009.

32 For more on the 1999 Group of Governmental Experts, see
    'The United Nations and Small Arms: The Role of The Group of
    Governmental Experts', Geneva Forum, February 1999, at www.
    geneva-forum.org/Reports/salw_vol1/19990225.pdf, last accessed 6
    April 2009.

33 The CASA mechanism can be found on the UN Small Arms website
    at http://disarmament2.un.org/cab/orgs/CASA-2003.pdf, last
    accessed 6 April 2009.

34 For more on the Firearms Protocol, see www.unodc.org/newsletter/
    en/200504/page005.html. For a list of states that are or are not
    parties to the Firearms Protocol, see IANSA, 'UN Firearms Protocol
    – Has Your Country Ratified?' at www.iansa.org/un/firearms-
    protocol.htm. Websites last accessed 6 April 2009.

35 See the report submitted by the Netherlands on the issue, at http://
    disarmament.un.org/cab/docs/trcngexperts/netherlandsview.pdf,
    last accessed 6 April 2009.

36 *Programme of Action to Prevent, Combat, and Eradicate the Illicit Trade of Small Arms and Light Weapons in All Its Aspects*, UN document A/ CONF.192/15, 2001, at http://disarmament2.un.org/cab/poa.html, last accessed 6 April 2009.

37 UN DDA, 'Conventional Weapons: Small Arms and Light Weapons', at http://disarmament2.un.org/cab/salw.html, last accessed 6 April 2009.

38 UN DDA, 'First Biennial Meeting', at http://disarmament2.un.org/ cab/salw-2003.html, last accessed 6 April 2009.

39 See the *Report of the Second Biennial Meeting of States to Consider the Implementation of the Programme of Action to Prevent, Combat, and Eradicate the Illicit Trade in Small Arms and Light Weapons in All Its Aspects*, at www.un.org/events/smallarms2005/report%20(e).pdf, last accessed 6 April 2009.

40 See the text of the agreement at http://disarmament2.un.org/cab/ Markingandtracing/InternationalIinstrumentEnglish.pdf, last accessed 6 April 2009.

41 The International Marking Instrument can be found on the UN SALW website at http://disarmament2.un.org/cab/salw.html, last accessed 6 April 2009.

42 See the UN Group of Government Experts report, at www.iansa.org/ un/documents/UNGGEBrokering.pdf, last accessed 6 April 2009.

43 UN 2006 Conference to Review Progress Made in the Implementation of the Programme of Action website, at www. un.org/events/smallarms2006/, last accessed 6 April 2009.

44 Owen Greene, *Promoting Effective Action on Small Arms: Emerging Agendas for the 2006 Review Conference* (London and Bradford: Biting the Bullet Project, July 2005), at www.international-alert.org/pdf/ btb_emerging_agendas.pdf, last accessed 6 April 2009.

45 UN E-Mine website, 'United Nations Mine Action Service', January 2008, www.mineaction.org/overview.asp?o=22, last accessed 6 April 2009.

46 UN E-Mine website, 'United Nations Inter-Agency Mine Action Strategy: 2006–2010', www.mineaction.org/downloads/1/UN_ IAMAS_online.pdf, last accessed 6 April 2009.

47 Associated Press, 'U.N. General Assembly Takes First Step Toward Establishing Treaty on Conventional Weapons', *International Herald Tribune*, 7 December 2006, at www.un.org/apps/news/story. asp?NewsID=20876&Cr=disornament&Cr1, last accessed 6 April 2009.

48 United Nations, 'Press Conference on Global Arms Trade Treaty', 23 April 2007, at www.un.org/News/briefings/docs/2007/070423_Arms.doc.htm, last accessed 6 April 2009.

49 See the EU statement on the Arms Trade Treaty in the *Bulletin of the European Union* at http://europa.eu/bulletin/en/200612/p126006.htm; and the ECOWAS statement at www.grip.org/bdg/g1649.html. Websites last accessed 6 April 2009.

50 See the Chinese and Russian statements in the UN Press Release, 'International Arms Trade Treaty Aim of Draft Resolution', 26 October 2006, at www.un.org/News/Press/docs/2006/gadis3335.doc.htm, last accessed 6 April 2009.

51 Ron Smith and Bernard Udis, 'New Challenges to Arms Export Control', in Paul Levine and Ron Smith, eds., *Arms Trade, Security and Conflict* (London and New York: Routledge, 2003), pp. 94–110.

52 Tamar Gabelnick and Rachel Stohl, *Challenging Conventional Wisdom: Debunking the Myths and Exposing the Risks of Arms Export Reform* (Washington, DC: Center for Defense Information and Federation of American Scientists, 2003), p. 174.

53 Wassenaar Arrangement, 'Best Practices for the Export of SALW', at www.wassenaar.org/publicdocuments/2007/docs/SALW_Guidelines.pdf, last accessed 6 April 2009.

54 Ibid.

55 Wassenaar Arrangement, 'Elements of Export Controls of Man-Portable Air Defence Systems (MANPADS)', pp. 25–8, at www.wassenaar.org/publicdocuments/2007/docs/Elements_for_Export_Controls_of_Manpads.pdf, last accessed 6 April 2009.

56 Wassenaar Arrangement, 'Elements for Effective Legislation on Arms Brokering', at www.wassenaar.org/2003Plenary/Brokering_2003.htm, last accessed 6 April 2009.

57 Federation of American Scientists, 'The OAS Firearms Convention', at www.fas.org/asmp/campaigns/smallarms/OAS_Firearms_Convention.html, last accessed 6 April 2009.

58 SIPRI, *Yearbook 2006*, Annex A.

59 Organization of American States, 'The Inter-American Convention Against the Illicit Manufacturing of and Trafficking in Firearms, Ammunition, Explosives, and Other Related Materials', at www.oas.org/juridico/english/treaties/a-63.html, last accessed 6 April 2009.

60 OAS Inter-American Drug Abuse Control Commision (CICAD) website, 'Model Regulations for Firearms', www.cicad.oas.org/

Desarrollo_Juridico/esp/Reglamentos/Reglamento%20Modelo/
RegModeloIdiomas/ReglArmseng.doc, last accessed 6 April 2009.

61 SIPRI, *Yearbook 2006*, Annex A.

62 Bureau of Western Hemisphere Affairs fact sheet website, www.
state.gov/p/wha/rls/fs/2009/114984.htm, last accessed 6 April
2009.

63 Organization of American States, 'Declaration on SALW
Resolution', 2 June 2000, at www.oas.org/Assembly2001/assembly/
docsaprovados/aprodocen/RES1743.htm, last accessed 6 April 2009.

64 Organization of American States, 'Amendments to the Model
Regulations for the Control of the International Movement of
Firearms, their Parts and Components and Ammunition', November
2003, at www.cicad.oas.org/Desarrollo_Juridico/ENG/Resources/32
2MRFirearmsBrokersEng.pdf, last accessed 6 April 2009.

65 Ian Davis, *Implementing and Deepening the OAS Agenda on Small
Arms and Light Weapons*, 2 May 2002, at www.basicint.org/WT/
smallarms/OAS-IDpres-0502.htm, last accessed 6 April 2009.

66 For a more detailed critique of OAS weapons activities, see Sarah
Meek, 'Combating Arms-Trafficking: The Need for Integrated
Approaches', *African Security Review*, 9 (2000), at www.iss.co.za/
pubs/asr/9No4/Meek.html; and BASIC, 'A Closer Examination
of the OAS Prototype', *One Size Fits All? Prospects for a Global
Convention on Illicit Trafficking by 2000* (Washington, DC: BASIC,
1999), at www.basicint.org/pubs/Research/1999onesize3a.htm.
Websites last accessed 6 April 2009.

67 European Union, Security-Related Export Control list
website, at www.consilium.europa.eu/cms3_fo/showPage.
asp?id=408&lang=EN&mode=g#exp4, last accessed 6 April 2009.

68 European Union, 'Code of Conduct of Arms Export', 5 June 1998,
at http://consilium.europa.eu/uedocs/cmsUpload/08675r2en8.pdf,
last accessed 6 April 2009.

69 See the European Union's Joint Action document at http://eur-lex.
europa.eu/LexUriServ/LexUriServ.do?uri=CELEX:31999E0034:EN:
HTML, last accessed 6 April 2009.

70 European Union Security-Related Export Control list
website, at www.consilium.europa.eu/cms3_fo/showPage.
asp?id=408&lang=EN&mode=g#exp4, last accessed 6 April 2009.

71 OSCE, 'Principles Governing Conventional Arms Transfers', 25
November 1993, at www.osce.org/documents/fsc/1993/11/460_
en.pdf, last accessed 6 April 2009.

72 OSCE, 'OSCE Document on Small Arms and Light Weapons', 24 November 2000, at www.osce.org/documents/fsc/2000/11/1873_ en.pdf, last accessed 6 April 2009.

73 OSCE, Forum for Security Cooperation website, at www.osce.org/ fsc/13087.html, last accessed 6 April 2009.

74 OSCE, 'OSCE Helps Kazakhstan to Secure Small Arms, Light Weapons and Conventional Ammunition', at www.osce.org/ item/14885.html, last accessed 6 April 2009.

75 OSCE, Handbook of Best Practices on Small Arms and Light Weapons (Vienna, 31 December 2003), at www.osce.org/fsc/item_11_13550. html; text at www.osce.org/publications/fsc/2003/12/13550_29_ en.pdf. Websites last accessed 6 April 2009.

76 OSCE, Assistance with Ammunition page, at www.osce.org/ fsc/13282.html, text of 'OSCE Document On Stockpiles of Conventional Arms' (19 November 2003), at www.osce.org/ documents/fsc/2003/11/1379_en.pdf, last accessed 6 April 2009.

77 Text of the ECOWAS Declaration is available at www.wcc-coe.org/ wcc/what/international/ecowas.html, last accessed 6 April 2009.

78 Adedeji Ebo, Small Arms Control in West Africa (London: International Alert, 2003), p. 19, at www.smallarmssurvey.org/ files/portal/spotlight/country/afr_pdf/africa-ben-bf-cotivo-gam-gha- guinbis-2003.pdf, last accessed 6 April 2009.

79 Ibid., p. 16.

80 Ibid., p. 29.

81 See Alhaji M. S. Bah, 'Micro-Disarmament in West Africa: The ECOWAS Moratorium on Small Arms and Light Weapons', African Security Review, 13(3) (2004), at www.iss.co.za/pubs/ASR/13No3/ FBah.htm, last accessed 6 April 2009.

82 Michael von Tangen Page, William Godnick and Janani Vivekananda, Implementing International Small Arms Controls: Some Lessons from Eurasia, Latin America and West Africa (London: International Alert, 2005), p. 27, at www.iansa.org/ documents/2005/misac-crossregionalreport.pdf, last accessed 6 April 2009.

83 SIPRI, 'International Arms Embargoes', at www.sipri.org/contents/ armstrad/embargoes.html.

84 Ilhan Berkol, 'Analysis of the ECOWAS Convention on SALW', GRIP, 1 April 2007, at http://grip.org/bdg/pdf/g1071en.pdf, last accessed 6 April 2009.

85 Stohl, Schroeder and Smith, The Small Arms Trade, p. 46.

86 IANSA, 'ECOWAS Convention on Small Arms and Light Weapons, Their Ammunitions and Other Related Materials' (June 2006), at www.iansa.org/regions/wafrica/documents/CONVENTION-CEDEAO-ENGLISH.PDF, last accessed 6 April 2009.
87 Geraldine O'Callaghan, Michael Crowley and Kathleen Miller, 'NATO and Small Arms: From Word to Deed', *GRIP*, October 2000, at www.basicint.org/pubs/Research/2000from_words(wt).htm, last accessed 6 April 2009.
88 NATO, 'Partnership for Peace Trust Funds: Promoting Security and Defence Reform', updated 31 July 2008, at www.nato.int/pfp/trust-fund.htm last accessed 6 April 2009.
89 Stability Pact, 'About Stability Pact' (2005), at www.stabilitypact.org/about/default.asp; and 'Task Force Status: Since May 2002 – Still Active' (2005), at www.stabilitypact.org/salw/default.asp. Websites last accessed 6 April 2009.
90 SEESAC, 'Background', at www.seesac.org/index.php?content=48&section=1, last accessed 6 April 2009.
91 See the SADC Firearms Protocol at www.smallarmsnet.org/docs/saaf09.pdf. For a specific assessment of the Nairobi Protocol, see Thokozani Thusi, 'Assessing Small Arms Control Initiatives: The Nairobi Declaration', *African Security Review*, 12(2) (2003), at www.iss.co.za/ASR/12No2/F2.html. Websites last accessed 6 April 2009.
92 Matt Schroeder and Rachel Stohl, 'Small Arms, Large Problem', *Arms Control Today*, June 2006, at www.armscontrol.org/act/2006_06/SmallArmsFeature.asp, last accessed 6 April 2009.
93 Suzette R. Grillot, *Small Arms Control in Central and Eastern Europe* (London: International Alert, 2003), p. 38.
94 Suzette R. Grillot, *Small Arms Control in the Black Sea Region* (London: International Alert, 2003), p. 39.
95 Ebo, *Small Arms Control in West Africa*, p. 19.
96 William Godnick and Helena Vasquez, *Small Arms Control in Central America* (London: International Alert, 2003), p. 34, at www.international-alert.org/pdf/CA_English_June.pdf, last accessed 6 April 2009.
97 Davis, *Implementing and Deepening the OAS Agenda*.
98 Stephanie Cooper, Michael von Tangen Page, Helena Vasquez and Lada Zimina, *Small Arms Control in Eurasia* (London: International Alert, 2004), p. 9, at www.international-alert.org/pdf/MISAC_eurasia_3.pdf, last accessed 6 April 2009.

99 Grillot, *Small Arms Control in Central and Eastern Europe*; and
    Suzette R. Grillot, 'Guns in the Balkans: Controlling Small Arms
    and Light Weapons in Six Western Balkan Countries', unpublished
    manuscript, October 2008.
100 Grillot, *Small Arms Control in the Black Sea Region*, p. 39.
101 Cooper et al., *Small Arms Control in Eurasia*, p. 9.
102 Grillot, *Small Arms Control in Central and Eastern Europe*; and
    Grillot, 'Guns in the Balkans'.
103 Grillot, *Small Arms Control in the Black Sea Region*; Ebo, *Small Arms
    Control in West Africa*; Godnick and Vasquez, *Small Arms Control in
    Central America*; and Edith M. Lederer, 'Security Along Lebanon–
    Syria Border Too Lax to Stop Arms Smuggling', *North Country
    Times*, 26 June 2007, at www.nctimes.com/articles/2007/06/27/
    news/nation/18_34_356_26_07.txt, last accessed 6 April 2009.
104 'More on Arms Seized at U.S.–Mexican Border Town',
    Northeast Intelligence Network, 23 February 2007, at www.
    homelandsecurityus.com/?m=200702; and Kevin Mooney,
    'Mexican Soldier Freelancing for Drug Cartels on US Soil',
    CNSNews.com, 21 December 2006, at bsimmons.wordpress.
    com/2006/12/21/mexican-soldiers-freelancing-for-drug-cartels-on-
    us-soil/. Websites last acessed 6 April 2009.
105 Jim Kouri, 'US Borders: Task Force Seizes Improvised Explosive
    Devices, Firearms Caches', *American Chronicle*, 5 February 2006,
    at www.americanchronicle.com/articles/view/5506, last accessed 7
    April 2009.
106 See 'End-Use Monitoring of Defense Articles and Defense Services
    Commercial Exports FY 2006', at pmddtc.state.gov/reports/
    documents/End_Use_FY2006.pdf, last accessed 6 April 2009.
107 Commission to Assess the Ballistic Missile Threat to the United
    States, 'Non-Proliferation Issues'.
108 United States Department of State, *U.S. Arms Export Compliance
    and Enforcement and the U.N. Programme of Action for Small Arms
    and Light Weapons*, 3 July 2006, at www.fas.org/asmp/resources/
    govern/109th/Statefactsheetzju106.htm.
109 'Four Indicted After Major Weapons Seizure', *The Local*, 22 January
    2008, at www.thelocal.se/9735/20080122/, last accessed 6 April
    2009.
110 Matt Schroeder, 'Transparency and Accountability in Arms Export
    Systems: The United States as a Case Study', *Disarmament Forum*,
    3 (2005), pp. 29–38, at www.unidir.org/pdf/articles/pdf-art2393.

pdf; and Maria Haug, Martin Langvandslien, Lora Lumpe and Nicholas Marsh, *Shining a Light on Small Arms Exports: The Record of State Transparency*, Occasional Paper 4 (Geneva: Small Arms Survey, 2002), available at www.smallarmssurvey.org/files/sas/publications/o_papers_pdf/2002-op04-exports.pdf. Websites last accessed 6 April 2009.

111 Grillot, *Small Arms Control in Central and Eastern Europe*, p. 22.

112 John Heathershaw, Emil Juraev, Michael von Tangen Page and Lada Zimina, *Small Arms Control in Central Asia* (London: International Alert, 2004), p. 30.

113 OAS Model Legislation, at www.oas.org/juridico/english/cifta_mod_leg_markings.pdf, last accessed 6 April 2009.

114 See Luis Alfonso de Alba, 'Certainly as Dangerous as a Cigarette', *Disarmament Watch*, at www.un.org/Pubs/chronicle/2003/issue2/0203p59.html; and The People's Republic of China, Department of Arms Control, Ministry of Foreign Affairs, *National Report of the People's Republic of China on Implementation of the UN SALW Programme of Action* (27 March 2003), at www.fmprc.gov.cn/eng/wjb/zzjg/jks/cjjk/2622/t22819.htm. Websites last accessed 6 April 2009.

115 Pierre, *Cascade of Arms*, p. 62. Also see Stohl, Schroeder and Smith, *The Small Arms Trade*.

116 Grillot, *Small Arms Control in Central and Eastern Europe*, p. 38, and Grillot, 'Guns in the Balkans'.

117 Cooper et al., *Small Arms Control in Eurasia*, p. 35.

118 See IANSA's report on Weapons for Development, at www.iansa.org/documents/development/weapons_for_dev.htm, last accessed 6 April 2009.

119 Von Tangen Page, *Implementing International Small Arms Controls*, p. 20.

120 Grillot, *Small Arms Control in Central and Eastern Europe*, p. 20.

121 Grillot, *Small Arms Control in the Black Sea Region*, p. 39.

122 Ebo, *Small Arms Control in West Africa*, p. 21.

123 United States Diplomatic Mission to Italy, 9 June 2006, at http://italy.usembassy.gov/viewer/article.asp?article=/file2006_06/alia/a6060907.htm, last accessed 6 April 2009.

124 Author's interview with State Department official, 15 January 2008.

125 Author's interview with DTRA official, 15 January 2008.

126 For more on the EXBS programme, see www.exportcontrol.org/links/1371c.aspx, last accessed 6 April 2009.

127 See the text of the Convention at www.icbl.org/treaty/text/english, last accessed 6 April 2009.

128 ICBL, 'What is the Mine Ban Treaty?' (March 2008), www.icbl.org/tools/faq/treaty/what, last accessed 6 April 2009.

129 ICBL, 'States Parties' (June 2006), www.icbl.org/treaty/members, last accessed 6 April 2009.

130 ICBL, 'States Not Parties' (January 2008), www.icbl.org/treaty/snp, last accessed 6 April 2009.

131 ICBL, 'How Did it All Start?' (February 2005), www.icbl.org/tools/faq/campaign/start, last accessed 6 April 2009.

132 See Kenneth R. Rutherford, 'Landmine Victim Assistance and Government Legal Obligation', *Journal of Mine Action*, 6 (1) (2002), at http://maic.jmu.edu/journal/6.1/features/rutherford/rutherford.htm; and United Nations, NGO Committee on Disarmament, Peace and Security, 'Events and Campaigns: Land Mines', at http://disarm.igc.org/landmine.html. Websites last accessed 6 April 2009.

133 IANSA, 'About IANSA' (2006), www.iansa.org/about.htm, last accessed 6 April 2009.

134 IANSA, 'Founding Document of IANSA', at www.iansa.org/about/m1.htm, last accessed 6 April 2009.

135 Suzette R. Grillot, Craig S. Stapley, and Molly E. Hanna, 'Assessing the Small Arms Movement: The Trials and Tribulations of a Transnational Network', *Contemporary Security Policy*, 27(1) (April 2006), pp. 60–84.

136 'Global Campaign Launched to Ban Cluster Bombs', Agence France Presse, 14 November 2003, at www.commondreams.org/headlines03/1114-04.htm, last accessed 6 April 2009.

137 CMC, 'The Coalition', at www.stopclustermunitions.org/the-coalition/, last accessed 6 April 2009.

138 See the Secretary-General's statement at www.un.org/apps/sg/sgstats.asp?nid=2844; and a discussion of his message at www.un.org/apps/news/story.asp?NewsID=24581&Cr=cluster&Cr1=munitions. Websites last accessed 6 April 2009.

139 See the Report on the Vienna Conference on Cluster Munitions at http://storage.paxchristi.net/PUBLIC/07-01374.pdf. See the report on the Oslo meeting and the Convention at www.stopclustermunitions.org/the-solution/. Websites last accessed 6 April 2009.

140 SIPRI, 'Arms Transfer Project', at www.sipri.org/contents/armstrad/, last accessed 6 April 2009.

141 SIPRI, 'Arms Control and Disarmament Documentary Survey', at www.sipri.org/contents/library/chronology.html, last accessed 6 April 2009.

142 For details about NISAT, see its website at www.prio.no/nisat, last accessed 6 April 2009.

143 Control Arms, 'Homepage', at www.controlarms.org, last accessed 6 April 2009.

144 See Human Rights Watch, 'Homepage', at www.hrw.org, last accessed 6 April 2009.

145 Small Arms Survey, 'Homepage', at www.smallarmssurvey.org, last accessed 6 April 2009.

146 Ebo, *Small Arms Control in West Africa*, p. 28.

147 Godnick and Vasquez, *Small Arms Control in Central America*, p. 9.

148 Ibid.

149 International Alert, 'Biting the Bullet', at www.international-alert.org/security/security_projects.php?t=2, last accessed 6 April 2009.

150 Lewis, 'Looking Back'.

151 See the Charter of the United Nations, at www.un.org/aboutun/charter/. Also see the UN Programme of Action, at http://disarmament.un.org/cab/poa.html, for a reiteration of these norms. Websites last accessed 6 April 2009.

152 Pierre, *Cascade of Arms*, p. 166.

153 Levine, *Arms Trade, Security and Conflict*, p. 95.

154 David Morton, 'Gunning for the World', *Foreign Policy*, online edition (January/February 2006), at www.foreignpolicy.com. For more on the WFSA, see their website at www.wfsa.net. Websites last accessed 6 April 2009.

155 Pierre, *Cascade of Arms*, p. 6.

156 Von Tangen Page, *Implementing International Small Arms Controls*, p. 20.

157 Pierre, *Cascade of Arms*, pp. 344–7, 350.

158 Davis, *Implementing and Deepening the OAS Agenda on Small Arms and Light Weapons*.

CHAPTER 7 CONCLUSION

1 See global trade data at http://stat.wto.org/StatisticalProgram/
   WSDBViewData.aspx?Language=E, last accessed 6 April 2009.
2 Control Arms, 'Towards an Arms Trade Treaty' (Control Arms, June
   2005), p. 3, at www.controlarms.org/en/documents%20and%20
   files/reports/english-reports/towards-an-arms-trade-treaty-next-
   steps-for-the-un, last accessed 6 April 2009.
3 On the WMD taboo, see Nina Tannenwald, *The Nuclear Taboo:
   The United States and the Non-Use of Nuclear Weapons since 1945*
   (Cambridge: Cambridge University Press, 2008); Nina Tannenwald,
   'Stigmatizing the Bomb: Origins of the Nuclear Taboo', *International
   Security*, 29(4) (2005), pp. 5–49; and Price, *The Chemical Weapons
   Taboo*.
4 See statements made at the Programme of Action meetings
   at the United Nations, such as the 2001 statements of China,
   Egypt, Germany, Indonesia, Russia and the United States, at
   http://disarmament.un.org/cab/smallarms/statements.htm.
   See statements of Egypt and Pakistan at www.un.org/events/
   smallarms2006/mem-states060628.html, and statement
   of Vietnam at www.un.org/events/smallarms2006/mem-
   states060627.html. Websites last accessed 6 April 2009.
5 Morton, 'Gunning for the World'.
6 One author's interviews with gun traders in Turkey (January 2003),
   Bulgaria (October 2000) and Macedonia (February–June 2003). See
   Grillot, *Small Arms Control in the Black Sea Region*, and Suzette R.
   Grillot, Shelly O. Stoneman, Hans Risser and Wolf-Christian Paes, *A
   Fragile Peace: Guns and Security in Macedonia* (Geneva: Small Arms
   Survey and the United Nations Development Program, January
   2004).

Bibliography

'African Troops Killed in Darfur', *BBC News*, 2 April 2007.

Agence France Presse, 'Global Campaign Launched to Ban Cluster Bombs', Agence France Presse, 14 November 2003.

—— 'Hungarian Tanks Leave for Iraq', *Defense News*, 17 October 2005.

—— 'Czech Republic Signs 835 Million Euro Contract for Armored Transporters', *Defense News*, 9 June 2006.

Alexander, Paul, 'Philippines Bus Siege Ends in Surrender', Associated Press, 28 March 2007.

Alpers, Philip, *Gun-running in Papua New Guinea: From Arrows to Assault Weapons in the Southern Highlands*, Special Report No. 5 (Geneva: Small Arms Survey, 2005).

Amnesty International, 'China: Secretive Arms Exports Stoking Conflict and Repression', 11 June 2006.

—— 'Arms Without Borders: Why a Globalised Trade Needs Global Controls', 2 October 2006.

—— 'People's Republic of China: Sustaining Conflict and Human Rights Abuses; The Flow of Arms Accelerates' (London: Amnesty International, 2007).

—— *Sudan: Arms Continuing to Fuel Serious Human Rights Violations in Darfur* (London: Amnesty International, 8 May 2007).

Anastasijevic, Dejan, *Organized Crime in the Western Balkans: Trafficking in Drugs, Trafficking in Weapons, Trafficking in Human Beings*, HUMSEC Working Paper for the European Commission (2006).

Anders, Holger, and Reinhilde Weidacher, 'The Production of Ammunition for Small Arms and Light Weapons', in *Targeting Ammunition: A Primer*, ed. Stéphanie Pézard and Holger Anders (Geneva: Small Arms Survey, 2006).

Anderson, Hil, 'F16s arrive in Poland; Renamed "Hawks"', UPI, 13 November 2006.

Anthony, Ian, ed., *Russia and the Arms Trade* (Oxford: Oxford University Press, 1998).

'Armed Conflict Report: Ethiopia–Eritrea', Ploughshares (February 2002).

Associated Press, 'U.N. General Assembly Takes First Step Toward Establishing Treaty on Conventional Weapons', *International Herald Tribune*, 7 December 2006.

Atwood, David, Anne-Kathrin Glatz and Robert Muggah, *Demanding Attention: Addressing the Dynamics of Small Arms Demand* (New York: Quaker United Nations Office, 2006).

Bah, Alhaji M. S., 'Micro-Disarmament in West Africa: The ECOWAS Moratorium on Small Arms and Light Weapons', *African Security Review*, 13(3) (2004).

BASIC, 'A Closer Examination of the OAS Prototype', in *One Size Fits All? Prospects for a Global Convention on Illicit Trafficking by 2000* (Washington, DC: BASIC, 1999).

Beehner, Lionel, 'Russia–Iran Arms Trade', *Council on Foreign Relations Backgrounder* (1 November 2006).

Berkol, Ilhan, 'Analysis of the ECOWAS Convention on SALW', *GRIP*, 1 April 2007.

Berman, Eric, and Robert Muggah, *Humanitarianism under Threat: The Humanitarian Impacts of Small Arms and Light Weapons* (Geneva: Small Arms Survey, March 2001).

'Boeing Arms Chief Warns Against "Peace Dividend"', *Reuters*, 24 May 2007.

Boutwell, Jeffrey, and Michael Klare, *Light Weapons and Civil Conflict: Controlling the Tools of Violence* (Lanham, MD: Rowman & Littlefield, 1999).

Brady Center to Prevent Gun Violence, *Guns and Terror* (Washington, DC: Brady Center to Prevent Gun Violence, 2001).

—— *Smoking Guns: Exposing the Gun Industry's Complicity in the Illegal Gun Market* (Washington, DC: Brady Center to Prevent Gun Violence, 2003).

—— *Shady Dealings: Illegal Gun Trafficking from Licensed Gun Dealers* (Washington, DC: Brady Center to Prevent Gun Violence, January 2007).

Brockway, Fenner, *The Bloody Traffic* (London: Victor Gollancz, 1933).

Brzoska, Michael, 'The Economics of Arms Imports After the End of the Cold War', *Defence and Peace Economics*, 15(2) (April 2004).

Brzoska, Michael, and Thomas Ohlson, eds., *Arms Production in the Third World* (London: Taylor & Francis, 1986).

Buchanan, Cate, and Robert Muggah, 'No Relief: Surveying the Effects of Gun Violence on Humanitarian and Development Personnel', Geneva: Centre for Humanitarian Dialogue and SAS, June 2005.

Bush, Jason, 'Russia's Back in the Arms Game', *Business Week*, 10 April 2007.

Byman, Daniel, and Roger Cliff, *China's Arms Sales: Motivations and Implications* (New York: RAND Corporation, 2000).

Campbell, Jason, Michael O'Hanlon and Amy Unikewicz, 'Op-Chart: The State of Iraq: An Update', *New York Times*, 10 June 2007.

Canadian Security Intelligence Service, *Weapons Proliferation and the Military–Industrial Complex of the PRC*, Ottawa, Ont., 27 August 2003.

Center for International Trade and Security, *Nonproliferation Export Controls: A Global Evaluation* (Athens, GA: Center for International Trade and Security).

Center for Public Integrity, 'U.S. Foreign Lobbying, Terrorism Influencing Post 9/11 U.S. Military Aid and Human Rights', Washington, DC, 18 May 2007.

Chamberlain, Gethin, 'Iran Fears Spark Sunni Arms Spree: $50 Billion Shopping List from Saudi Arabia Alone', *The Gazette (Montreal)*, 11 February 2007.

'China Always Prudent in Arms Trade: FM Spokeswoman', *People's Daily Online*, 13 June 2006.

'China Refutes Amnesty International's Slams on Arms Trade', *People's Daily Online*, 12 June 2006.

'China Voices Firm Opposition to Illegal Trade in Small Arms', *People's Daily Online*, 10 July 2001.

'Chinese Fighter Jets to Reach Pakistan', *Kommersant: Russia's Daily Online*, 26 April 2007.

Chuter, Andrew, and Martin Agüera, 'Copper Helps Chile Make Deals for Ships, Planes', *Defense News*, 24 June 2005.

'Civil Society Consultation on the ECOWAS Moratorium: Beyond the UN 2001 Conference', Center for Democratic Development, June 2001.

Cliff, Roger, and Evan S. Medeiros, 'Keep the Ban on Arms for China: Europe's Embargo', *International Herald Tribune*, 23 March 2004.

Cloud, David S., 'Inquiry Opened Into Israeli Use of U.S. Bombs', *New York Times*, 25 August 2006.

Cloud, David S., and Greg Myre, 'Israel May Have Violated Arms Pact, U.S. Says', *New York Times*, 28 January 2007.

Cohen, Ariel, 'The Russian Effect', *FrontPageMagazine.com*, 20 March 2007.

Collier, Basil, *Arms and the Men: The Arms Trade and Governments* (London: Hamish Hamilton, 1980).

Commission to Assess the Ballistic Missile Threat to the United States, Appendix III: Unclassified Working Papers, System Planning Corporation: 'Non-Proliferation Issues', France, Executive Summary.

Congressional Research Service, *Foreign Terrorists and the Availability of Firearms and Black Powder in the United States*, Washington, DC: Congressional Research Service, 16 May 2003, p. CRS-5.

Control Arms Briefing Note, 'UN Arms Embargoes: An Overview of the Last Ten Years' (16 March 2006).

'Convention on Certain Conventional Weapons (CCW) at a Glance', *Arms Control Association*, October 2007.

Coonan, Clifford, 'China is Arming World's Regimes to Fuel Economic Boom, says Amnesty', *The Independent*, 12 June 2006.

Cooper, Stephanie, Michael von Tangen Page, Helena Vasquez and Lada Zimina, *Small Arms Control in Eurasia* (London: International Alert, 2004).

Cortright, David and George A. Lopez, with Linda Gerber, 'Sanctions *Sans* Commitment: An Assessment of UN Arms Embargoes', Project Ploughshares Working Paper (Waterloo, Ont.: May 2002).

Cox, Matthew, 'Better Than M4, But You Can't Have One', *Army Times*, 1 March 2007.

Craft, Cassady, *Weapons for Peace, Weapons for War: The Effect of Arms Transfers on War Outbreak, Involvement, and Outcomes* (New York: Routledge, 1999).

—— 'Military Diplomacy: The Myth of Arms for Influence', in *Challenging Conventional Wisdom: Debunking the Myths and Exposing the Risks of Arms Export Reform*, ed. Tamar Gabelnick and Rachel Stohl (Washington, DC: Center for Defense Information and Federation of American Scientists, June 2003).

Cupitt, Richard T., and Suzette R. Grillot, 'COCOM Is Dead, Long Live COCOM: Persistence and Change in Multilateral Security Regimes', *British Journal of Political Science*, 27 (July 1997).

Curtis, Glenn E., and Tara Karacan, *The Nexus Among Terrorists, Narcotics Traffickers, Weapons Proliferators, and Organized Crime Networks in Western Europe*, study prepared by the Federal Research Division, Library of Congress, December 2002.

Curtis, Mark, Helen Close, Vanessa Dury and Roy Isbister, *The Good, the Bad, and the Ugly: A Decade of Labour's Arms Exports* (London: Saferworld, May 2007).

'Damaged U.S. Spy Plane Arrives in Georgia', CNN 5 July 2001.

Davis, Ian, *Implementing and Deepening the OAS Agenda on Small Arms and Light Weapons*, May 2002.

DeHaas, Marcel, 'Russia–China Security Cooperation', *Power and Interest News Report* (27 November 2006).

Diaz, Tom, 'Credit Card Armies – Firearms and Training for Terror in the United States', Violence Policy Center, November 2002.

Dorsey, James M., 'Sandinista Buildup at Border Stirs U.S. Concern', *Washington Times*, 6 December 1989.

Dougherty, Jill, 'Chechen "claims Beslan attack"', CNN.com, 17 September 2004.

Dreyfus, Pablo, Benjamin Lessing and Júlio César Purcena, 'The Brazilian Small Arms Industry: Legal Production and Trade', in *Brazil: The Arms and the Victims*, ed. Rubem César Fernandes (Rio de Janeiro: 7 Letras/Iser, 2005).

Ebo, Adedeji, *Small Arms Control in West Africa* (London: International Alert, 2003).

Edmonds, Martin, ed., *International Arms Procurement: New Directions* (New York: Pergamon Press, 1981).

Engelmann, Bernt, *The Weapons Merchants* (New York: Crown, Inc., 1964).

Epstein, Keith, 'F-14 Parts Anyone? How Iran Obtains Restricted Military Technology from the Defense Department', *Business Week*, 11 June 2007.

Evans, Rob, 'Export Department Closure Leaves Defence Firms Out in the Cold', Thursday 26 July 2007, www.guardian.co.uk.

Farah, Douglas, 'Liberian Leader Again Finds Means to Hang On; Taylor Exploits Timber to Keep Power', *The Washington Post*, 4 June 2002.

—— *Blood From Stones: The Secret Financial Network of Terror* (New York: Broadway Books, 2004).

—— 'Standing By as a Brutal Warlord Plots his Return', *The Washington Post*, 2 October 2005.

Farah, Douglas, and Stephen Braun, *Merchant of Death: Money, Guns, Planes, and the Man Who Makes War Possible* (Hoboken, NJ: John Wiley & Sons, Inc., 2007).

Faulconbridge, Guy, 'No One Can Limit Russian Arms Exports: Putin', Reuters, 31 October 2007.

Fedynsky, Peter, 'Russia's Parliament Suspends Arms Control Treaty Compliance', *Global Security.org*, 7 November 2007.

Finn, Peter, 'Al Qaeda Arms Traced to Saudi National Guard; 3 Attackers Identified in Riyadh Bombings', *The Washington Post*, 19 May 2003, p. A1.

Fite, David, 'A View from Congress', in *Challenging Conventional Wisdom: Debunking the Myths and Exposing the Risks of Arms Export Reform*, ed. Tamar Gabelnick and Rachel Stohl (Washington, DC: Center for Defense Information and Federation of American Scientists, June 2003.

'Four Indicted After Major Weapons Seizure', *The Local*, 22 January 2008.

French Ministry of Defence, 'Press Kit: Report to the French Parliament Regarding Defence Equipments Exports in 2006', 4 December 2007.

French Ministry of Defence, 'Export of Defense and Security Equipment: A Strategy for Growth', 13 December 2007, unofficial translation by www.defense-aerospace.com.

Fund for Peace, 'Model Convention on the Registration of Arms Brokers and the Suppression of Unlicensed Arms Brokering' (Washington DC: Fund for Peace, July 2001).

Gander, Terry, *Guerrilla Warfare Weapons: The Modern Underground Fighter's Armoury* (New York: Sterling Publishing Co., 1990).

Gill, Bates, and Evan S. Medeiros, 'Foreign and Domestic Influences on China's Arms Control and Nonproliferation Policies', *The China Quarterly*, 161 (March 2000), pp. 66–94.

Gilson, Dave, 'Ukraine: Cashing in on Illegal Arms', *Frontline World*, May 2002.

Glatz, Anne-Kathrin, 'Buying the Bullet: Authorized Small Arms Ammunition Transfers', in *Targeting Ammunition: A Primer*, ed. Stéphanie Pézard and Holger Anders (Geneva: Small Arms Survey, 2006).

Godnick, William, Robert Muggah and Camilla Waszink, *Stray Bullets: The Impact of Small Arms Misuse in Central America* (Geneva: Small Arms Survey, October 2002).

Godnick, William, and Helena Vasquez, *Small Arms Control in Central America* (London: International Alert, 2003).

Gold, David, 'The Changing Economics of the Arms Trade', in *Arming the Future: A Defense Industry for the 21st Century*, ed. Sean S. Costigan and Ann R. Markusen (New York: Council on Foreign Relations Press, 1999).

Greene, Owen, *Promoting Effective Action on Small Arms: Emerging Agendas for the 2006 Review Conference* (London and Bradford: Biting the Bullet Project, July 2005).

Grimmett, Richard F., *CRS Report for Congress: Trends in Conventional Arms Transfers to the Third World by Major Supplier, 1982–1989* (Washington, DC: Congressional Research Service, 19 June 1990).
—— *CRS Report for Congress: Conventional Arms Transfers to the Third World, 1983–1990* (Washington, DC: Congressional Research Service, Library of Congress, 2 August 1991).
—— *CRS Report for Congress: Conventional Arms Transfers to Developing Nations, 1992–1999* (Washington, DC: Congressional Research Service, Library of Congress, 18 August 2000).
—— *Conventional Arms Transfers to Developing Nations 1993–2000* (Washington, DC: Congressional Research Service, Library of Congress, 16 August 2001).
—— *CRS Report for Congress: Conventional Arms Transfers to Developing Nations, 1998–2005* (Washington, DC: Congressional Research Service, Library of Congress, 23 October 2006).
—— *CRS Report for Congress: Trends in Conventional Arms Transfers to the Third World by Major Supplier, 1999–2006* (Washington, DC: Congressional Research Service, Library of Congress, 26 September 2007).
—— *Conventional Arms Transfers to Developing Nations 2000–2007* (Washington, DC: Congressional Research Service, Library of Congress, 23 October 2008).
—— *CRS Report for Congress, U.S. Arms Sales: Agreements with and Deliveries to Major Clients* (Washington, DC: Congressional Research Service, Library of Congress, 15 December 2006).
—— *CRS Report for Congress, U.S. Arms Sales: Agreements with and Deliveries to Major Clients, 1999–2006* (Washington, DC: Congressional Research Service, Library of Congress, 20 December 2007).
Grillot, Suzette R., *Small Arms Control in Central and Eastern Europe* (London: International Alert, 2003).
—— *Small Arms Control in the Black Sea Region* (London: International Alert, 2003).
—— 'Guns in the Balkans: Controlling Small Arms and Light Weapons in Six Western Balkan Countries', unpublished manuscript, October 2008.
Grillot, Suzette R., Craig S. Stapley and Molly E. Hanna, 'Assessing the Small Arms Movement: The Trials and Tribulations of a Transnational Network', *Contemporary Security Policy*, 27(1) (April 2006), pp. 60-84.
Gripen International, 'Latest Hungarian Gripen Offset Claim Approved', defense-aerospace.com, 5 August 2005.

Haddad, Musue N., 'Arms Proliferation Increases Repression' (New York: United Nations, 20 July 2002).

Harding, Andrew, 'UN Warns of Somali Terror Link', BBC, 4 November 2003.

Harkavy, Robert E., *The Arms Trade and International Systems* (Cambridge, MA: Ballinger Publishing Company, 1975).

Hartung, William D., *And Weapons for All* (New York: HarperCollins, 1994).

Haug, Maria, Martin Langvandslien, Lora Lumpe and Nicholas Marsh, *Shining a Light on Small Arms Exports: The Record of State Transparency*, Occasional Paper 4 (Geneva: Small Arms Survey, 2002).

Heathershaw, John, Emil Juraev, Michael von Tangen Page and Lada Zimina, *Small Arms Control in Central Asia* (London: International Alert, 2004).

Hill, Symon, 'How to Get Ahead in Arms Dealing', *Morning Star*, 6 October 2006.

Hoagland, Jim, 'No More Frankensteins', *The Washington Post*, 13 July 1993, p. A15.

'HRW Questions U.S. Laser Programs as Blinding Laser Weapon Ban Becomes International Law', *Human Rights News*, 29 July 1998.

Human Rights Watch, 'Arsenals on the Cheap: NATO Expansion and the Arms Cascade', April 1999.

Human Security Center, *Human Security Report 2005: War and Peace in the 21st Century* (New York: Oxford University Press, 2005).

IANSA, 'ECOWAS Convention on Small Arms and Light Weapons, Their Ammunitions and Other Related Materials' (June 2006).

IANSA, *Reviewing Action on Small Arms 2006: Assessing the First Five Years of the Programme of Action* (London and Bradford: IANSA and Biting the Bullet Project, 2006).

'ICE-Led Border Task Force Seizes IEDs, Weapons in Major Arrest', *Inside ICE*, 3(2) (2006).

Internal Displacement Monitoring Center, 'Internal Displacement: Global Overview of Trends and Developments in 2006', April 2007.

International Criminal Court, 'Background Information on the Situation in Uganda', 29 January 2004.

International Monetary Fund, *Chile: Report on Observance of Standards and Codes – Fiscal Transparency* (Washington, DC: International Monetary Fund, August 2003).

Izyumov, Alexei, 'The Soviet Union: Arms Control and Conversion

– Plan and Reality', in *Arms Industry Limited*, ed. Herbert Wulf (Stockholm and Oxford: SIPRI and Oxford University Press, 1993).

Jackson, Thomas, Nicholas Marsh, Taylor Owen and Anne Thurin, *Who Takes the Bullet: The Impact of Small Arms Violence* (Oslo: Norwegian Church Aid and the International Peace Research Institute, March 2005).

'Joint Strike Fighter', *Federation of American Scientists*, 30 May 2008.

Kahaner, Larry, 'Lessons of the Ak-47', defensetech.org, 25 October 2006.

Katumanga, Musambayi, with Lionel Cliffe, *Nairobi – A City Besieged: The Impact of Armed Violence on Poverty and Development* (Bradford: University of Bradford, Centre for International Cooperation and Security, March 2005).

Kelly, Robert J., Jess Maghan and Joseph D. Serio, *Illicit Trafficking: A Reference Handbook* (Santa Barbara: ABC-CLIO, Inc., 2005).

Kemp, Geoffrey, 'Introduction: The Global Arms Trade: Past and Present', in *The Global Arms Trade*, ed. Gary E. McCuen (Hudson: Gary E. McCuen, Inc., 1992).

Kent, John R., and John Smith, 'Denmark Joins F-35 Program's Next Phase, Completes JSF Partner Participation', Lockheed Martin, 27 February 2005.

Klare, Michael T., and Robert I. Rotberg, *The Scourge of Small Arms* (Cambridge, MA: World Peace Foundation, 1999).

Koch, Andrew, 'The Nuclear Network – Khanfessions of a Proliferator', *Jane's Defense Weekly*, 26 February 2004.

Kolodziej, Edward A., 'Arms Transfers and International Politics: The Interdependence of Independence', in *Arms Transfers in the Modern World*, ed. Neuman and Harkavy.

Kouri, Jim, 'US Businessmen Illegally Sell Military Technology', *PHW News.com*, 23 June 2005.

Krause, Keith, *Arms and the State: Patterns of Military Production and Trade* (Cambridge: Cambridge University Press, 1992).

Kristof, Nicholas D., 'China's Genocide Olympics', *International Herald Tribune*, 24 January 2008.

Kuzio, Taras, 'Ukraine: Look into Arms Exports', *The Christian Science Monitor*, 12 February 2002.

Kwayera, Juma, 'Kenya Will Not Close Eldoret Bullet Factory, Says Murungaru', *The East African*, 20 October 2003.

Lague, David, 'Russia and China Rethink Arms Deals', *International Herald Tribune* (2 March 2008).

'Lasers Burn U.S. Pilots' Eyes', *ABC News.com*, 4 November 1998.

Lederer, Edith M., 'Security Along Lebanon–Syria Border Too Lax to Stop Arms Smuggling', *North Country Times*, 26 June 2007.

Lewis, James A., 'Looking Back: Multilateral Arms Transfer Restraint: The Limits of Cooperation', *Arms Control Today*, November 2005.

Lipson, Michael, 'The Reincarnation of CoCom: Explaining Post-Cold War Export Controls', *The Nonproliferation Review* (Winter 1999).

Litovkin, Viktor, 'Russia Arms Exports Break Records', *RIA Novosti* (8 March 2007).

—— 'An Arms Export Bonanza for Russia', UPI Moscow, 20 March 2007.

Lodgaard, Sverre, 'Chronology of Events Relating to the ECOWAS Moratorium' (Oslo: NISAT, 4 June 1999).

''Lord of War' Arms Dealer Victor Bout Arrested in Thailand', *Times Online*, 6 March 2008.

Luckham, Robin, Ismail Ahmed, Hobert Myggah and Sarah White, *Conflict and Poverty in Sub-Saharan Africa: An Assessment of the Issues and Evidence*, IDS Working Paper 128, March (Brighton: Institute of Development Studies, 2001).

Lumpe, Lora, *Running Guns: The Global Black Market in Small Arms* (London: Zed Books, 2000).

Lumpe, Lora and Jeff Donarski, *The Arms Trade Revealed: A Guide for Investigators and Activists* (Washington, DC: Federation of American Scientists Arms Sales Monitoring Project, 1998).

Mackay, Neil, 'Revealed: The Extent of Britain's Arms Trade', *The Sunday Herald*, 8 July 2006, p. 8.

Manchester, William, *The Arms of Krupp* (Boston: Little, Brown and Company, 1968).

Marshall, Jonathan, Jane Hunter and Peter D. Scott, *The Iran–Contra Connection* (Toronto: University of Toronto Press, 1987).

Mastanduno, Michael, *Economic Containment: CoCom and the Politics of East–West Trade* (Ithaca, NJ: Cornell University Press, 1992).

McCuen, Gary E., ed., *The Global Arms Trade* (Hudson: Gary E. McCuen, Inc., 1992).

Medeiros, Evan S., *Chasing the Dragon: Assessing China's System of Export Controls for WMD-Related Goods and Technologies* (Santa Monica: RAND Corporation, 2005).

Meek, Sarah, 'Combating Arms-Trafficking: The Need for Integrated Approaches', *African Security Review*, 9 (2000).

'Middle East Tourists Return to Luxor', *BBC News*, 17 November 1998.

Mooney, Kevin, 'Mexican Soldier Freelancing for Drug Cartels on US Soil', *CNSNews.com*, 21 December 2006.

'More on Arms Seized at U.S.–Mexican Border Town', *Northeast Intelligence Network*, 23 February 2007.

Morton, David, 'Gunning for the World', *Foreign Policy*, online edition (January/February 2006).

Mthembu-Salter, Gregory, 'The Wheel Turns Again: Militarization and Rwanda's Congolese Refugees', in *No Refuge: The Crisis of Refugee Militarization in Africa*, ed. Robert Muggah (London: Zed Books, 2006).

Muggah, Robert, and Edward Mogire, 'Introduction', in *No Refuge: The Crisis of Refugee Militarization in Africa*, ed. Robert Muggah (London: Zed Books, 2006).

Naím, Moisés, *Illicit: How Smugglers, Traffickers and Copycats are Hijacking the Global Economy* (New York: Random House, 2005).

Naylor, R. T., 'The Structure and Operation of the Modern Arms Black Market', in *Lethal Commerce: The Global Trade in Small Arms and Light Weapons*, ed. Jeffrey Boutwell, Michael T. Klare and Laura W. Reed (Cambridge, MA: American Academy of Arts and Sciences, 1995).

Neuman, Stephanie G., and Robert E. Harkavy, eds. *Arms Transfers in the Modern World* (New York: Praeger, 1979).

Nikolsky, Alexi, 'The Defense Industry Switches to Euros', *Vedemosti*, 4 June 2007.

Norton-Taylor, Richard, 'Countries Listed by Foreign Office as Poor on Human Rights Invited to Arms Trade Fair', *The Guardian*, 13 September 2005.

Nunn-Lugar Report, *Lugar, Obama Urge Destruction of Conventional Weapons Stockpiles*, August 2005, at http://lugar.senate.gov/reports/Nunn-Lugar_Report_2005.pdf.

O'Callaghan, Geraldine, Michael Crowley and Kathleen Miller, 'NATO and Small Arms: From Word to Deed', *GRIP*, October 2000.

Office of the US Secretary of Defense, *Annual Report to Congress: Military Power of the People's Republic of China* (May 2007).

OSCE, 'OSCE Helps Kazakhstan to Secure Surplus Small Arms, Light Weapons and Conventional Ammunition,' 3 June 2005.

OSCE, *Handbook of Best Practices on Small Arms and Light Weapons*, 31 December 2003.

Pan, Esther, *China, Africa and Oil* (Washington, DC: Council on Foreign Relations, 2007).

Paris, Roland, 'Human Security: Paradigm Shift or Hot Air?' *International Security*, 26(2) (2001), pp. 87–102.

Pearson, Frederic S., *The Global Spread of Arms: Political Economy of International Security* (Oxford: Westview Press, 1994).

People's Republic of China, Department of Arms Control, Ministry of Foreign Affairs, *National Report of the People's Republic of China on Implementation of the UN SALW Programme of Action* (27 March 2003), available at www.fmprc.gov.cn/eng/wjb/zzjg/jks/cjjk/2622/t22819. htm.

People's Republic of China, Ministry of Foreign Affairs, *UN Register of Conventional Arms*, 21 May 2005.

'Petraeus: Increased U.S. Troops Yielding Results', *National Public Radio*, 19 July 2007, at www.npr.org/templates/story/story. php?storyId=12099511.

Peźard, Stéphanie, and Holger Anders, eds., *Targeting Ammunition: A Primer* (Geneva: Small Arms Survey, 2006).

Pierre, Andrew J., *The Global Politics of Arms Sales* (Princeton: Princeton University Press, 1982).

Plowright, Adam, ed., 'OECD has "serious concerns" about halt to BAE–Saudi probe', *Cascade of Arms: Managing Conventional Weapons Proliferation* (Washington, DC: Brookings Institution Press, Agence France Presse, 18 January 2007).

Prenzler, Tim, 'The Human Side of Security', *Security Journal*, 20(1) (2007), pp. 35–9.

Price, Richard M., *The Chemical Weapons Taboo* (Ithaca, NY: Cornell University Press, 1997).

'Putin to Reform Russian Arms Exporter', Reuters, 20 June 2005.

Queen's Printer of Acts of Parliament, *Explanatory Notes to Export Control Act 2002* (London: The Stationery Office, 2002).

Randle, Jim, 'Bosnia Laser Attack', *Federation of American Scientists*, 4 November 1998.

Reingold, Jonathan, 'U.S. Arms Sales to Israel End Up in China, Iraq', *CommonDreams.org*, 9 May 2002.

Rivlin, Paul, 'The Russian Economy and Arms Exports to the Middle East', *Jaffee Center for Strategic Studies, Memorandum 79*, September 2005.

Robertson, Jordan, 'Dual-use Technologies Vex Export Regulators; Salesman Facing 100 years', Associated Press, 13 May 2007.

'Rosoboronexport to Sue Over Illegal Arms Production Abroad' 27 June 2006. Alexandria, VA: Global Security; Moscow: RIA Novosti.

Ross, Andrew L., 'On Arms Acquisitions and Transfers', in *Security and Arms Control*. Vol. I, ed. Edward A. Kolodziej and Patrick M. Morgan (New York: Greenwood Press, 1989).

Rossant, John, with Dexter Roberts, 'An Arms Cornucopia for China?' *Business Week*, 21 February 2005.

'Russia to Supply over $2.2bln Weapons to Libya', *Iran Defence Forum*, 4 May 2007.

'Russian Charged with Trying to Sell Arms', *New York Times*, 7 March 2008.

'Russia's Sukhoi Fighter is State-of-the-Art Warplane – Chavez', AItar-Tasr, 18 April 2007.

Rutherford, Kenneth R., 'Landmine Victim Assistance and Government Legal Obligation', *Journal of Mine Action*, 6(1) (2002).

Saferworld, *Turning the Page: Small Arms and Light Weapons in Albania* (London and Belgrade: Saferworld and the Southeastern and Eastern Europe Clearinghouse for the Control of Small Arms and Light Weapons (SEESAC), 2005).

Sampson, Anthony, *The Arms Bazaar* (New York: Viking Press, 1977).

Schroeder, Matt, 'Issue Brief 3: The Illicit Arms Trade', *Federation of American Scientists*, 15 September 2005.

—— 'Transparency and Accountability in Arms Export Systems: The United States as a Case Study', *Disarmament Forum*, 3 (2005), 29–38.

Schroeder, Matthew, and Rachel Stohl, 'U.S. Export Controls', in SIPRI, *Yearbook 2005, Armaments, Disarmament and International Security* (New York: Oxford University Press, 2005), Appendix 17A.

Segal, Adam, 'New China Worries', *The International Economy* (Fall 2007).

Shrader, Katherine, 'U.S.: Hezbollah Recovers, and Iran Helps', *The Washington Post*, 18 December 2006.

SIPRI, *Yearbook 1994, Armaments, Disarmament and International Security* (New York: Oxford University Press, 1994).

—— *Yearbook 1995, Armaments, Disarmament and International Security* (New York: Oxford University Press, 1995).

—— *Yearbook 1999, Armaments, Disarmament and International Security* (New York: Oxford University Press, 1999).

—— *Yearbook 2000, Armaments, Disarmament and International Security* (New York: Oxford University Press, 2000).

—— *Yearbook 2003, Armaments, Disarmament and International Security* (New York: Oxford University Press, 2003).

—— *Yearbook 2006, Armaments, Disarmament and International Security* (New York: Oxford University Press, 2006).

—— *Yearbook 2007, Armaments, Disarmament and International Security* (New York: Oxford University Press, 2007).

—— *Yearbook 2008: Armaments, Disarmament and International Security* (New York: Oxford University Press, 2008).

Skedsmo, Arild, Kwong Danhier and Hoth Gor Luak, 'The Changing Meaning of Small Arms in Nuer Society', *African Security Review*, 12(4) (2003), pp. 57–67.

Small Arms Survey, *Small Arms Survey 2001: Profiling the Problem* (Oxford: Oxford University Press, 2001)

—— *Small Arms Survey 2002: Counting the Human Cost* (Oxford: Oxford University Press, 2002).

—— *Small Arms Survey 2003: Development Denied* (Oxford: Oxford University Press, 2003).

—— *Small Arms Survey 2004: Rights at Risk* (Oxford: Oxford University Press, 2004).

—— *Small Arms Survey 2005: Weapons at War* (Oxford: Oxford University Press, 2005).

—— *Small Arms Survey 2006: Unfinished Business* (Oxford: Oxford University Press, 2006).

—— *Small Arms Survey 2007: Guns and the City* (Cambridge: Cambridge University Press, 2007).

Smith, Col. Daniel M. (USA, ret.), 'U.S Arms Exports and Interoperability: Fighting with Each Other', in *Challenging Conventional Wisdom: Debunking the Myths and Exposing the Risks of Arms Export Reform*, ed. Tamar Gabelnick and Rachel Stohl (Washington, DC: Center for Defense Information and Federation of American Scientists, June 2003).

Smith, Ron, and Bernard Udis, 'New Challenges to Arms Export Control', in *Arms Trade, Security and Conflict*, ed. Paul Levine and Ron Smith (London and New York: Routledge, 2003).

Special Inspector General for Iraq Reconstruction, 'Iraqi Security Forces: Weapons Provided by the U.S. Department of Defense Using the Iraqi Relief and Reconstruction Fund' (Washington, DC: Office of the Special Inspector General for Iraq Reconstruction, 28 October 2006).

Speers, Kevin, and RADM Stephen H. Baker (ret.), 'Economic Arguments for Arms Export Reform', in *Challenging Conventional Wisdom: Debunking the Myths and Exposing the Risks of Arms Export Reform*, ed. Tamar Gabelnick and Rachel Stohl (Washington, DC: Center for Defense Information and Federation of American Scientists, June 2003).

Speier, Richard, Robert Gallucci, Robbie Sobel and Victor Mizin, 'Iran–Russia Missile Cooperation', in *Repairing the Regime: Preventing the Spread of Weapons of Mass Destruction*, Carnegie Endowment for International Peace and Routledge, May 2000.

Spiegel, Peter, and Laura King, 'Israel Says Syria, Not just Iran, Supplied Missiles to Hezbollah', *Los Angeles Times*, 31 August 2006.

Stanley, John, and Maurice Pearton, *The International Trade in Arms* (New York: Praeger, 1972).

Stern, Marcus, 'Terrorism Takes Root in Jungle of S. America: Region Linked to Funds for Hezbollah, Hamas', *San Diego Union-Tribune*, 15 June 2003.

Stewart, Frances, and Valpy FitzGerald, 'Introduction: Assessing the Economic Costs of War', in *War and Underdevelopment*. Vol. I *The Economic and Social Consequences of Conflict* (Oxford: Oxford University Press, 2000).

Stohl, Rachel, 'Wrangling Over Arms Sales to China', *Foreign Policy in Focus* (December 2006).

Stohl, Rachel, Matt Schroeder and Dan Smith, *The Small Arms Trade* (Oxford: Oneworld, 2006).

Stohl, Rachel, and Doug Tuttle, '"Merchant of Death" Arrested in Thailand', Center for Defense Information, March 10, 2008.

Stoker, Donald J., and Jonathan A. Grant, eds., *Girding for Battle: The Arms Trade in a Global Perspective, 1815–1940* (London: Praeger, 2003).

Stokes, Lee, 'Kuwait–Soviet Arms Deal Signals Shift from U.S.', UPI, 10 July 1988.

Stowsky, Jay, 'The History and Politics of the Pentagon's Dual-Use Strategy', in *Arming the Future: A Defense Industry for the 21st Century*, ed. Ann R. Markusen and Sean Costigan (New York: Council on Foreign Relations Press, 1999).

Sullivan, Mark P., *CRS Report for Congress: Chile: Political and Economic Conditions and U.S. Relations* (Washington, DC: Congressional Research Service, Library of Congress, updated 5 August 2003).

Sunnucks, Mike, 'Red Flags Rise Over Military Surplus Sales', *Phoenix Business Journal*, 27 April 2007.

Tannenwald, Nina, 'Stigmatizing the Bomb: Origins of the Nuclear Taboo', *International Security*, 29(4) (2005), pp. 5–49.

—— *The Nuclear Taboo: The United States and the Non-Use of Nuclear Weapons Since 1945* (Cambridge: Cambridge University Press, 2008).

'The First Two Serially Produced Su-30MKM Fighters for the Royal Malaysian Air Force Have Been Demonstrated', Irkut Corporation Press Release, 24 May 2007.

'The Small Arms Manufacturing Industry's Revenue for the Year 2006 Was Approximately $2,150,000,000', *Business Wire*, 11 April 2007.

'The United Nations and Small Arms: The Role of the Group of Governmental Experts', *Geneva Forum*, February 1999.

Theimer, Sharon, 'Pentagon Suspends Sale of F-14 Fighter Jet Parts Sought by Iran', *ABC News*, 31 January 2007.

—— 'Jets Shredded, Kept Away from "Bad Guys"', *ABC News*, 2 July 2007.

Thucydides, *The History of the Peloponnesian War*, trans. by Steven Lattimore (Indianapolis: Hackett Publishing Co. 1998).

Thusi, Thokosani, 'Assessing Small Arms Control Initiatives in East Africa: The Nairobi Declaration', *African Security Review*, 12(2) (2003).

Tierney, Dominic, 'Irrelevant or Malevolent? UN Arms Embargoes in Civil Wars', *Review of International Studies*, 31 (2005), 645–64.

Tigner, Brooks, 'EDA Strives to Rein in Offsets', *Defense News*, 28 August 2006.

'Towards an Arms Trade Treaty: Next Step for the UN Programme of Action', Control Arms (June 2005).

Tran, Pierre, 'France Works to Review Flagging Arms Exports', *Defense News*, 17 December 2007.

'UK Breaks EU Rule, Trains Chinese Officer', *UPI.com* (7 September 2008).

'UN Conference on Illicit Trade in Small Arms', *The American Journal of International Law*, 95 (2001), 901–3.

United Nations, *Final Report of the Monitoring Group on Somalia Pursuant to Security Council Resolution*, S/1670 (2006)/913 (New York: United Nations, 22 November 2006).

—— *Programme of Action to Prevent, Combat and Eradicate the Illicit Trade in Small Arms and Light Weapons in All Its Aspects*, A/CONF.192/15, 2001.

—— *Report of the Disarmament Commission*, A/51/42 (1996).

United Nations Department for Disarmament Affairs, *United Nations Register of Conventional Arms: Information Booklet 2007*, New York: United Nations.

United Nations Food and Agriculture Organization, 'Study on the Impact of Armed Conflicts on the Nutritional Situation of Children', Rome, 1996.

United Nations General Assembly, *Report of the Panel of Governmental Experts on Small Arms*, A/52/298 (New York: United Nations, 27 August 1997).

United Nations High Commissioner for Refugees, *The State of the World's Refugees 2006* (Oxford: Oxford University Press, 2007).

United Nations Office on Drugs and Crime, 'Brazil 2006–2009, Strategic Programme Framework' (Vienna, August, 2006).

United Nations Press Release, 'Security Council Extends Sanctions Against Liberia Until 7 May 2004, Unanimously Adopted Resolution 1478 (2003)', SC/7752, 5 June 2003.

'United States: New Allegations of Nicaraguan Arms Buildup', Inter Press Service, 19 April 1985.

United States Bureau of Industry and Security, *Annual Report Fiscal Year 2007* (Washington, DC: United States Department of Commerce, 2006).

United States Department of Commerce, *Offsets in Defense Trade*, 10th study (Washington, DC: United States Department of Commerce, 2005).

United States Department of Defense, *Joint Publication 1–02, Department of Defense Dictionary of Military and Associated Terms* (Washington, DC, 12 April 2001, as amended through 22 March 2007).

United States Department of State, *U.S. Arms Export Compliance and Enforcement and the U.N. Programme of Action for Small Arms and Light Weapons*, 3 July 2006.

—— *End-Use Monitoring of Defense Articles and Defense Services Commercial Exports FY 2007* (Washington, DC: Directorate of Defense Trade Controls).

United States Department of State, Bureau of Political–Military Affairs, 'Background Paper: The U.S. Approach to Combating the Spread of Small Arms', 2 June 2001.

United States Department of State, Bureau of Political–Military Affairs, *Foreign Military Training: Joint Report to Congress, Fiscal Years 2006 and 2007* (Washington, DC: United States Department of State, August 2007).

United States Department of State, Bureaus of International Information Programs, 'Shoulder-Fired Anti-Aircraft Missiles Threaten Global Aviation', Washington, DC, 21 September 2005.

United States Department of State, Office of the Spokesman, 'Fact Sheet: Sanctions on Pakistan and India' (Washington, DC, 28 September 2001).

United States Government Accountability Office, 'Defense Industry: Trends in DOD Spending, Industrial Productivity, and Competition', January 1997

—— 'Gun Control and Terrorism: FBI Could Better Manage

Firearm-related Background Checks involving Terrorist Watch List Records', January 2005.
—— *Operation Iraqi Freedom* (Washington, DC: 22 March 2007).
'U.S. "Targets Al Qaeda" in Somalia', BBC, 9 January 2007.
van Schendel, Willem, and Itty Abraham, *Illicit Flows and Criminal Things* (Bloomington: Indiana University Press, 2005).
'Victor Infante Charged with Weapons Exportation and Methamphetamine Distribution Arrested in the Philippines', US Drug Enforcement Administration, (Washington, DC: 6 November 2003).
Von Tangen Page, Michael, William Godnick and Janani Vivekananda, *Implementing International Small Arms Controls: Some Lessons from Eurasia, Latin America and West Africa* (London: International Alert, 2005).
Walsh, Lawrence, *Firewall: The Iran–Contra Conspiracy and Cover-Up* (New York: W.W. Norton, 1998).
Walsh, Lawrence E., *The Final Report of the Independent Counsel for Iran/Contra Matters* (Washington DC: US Court of Appeals for the DC Circuit).
Ward, Olivia, 'Congo's Women under Siege', *Toronto Star*, 8 June 2007.
Wassenaar Arrangement, 'French Policy On Export Controls for Conventional Arms and Dual-Use Goods and Technologies'.
Wayne, Leslie, 'A Well-Kept Military Secret', *New York Times*, 16 February 2003.
—— 'Free To A Good Country', *New York Times*, 31 October 2006.
Weinberger, Sharon, 'Seller's Market', *Aviation Week*, 19 November 2006.
White House, Office of the Press Secretary, 'Fact Sheet: Criteria for Decision making on U.S. Arms Exports', (Washington, DC: 17 February 1995).
—— 'White House Memo For The Secretary of State on Waiver of Nuclear-Related Sanctions on India and Pakistan', (Washington, DC, 23 September 2001).
Wolf, Jim, 'U.S. Looks to Arm Iran's Neighbors: General', Reuters, 18 May 2006.
—— 'Iran, North Korea Spur PAC-3 Missile Demand: Lockheed', Reuters, 24 August 2006.
Wood, Brian, and Johan Peleman, 'Brokering Arms for Genocide', in *The Arms Fixers: Controlling the Brokers and Shipping Agents* (Oslo and Washington, DC: PRIS, NISAT and BASIC, 1999).
Zaharia, Marius, 'Romania To Buy 48 New Fighter Jets: Official', *Defense News*, 22 February 2007.

Index